Closing the Coverage Gap

The University of New Mexico
At Gallup

Zollinger Library

Closing the Coverage Gap

THE ROLE OF SOCIAL PENSIONS
AND OTHER RETIREMENT INCOME TRANSFERS

Robert Holzmann, David A. Robalino,
and Noriyuki Takayama, editors

THE WORLD BANK
Washington, DC

© 2009 The International Bank for Reconstruction and Development / The World Bank
1818 H Street, NW
Washington, DC 20433
Telephone 202-473-1000
Internet www.worldbank.org
E-mail feedback@worldbank.org

1 2 3 4 :: 12 11 10 09

ISBN: 978-0-8213-7971-4
eISBN: 978-0-8213-7980-6
DOI: 10.1596/978-0-8213-7971-4

Cataloging-in-Publication data for this title is available from the Library of Congress.

Contents

Boxes

Figures

Tables

Preface and Acknowledgments

Closing the coverage gap for key contingencies such as income requirements for the elderly is the ultimate frontier for social policy throughout the world. In high-income countries, old-age pension coverage is typically high but in many cases far from complete; across OECD countries, it tends to decline. And this decline occurs at a time of continued increases in life expectancy that, together with low fertility rates, accelerate overall aging of the population. In low- and middle-income countries, the percent of the population covered under mandatory schemes is typically low and has stagnated for some time, even in those countries that have enacted structural reforms strengthening the link between contributions and benefits. At the same time, due to the weakening of traditional family structures, caused by such factors as urbanization or HIV/AIDS, individuals are less and less able to rely on support from their children or communities and lack access to formal employment, resources, instruments, and incentives to prepare for their old age. These developments raise the risk of increasing poverty and marginalizing a rising share of the elderly in the world.

The options to address these challenges are limited. They include increasing the coverage of contributory schemes (independently of benefit type, type of funding, or administration), increasing coverage through access to social assistance-type benefits (financed from budgetary resources), and increasing access to voluntary savings instruments for old age.

This book investigates the second option and the various forms of retirement income transfers that aim to prevent poverty and guarantee a minimum level of income during old age. Well-known, and less well-known, examples of such general budget-financed income transfers include social pensions, minimum pension guarantees, and matching contributions. While the popularity of such transfers is increasing, the amount of research done to assess their performance in extending coverage and preventing poverty has been limited.

For this reason, the World Bank, Hitosubashi University, and the Japanese Ministry of Finance joined forces and organized a workshop in Tokyo in February 2008 to assess the need for retirement income transfers, to take stock of the international experience with social pensions, to review design and implementation issues, and to explore the scope for subsidized contributory systems. The conference brought together academics, staff from international organizations, and development practitioners. Based on their presentations and the discussions at the meeting, 14 papers were prepared and compiled, and are presented in this publication. The papers look at the extent of the coverage gap worldwide, poverty among the elderly, experiences in low- and high-income countries with the implementation of social pensions, and issues related to financing, incentive effects, targeting, and institutional organization and administration. We hope that together, these papers will help to close the knowledge gap regarding the design of policies to extend old-age income security to all citizens.

This publication would not have been possible without the generous financial support of the Japanese Ministry of Finance, the great editorial support provided by David Robalino, and superb administrative support at both Hitotsubashi University and at the World Bank. We also acknowledge inputs and comments provided by Landis Mackeller, Salvador Valdez Prieto, David Lindeman, Dalmer Hoskins, Andrew Stone, Helena Ribe, Rafael Rofman, Gustavo Demarco, and Michal Rutkowski. To all we are deeply thankful.

Professor Robert Holzmann   Professor Nuriyuki Takayama
Director for Social Protection & Labor   Head of Project on International Equity
The World Bank   Hitotsubashi University

Contributors

Mukul G. Asher is professor of public policy at the Lee Kuan Yew School of Public Policy, National University of Singapore. He specializes in public finance, social security reforms, and India's external economic relations. He has published extensively in national and international journals and has authored or edited several books. He has been a consultant to many governments and multilateral institutions, including the World Bank and the International Labour Organization (ILO). He is on the International Editorial Advisory Board of the International Social Security Review and Policy Society.

Armando Barrientos is senior research fellow and associate director at the Brooks World Poverty Institute at the University of Manchester, United Kingdom. He is also a senior researcher with the Chronic Poverty Research Centre, leading research on insecurity, risk, and vulnerability. His research interests focus on the linkages existing between social protection and labor markets in developing countries and policies addressing poverty, vulnerability, and population aging. His work has appeared in such publications as *World Development* and *Applied Economics.* His most recent book is *Social Protection for the Poor and Poorest: Concepts, Policies and Politics* (Palgrave, 2008, edited with David Hulme).

Alvaro Forteza is professor of economics at the Universidad de la República (Uruguay) and visiting professor at the universities of Antwerp (Belgium), Aarhus (Denmark), Cergy (France), and Murcia and Vigo (Spain). He is an expert on social security. He has been a consultant to the World Bank, the Inter-American Development Bank, the ILO, the Inter-American Conference on Social Security, and the Economic Commission for Latin America and the Caribbean. He has published work in the *Journal of Pension Economics and Finance, the Journal of Macroeconomics*, and the *European Journal of Political Economy*. He holds a PhD in economics from Gothenburg University, Sweden.

Margaret Grosh is lead economist in the World Bank's Social Protection Department under the Bank's Human Development Network, where she is presently the lead specialist for safety nets and practice leader for the Safety Nets Global Expert Team. Her most recent book (co-authored) is *For Protection and Promotion: The Design and Implementation of Effective Safety Nets* (2008). She led the Living Standards Measurement Study survey team for 6 years, fostering the collection and analysis of survey data to inform social policy, including social safety net programs. She holds a PhD in economics from Cornell University.

Krzysztof Hagemejer is chief of policy development and research group in the Social Security Department of the ILO and actively participates in fieldwork on extension of social security coverage, particularly in Africa (Mozambique, Tanzania, and Zambia). From 1998 to 2005, he served as research and statistics coordinator and deputy chief of the Social Security Financial, Actuarial, and Statistical Services Branch. Before joining the ILO in 1993, he was an assistant professor at the Department of Economics of Warsaw University, adviser on social and economic policies to the National Committee of the Independent Trade Union Solidarnosc (1980 to 1991), and adviser to the Minister of Labour and Social Affairs in Poland (1991 to 1993). He holds a master's degree in econometrics and a PhD in economics from Warsaw University. He writes on various economic issues in social security, particularly on problems related to affordability of basic social protection in developing countries and on social reforms in the transition countries of Central and Eastern Europe. He teaches social budgeting at Maastricht University, Netherlands.

Robert Holzmann is director of the World Bank's Social Protection Department under the Bank's Human Development Network. This unit is in charge of the conceptual and strategic work of the World Bank in the area of social risk management, covering labor market interventions, social insurance (including pensions), and social safety nets. Before joining the Bank in 1997, he was professor of economics and the director of the European Institute at the University of Saarland, Germany; professor of economics at the University of Vienna; and senior economist at both the International Monetary Fund (IMF) and the Organisation for Economic Co-operation and Development (OECD). He has published 28 books and over 150 articles on social, fiscal and financial policy issues.

Sergi Jimenez-Martin graduated from the Universitat Pompeu Fabra and currently is associate professor of economics at Universitat Pompeu Fabra and Barcelona GSE. He is also director of the LaCaixa-FEDEA chair on health economics and of the Cuadernos Económicos de ICE. For the last 15 years, he has been an active member of the International Social Security Group of the National Bureau of Economic Research (NBER) and has contributed to each of the volumes in NBER's "Social Security and Retirement around the World" series of working papers. His current topics of interest are health economics and social security and retirement.

Alain Jousten is professor of economics at HEC—University of Liège. He holds a PhD in economics from the Massachusetts Institute of Technology. His research centers on public economics and the economics of aging. He is highly interested in questions relating to the viability of pension systems, as well as the incentive issues created by them. He has extensive national and international experience as a policy adviser. From 2006 to 2008, he served as a tax policy expert for the IMF. Professor Jousten is a research fellow with the Institute for the Study of Labor (Bonn), Netspar (Tilburg), and the Centre for Economic Policy Research (London). He is also a member of the panel of experts of the Fiscal Affairs Department at the IMF. He has held visiting positions at the Center for Operations Research and Econometrics in Louvain-la-Neuve, the Department of Economics at the Free University of Brussels (ULB), and the Université des Sciences Sociales in Toulouse.

Stephen Kidd is director of policy and communications at HelpAge International. Before joining HelpAge International in 2007, Stephen worked for the UK's Department for International Development (DFID) where, during his last three years, he led policy work on social protection. Previously, he worked on DFID's China and Latin America programs. Stephen has a PhD in social anthropology (which he taught for two years at the University of Edinburgh) and has worked for over 10 years in Latin America supporting the rights of indigenous people.

Phillippe G. Leite is an economist in the World Bank's Social Protection Department under the Bank's Human Development Network. He holds BA and MS degrees in statistics (sampling and modeling) from the Brazilian Statistics School and an MS degree in economics from École des Hautes Études en Sciences Sociales (Paris), where he is finishing his PhD. His topics of interest are determinants of poverty and inequality, poverty maps, evaluation and design of social safety net programs to poor families, and microeconometric simulation models.

Leonardo Lucchetti is a PhD candidate in economics at the University of Illinois at Urbana–Champaign. He holds a master's degree in economics from the Universidad Nacional de La Plata, Argentina. Previously, he worked as a junior professional associate for the World Bank (Social Protection Department, Human Development Network), as a researcher for CEDLAS in Argentina, and as a trainee for the European Commission (economic and finance general direction, econometric research). His work has focused on social security, nutrition, subjective poverty, and the evaluation of conditional cash transfer programs in Latin America.

Hyungpyo Moon is a senior research fellow at the Korea Development Institute and the director of its Economic Information and Education Center. He received a PhD in economics from the University of Pennsylvania. Previously he was deputy assistant secretary for social welfare for the Republic of Korea. He is a leading scholar on pensions in Korea and has published numerous books and articles on various issues in public economics. In 2008, he chaired the Actuarial Valuation Committee of the National Pension Scheme in Korea. His recent publications include two edited volumes, *Comprehensive Study on the Establishment of Old-Age Income Security System in Korea* and *Socio-Economic Impacts of Population Aging and Policy Issues*.

Montserrat Pallares-Miralles is a social protection economist with the Pensions Team in the World Bank's Social Protection Department under the Bank's Human Development Network, where she currently works on research and the modeling of pension systems and reforms. She has worked on pension reforms in more than 70 countries in Africa, Eastern Europe, Latin America, the Middle East, and Asia. She graduated from the University of Barcelona and received other specialized training in France, Italy, and the United States.

Robert Palacios is senior pension economist in the World Bank's Social Protection Department under the Bank's Human Development Network. Between 1992 and 1994 he was a member of the team that produced the World Bank's influential volume on international pension systems, *Averting the Old Age Crisis: Policies to Protect the Old and Promote Growth*. Between 1995 and 1997, he worked in the department responsible for Eastern Europe and was intimately involved in the reform of the Hungarian pension system. Since 1997, he has divided his time between applied research and operational work in two dozen countries in Asia, Eastern Europe, Africa, and Latin America. He is the author of many articles and papers on pension reform. He is currently working in India, the Maldives, Nepal, and Pakistan.

Mark Pearson is head of the Health Division at the OECD; previously, he headed up work on social policy at the OECD. He has written a number of books for the OECD, including *Making Work Pay: The Caring World,* a series of studies of social assistance policies (*The Battle against Exclusion*) and family policies (*Babies and Bosses*). He initiated the renewal of the OECD social indicators program (*Society at a Glance*) and introduced international monitoring of benefit policies (*Benefits and Wages*) and pensions (*Pensions at a Glance*). He has written books on tax, environmental, and disability policies; education and work; income distribution; the relationship between inequality and growth; projections of health and social expenditures; and the interactions between tax and benefit systems. He has been a consultant to the World Bank, the IMF, and the European Commission.

John Piggott is professor of economics and associate dean research in the Australian School of Business, University of New South Wales, where he is also director of the Australian Institute for Population Ageing Research. He has long-standing interests and has published extensively in the areas of public finance and the economic and financial aspects of retirement and pension. In recent years he has worked on ageing issues with the Government of Japan's Cabinet Office; he has also advised on pension issues in the Asian region more generally. In 2007 he was appointed Visiting Professor, Zhejiang University, China. He is a member of Australia's Future Tax System Review Panel, and serves on the Australian Ministerial Superannuation Advisory Committee. He is on the editorial board of the *Journal of Pension Economics and Finance.*

David A. Robalino is a senior economist in the World Bank's Human Development Network. He works on issues related to social security, labor markets, and fiscal policy, and has advised several countries in Africa, East Asia, the Middle East, and Latin America. He has published on issues related to macroeconomics and labor markets, social insurance and pensions, health financing, the economics of HIV/AIDS, and the economics of climate change. Prior to joining the Bank, he was a researcher at the RAND Corporation, where he was involved in the development of quantitative methods for economic analysis under conditions of deep uncertainty, and served in Ecuador's Presidential Committee for Social Security Reform. He holds a PhD in economic analysis from the RAND Graduate School in Santa Monica, California; a DESUP in macroeconomics from the University of Paris (Sorbonne); and a BA degree in economics and finance from the Central University of Ecuador.

Oleksiy Sluchynsky is a senior economist at the World Bank with extensive international experience in design and implementation issues of the social insurance program. At the Bank, he has worked on social protection issues in the South Asia, Middle East and North Africa, and Europe and Central Asia regions. Prior to joining the Bank, he was a resident adviser in Kosovo, providing support for the implementation of a new pension program. He has worked on operational issues on both DB and DC pension schemes, having researched and written on international best practices of various administrative models. He holds an MA degree in public administration from Harvard University's Kennedy School of Government, as well as an MA in economics and an MSc in computer science.

Noriyuki Takayama is professor of economics at the Institute of Economic Research, Hitotsubashi University, Tokyo. He holds a PhD from the University of Tokyo and is director general and CEO of the Project on Intergenerational Equity (PIE). He is known as a distinguished key player in the area of pensions in Japan. He has published numerous books and articles in international publications including *Econometrica* and the *American Economic Review*. His books include *Taste of Pie: Searching for Better Pension Provisions in Developed Countries* and *Pensions in Asia: Incentives, Compliance and their Role in Retirement*. He is also the author of a Japanese book, *Saving and Wealth Formation*, which was awarded the 1996 Nikkei Prize for the best book on economic issues.

Edward Whitehouse heads the pensions team in the social policy division of the OECD. He is coauthor of the OECD's flagship report on retirement incomes, *Pensions at a Glance*. He also works with the World Bank on designing and implementing pension reforms. He wrote the joint World Bank/OECD report, *Pensions Panorama: Retirement-Income Systems in 53 Countries*. Previously, he was leader writer and social affairs correspondent for the *Financial Times* and worked at the Institute for Fiscal Studies in London. He has taught at University College, London, and Oxford University.

CHAPTER 1

Overview and Preliminary Policy Guidance

David A. Robalino and Robert Holzmann

Many countries have implemented, or are considering, various forms of retirement income transfers that aim to guarantee a minimum level of income during old age and to prevent poverty; examples are social pensions, minimum pension guarantees, and matching contributions. Despite the growing popularity of these programs, only limited research has been carried out to assess their performance in extending coverage and preventing poverty, and policy analysis that could inform governments on key design and implementation issues is sparse. Programs in various countries have been studied from different angles, but to our knowledge, there is to date no source that systematically analyzes international experience and proposes an integrated policy framework to guide choices about when and how to implement such programs. This book is an effort to start filling the void.

The focus is on social pensions broadly defined—cash transfers, not linked to contributions, that take place after retirement or after a given eligibility age—and on their potential role as instruments for expanding access to old-age income security. The book also discusses, albeit in less depth, issues related to the design of minimum pension guarantees and matching contributions within contributory systems. The main reason for including these other types of transfer is that there are important interactions; when the three kinds of program coexist, the performance of one depends on the design of the others, and they jointly affect individuals' behaviors. Thus, when deciding about the best arrangement for securing a minimum level of income during old age for a given population group, it is necessary to carefully coordinate the design of the three types of program.

The book has four specific objectives: (a) to discuss the role of retirement income transfers in the context of a strategy for expanding old-age income security and preventing poverty among the elderly; (b) to take stock of international experience with the design and implementation of these programs; (c) to identify key policy issues that need to receive attention during the design and implementation phases; and (d) to offer some preliminary policy recommendations and propose next steps.

The organization of the book reflects these objectives. The first chapters discuss the rationale for retirement income transfers. The main justifications are the limited coverage of the mandatory pension systems (chapter 2) and the risk of poverty during old age (chapter 3). Chapter 4 then examines the rights-based approach to expansion of social security coverage based on the conventions and recommendations of the International Labour Organization (ILO). The middle part of the book deals with international experience. Chapters 5, 6, and 7 review selected programs in low-, middle-, and high-income countries, respectively, and chapters 8 and 9 discuss in greater depth the cases of Japan and the Republic of Korea.

The five concluding chapters are concerned with policy issues as related to design. Chapter 10 presents a typology of retirement income transfers and analyzes the potential economic impacts of the programs. Chapter 11 deals with financing mechanisms and the problem of allocative efficiency, given limited resources. Chapter 12 addresses two key issues related to institutional arrangements and targeting systems: Should countries consider separate programs to target the elderly poor instead of using the general social assistance system to target all poor? And, how can current proxy means-test systems be adapted to target the elderly poor? Chapter 13 explores in more detail the links between social pensions and matching contributions in the context of a general strategy for expanding coverage. Finally, chapter 14 provides guidelines for the design of the administrative systems needed to operationalize the various programs.

The remainder of this overview summarizes the main messages from the subsequent chapters and outlines an agenda for future research and policy analysis. For clarity, it starts by presenting some definitions pertinent to the retirement income transfers discussed in the book.

Some Definitions

The subject of this book is cash transfers or explicit subsidies that aim to guarantee a minimum level of income during old age and to prevent poverty. We refer to these transfers as *retirement income transfers* or *old-age subsidies*.

Transfers can take place on retirement and on reaching a certain eligibility age (*ex post interventions*), or during active life (*ex ante interventions*). The taxonomy analyzed in chapter 10 distinguishes two main types of ex post intervention: (a) transfers that are not linked to contribution histories, often called *social pensions,* and (b) transfers to guarantee a *minimum pension* within mandatory contributory pension systems, which most of the time are conditional on a given contribution history or vesting period.

Social pensions can be *universal* or *resource tested.* Universal pensions—also referred to as basic pensions—are paid to all individuals who reach eligibility age, sometimes with residency restrictions. Resource-tested pensions are, in addition, conditional on a maximum level of income (pension income or a broader definition), or of asset holdings, or both.

Minimum pensions are always tested on pension income—more precisely, on the value of the contributory pension. In a way, minimum pensions are a form of resource-tested pension that differs from a social pension only to the extent that eligibility is subject to a vesting period. In fact, chapter 7, which deals with member countries of the Organisation for Economic Co-operation and Development (OECD), treats minimum pensions as a form of social pension.[1]

Under ex ante interventions, this book discusses *matching contributions.* These are transfers that are given to individuals conditional on their contributions to a given pension plan. For instance, a government can decide to pay a 50 percent or a 100 percent match for each monetary unit deposited in a pension account, which can be funded or notional, publicly or privately managed. Matching contributions are included in the

FIGURE 1.1 **Taxonomy of retirement income transfers**

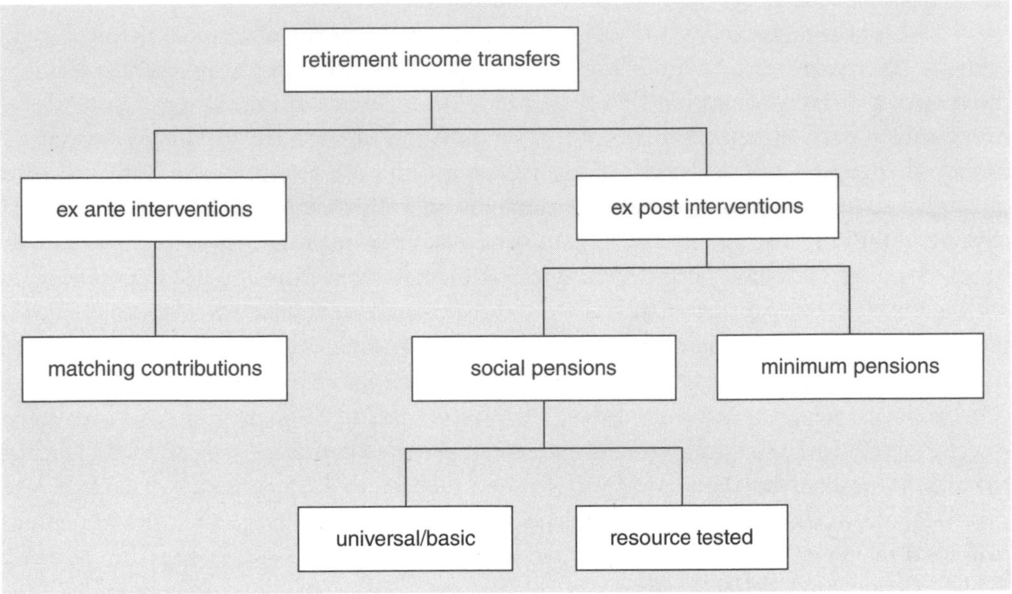

SOURCE: Authors' elaboration.

discussion because of their potential role in stimulating long-term saving (and therefore increase income during old age) and in providing incentives for formal sector work among individuals with limited saving capacity. These contributions can have a significant role in the context of an integrated strategy for expanding coverage, and their interactions with ex post retirement income transfers need to be analyzed. (Other forms of ex ante intervention, such as contribution credits during periods of unemployment, or maternity leave, fall outside the scope of this book.) Figure 1.1 summarizes the relevant taxonomy of retirement income transfers that is used across chapters.

Rationale for Retirement Income Transfers

As previously noted, the main function of social pensions and other retirement income transfers is to prevent poverty during old age. In high-income countries the transfers benefit individuals who, for the most part, are also covered by contributory systems. In middle- and low-income countries, by contrast, transfers are for many the only source of cash income during old age and therefore are often considered key instruments for expanding access to old-age income security.

THE COVERAGE GAP

The authors of chapter 2 estimate that only 25 percent of the world's labor force is covered by a mandatory contributory pension system.[2] Even countries such as Argentina, Chile, and Mexico—which in the 1980s and 1990s moved toward funded defined-contribution pension arrangements that were expected to improve incentives to enroll and contribute—have failed to expand coverage in a meaningful way, and only around half of their labor force is under the mandatory pension system.

Except for high-income OECD countries, the share of the labor force enrolled in the mandatory system remains quite low, and in OECD countries pension coverage seems to be stagnant or even decreasing (Holzmann 2003). As discussed in chapters 8 and 9, even in countries such as Japan and Korea, universalization of coverage remains an important policy challenge. Coverage rates in Eastern Europe and the former Soviet Union tend to be higher than average, in part because of the role of public sector employment and collective agriculture in the past. As these countries make the transition toward market economies, coverage rates have been declining (see Holzmann and Guven 2009), and today the average is close to 65 percent. In East Asia the average coverage rate is 44 percent, but in China it reaches only 20 percent. In the Middle East and North Africa and in Latin America and the Caribbean coverage rates are low to moderate, averaging 34 and 32 percent of the labor force, respectively. Moving to South Asia and Sub-Saharan Africa, coverage rates drop substantially. In South Asia the average across countries is close to 13 percent. In Sub-Saharan Africa the average is 6 percent; the already historically low coverage rates deteriorated during the 1980s. Mauritius has the highest coverage rate, at 50 percent, followed by Cape Verde, with 27 percent. Most Sub-Saharan African countries, however, have coverage rates below 5 percent, with contributory systems that often extend only to civil servants and employees in public and large private enterprises.

What are the main factors that determine coverage? Not surprisingly, a country's income per capita is a good predictor of coverage rates—the higher the level of income, the higher the share of the labor force enrolled in the mandatory pension system. This is to be expected; with economic development, institutional and enforcement capacity increase, and total output and employment become less dependent on the agriculture sector, where coverage rates are usually lower. Higher average earnings and greater saving capacity can contribute, as well.

At a given income level, however, large variations in coverage rates can still be observed. These ultimately reflect differences in the structure of the economy and the labor market, as well as in the distribution of income: large informal sectors go hand in hand with low coverage rates, and the poor seldom enroll in contributory systems. For instance, data from Latin America show that coverage rates are lower in the construction sector and in agriculture. Coverage rates tend to be higher in the public sector, the services sector, and the manufacturing sector, although they have been declining in manufacturing. Another finding is that the self-employed and wage earners in small enterprises are less likely to be enrolled in the mandatory pension system. The same is true for low-skilled and low-income workers.

Chapter 2 develops a dynamic analysis of coverage rates that raises additional policy issues. Using social security records for Uruguay, the authors show that very few individuals contribute continuously to the mandatory pension system. Most people move in and out of the system and have sparse contribution densities. Interestingly, transition rates decline over time, so that the chances that individuals who do not contribute will stay out of the system increase with time. As before, low-income workers face a higher risk of dropping out of the system than high-income workers and have a lower probability of reentry. Economic downturns thus raise the risk that private workers may stop contributing and lower the chances that contributions will be resumed. As a result, it is projected that, on average, only 25 percent of contributors in Uruguay will have put in the 35 years of payments required to access an ordinary pension at the normal retirement age; only 1 percent of those belonging to the poorest quintile will do so.

Until the reforms introduced in 2008, a similar problem existed in Chile: those who did not accumulate funds sufficient to self-finance a pension above the minimum pension guarantee would not attain the 20 years of contributions required to access benefits. About half of the retirees would not receive a pension above the minimum, and only about 2 percent would be eligible for the guarantee. Evidence of low contribution densities also exists for Argentina and Brazil (see Robalino and others, forthcoming).

But do low coverage rates and sparse contribution densities justify the implementation of retirement income transfers financed by general government revenues? After all, to prevent poverty during old age, individuals have access to sources of income outside the mandatory system, including voluntary savings and implicit or explicit family transfers. In fact, the share of the elderly living with their children tends to be higher in low-income countries, where coverage rates are expected to be lower (see figure 1.2).

The usual justification for public intervention is that the average citizen is not a good financial planner and might fail to set aside sufficient and well-diversified savings

FIGURE 1.2 **Share of the elderly living with their children**

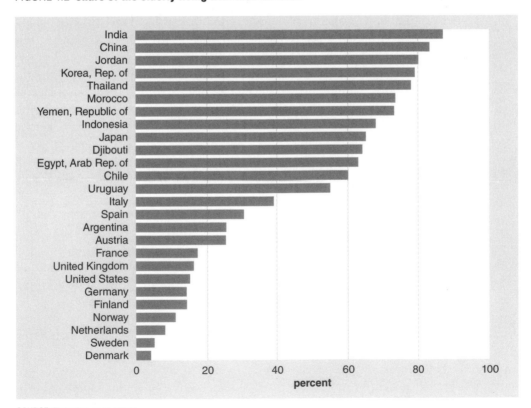

SOURCE: Robalino et al. 2005.

while young, thus running the risk of falling into poverty when old. Family support is not always there, and it tends to decline as a result of economic development (with the accompanying urbanization, migration, and greater labor force mobility). The obvious question is, what happens to the elderly who do not receive a public pension? What is their socioeconomic situation? Do they face a higher risk of poverty than the rest of the population? If not, the rationale for retirement income transfers would be weakened—the elderly poor could simply become part of the general social assistance system that targets *all* the poor (if, of course, such a system exists). These questions are addressed in chapters 3 and 12.

POVERTY AMONG THE ELDERLY

As is pointed out in the chapters, the world's population is aging rapidly. Today, there are around 670 million people over age 60, or 10.4 percent of the global population. By 2050 the number is expected to have increased to almost 2 billion, or 21.7 percent of the population. Consistent with the low coverage of the labor force, only a minority of the elderly, around 20 percent, has access to some form of public pension (see figure 2.1 in chapter 2). Yet, the authors of chapter 3 argue, the elderly could be more exposed to the risk of poverty than the rest of the population, in part because of their higher vulnerability to sickness and disability.

The international evidence is mixed. In Sub-Saharan Africa, Kakwani and Subbarao (2005) show that in 9 of the 15 countries they analyze, poverty rates among the elderly are higher than in the general population. (In the other six, differences were not statistically significant.) Similarly, Gasparini et al. (2007) find that in 14 of the 18 Latin American countries that they studied, poverty rates among the elderly would be higher in the absence of pension transfers. In three of the four countries analyzed in chapter 12 of this volume—the Kyrgyz Republic, Niger, and Panama—poverty rates are higher among the elderly. (The exception is the Republic of Yemen.) But other studies for Asia (Sri Lanka and India) and the Middle East and North Africa (Djibouti, the Arab Republic of Egypt, Jordan, Morocco, and the Republic of Yemen) tell a different story: poverty rates among the elderly are equal to or lower than those of the general population. There are cases of higher poverty rates among elderly persons living alone with children, but the share of these households is quite small (see also Palacios and Sluchynsky 2006; see Robalino, Rao, and Sluchynsky 2007 for a review).

Clearly, one should not be surprised that the results vary by country; they should. The authors of chapter 3 point out, however, that some of the differences could stem from differing assumptions regarding economies of scale and the distribution of income and consumption within the household. For instance, most studies assume an equal distribution, yet there is evidence of weakened family support and cases in which income and consumption are allocated disproportionally to children and individuals of working age. Some studies may thus underestimate poverty among the elderly.

There are three main messages from the review. First, care is needed in interpreting the results of studies that assess poverty among the elderly. Second, new methodologies and standards for measuring poverty among household members need to be developed and applied to adequately inform policy. Third, studies need to be country specific; broad generalizations about the relative socioeconomic situation of the elderly are not enough to motivate and guide the design of retirement income transfers. Even within countries, there can be large regional differences in relative poverty rates.

Chapter 12 discusses these issues in more detail.

RIGHT TO INCOME SECURITY DURING OLD AGE

There is also a view that public intervention in providing income security to the elderly is simply justified by the fact that social security is a human right, as stated in the 1948 Universal Declaration of Human Rights. This right is made specific in respective ILO Conventions and Recommendations. Countries ratifying these instruments accept that the state is responsible for guaranteeing, through various means, income security to the elderly, along with other elements of social security.

Thus, for the ILO, the universalization of the right to affordable retirement is part of a wider objective to guarantee basic social security to all in need. Chapter 4 discusses the principles that sustain this vision, as well as issues related to its design and implementation. The chapter shows that in order to provide at least minimum income security to all during old age, one has to go beyond purely earnings-related contributory pensions and introduce various noncontributory interventions, both within contributory schemes and outside them. This is necessary to adapt to the labor market patterns of informality, self-employment, and short contribution densities to social security. The chapter also discusses the need to carefully balance adequacy and cost concerns in order to arrive at affordable and viable pension polices.

Some of the policy considerations to achieve this balance are discussed in chapters 10 to 14, and we will come back to them later in this overview. Before doing so, however, it is useful to briefly review the types of retirement income transfers that have been implemented around the world and their impact on poverty rates among the elderly.

Retirement Income Transfers around the World

The prevalence of retirement income transfers, their mandates, and their designs vary widely across regions. Nonetheless, from the reviews in chapters 5 to 9 certain patterns emerge that are correlated with countries' income levels.

OECD COUNTRIES

Chapter 7 shows that most high-income OECD countries have implemented social pensions or minimum pensions (or both) within the contributory system, but to our knowledge, no matching contributions programs exist among these countries. In the majority of cases, most people who receive some form of social pension or minimum pension also receive at least some benefit from the earnings-related schemes to which around 90 percent of the labor force contributes. Arrangements vary by country. Around half of the countries have only one kind of program. Germany and the United States, for example, have only a resource-tested scheme; Japan, the Netherlands, and New Zealand rely on universal pensions; and Finland and Sweden have only minimum pensions. In most countries, however, we find two of the four types, and in the United Kingdom, three (all except matching contributions). Overall, resource-tested and minimum pensions are equally prevalent and exist in 17 of the 30 countries analyzed. Universal schemes are less prevalent but are still found in 13 of the 30 countries.

But even if most countries have implemented some type of retirement income transfer, there are differences as to whether the programs are being expanded or contained. For instance, France, Korea, Mexico, and Sweden have introduced reforms that have strengthened the role of social pensions. Finland, Hungary, and Poland, by contrast, have moved in the opposite direction. Finland went from mixed basic and pension-tested benefits to a pure pension-tested benefit; Hungary and Poland abolished the minimum pension. The main concern in these three cases has been to strengthen the link between contributions and benefits and so improve incentives.

Benefits from social pensions and minimum pensions are worth, on average, about 30 percent of economywide average earnings. In 18 of the 30 countries reviewed in chapter 7, the value of these transfers ranges between 25 and 35 percent of average earnings. Some exceptions are Finland, Germany, and Japan, where the value of the transfer is lower (less than 20 percent), and New Zealand and Portugal, where the transfer represents more than 40 percent of average earnings.

The coverage of retirement income transfers varies more widely. For instance, whereas the U.S. program covers less than 6 percent of the population of pension age, in Australia coverage is a little over 75 percent. In Canada, Ireland, Italy, Finland, France, Sweden, and the United Kingdom coverage rates are within, or close to, the 25–50 percent range. These coverage rates ultimately depend on eligibility rules, in particular, the type of income test.

MIDDLE- AND LOW-INCOME COUNTRIES

Social pensions (universal and resource-tested pensions) are less prevalent, and also of more recent date, in middle- and low-income countries. In the Middle East and North Africa only Algeria and Egypt have noncontributory or quasi-noncontributory systems that could be assimilated to a social pension. In Latin America and the Caribbean only nine countries have implemented noncontributory programs, and in Sub-Saharan Africa, Eastern Europe, and Asia, not more than an additional dozen programs can be counted. On the other hand, most countries that have mandatory contributory systems have implemented a minimum pension guarantee. Matching contributions, by contrast, are only recently emerging. The Dominican Republic (law passed), India (program implemented in West Bengal, pilot soon to be launched in Andhra Pradesh), Mexico (program implemented), and Vietnam (law under consideration) are leaders in the design of this type of program (see chapter 13 for a more detailed discussion).

Minimum pensions within contributory systems usually take the form of a top-up: individuals who on retirement have a contributory pension below the minimum guaranteed receive the difference from the plan or from the government. Eligibility conditions are the same as for the contributory pension. Thus, on top of a minimum retirement age, there is usually also a minimum vesting period. Nonetheless, in many instances, eligible individuals who apply for early retirement are also eligible for the minimum pension guarantee.

Overall, the level of benefits ranges between 25 and 35 percent of average earnings (see figure 1.3). In most cases the cost of the minimum pension is financed, implicitly,

FIGURE 1.3 **Minimum pensions in middle- and low-income countries**

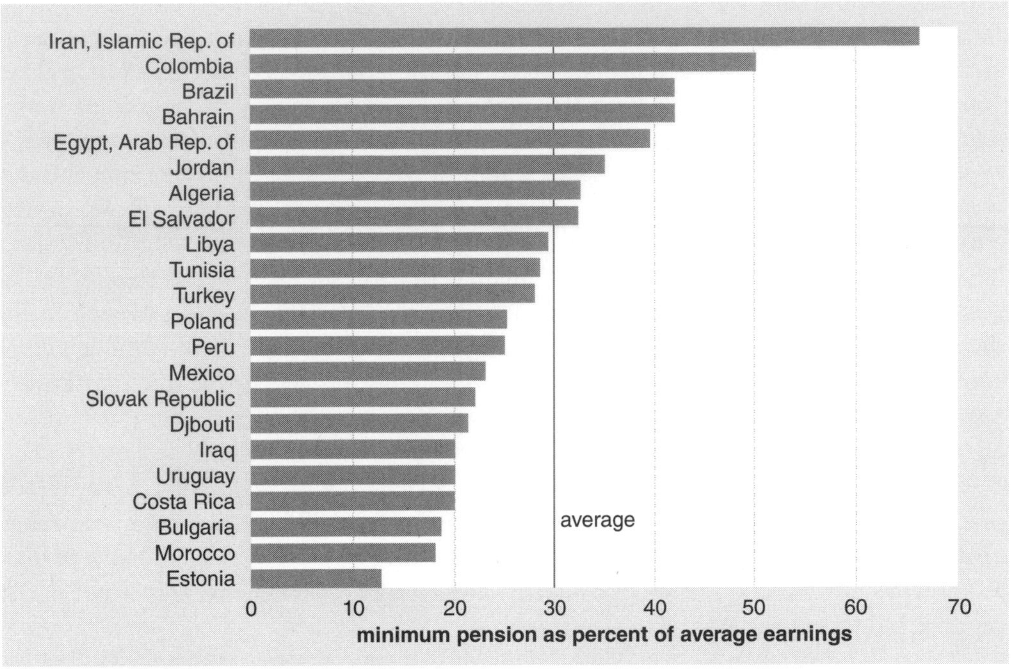

SOURCE: Authors' calculations.

through payroll taxes and social security contributions. Also, in most countries that have implemented both a social pension and a minimum pension (e.g., Algeria and Brazil), the programs have been designed with little or no coordination, as if applying to very different population groups. There are thus marked differences in benefit levels and/or eligibility conditions.

In contrast to OECD countries, social pensions in most middle- and low-income countries cover a population group that, for the most part, is not under the contributory system. Thus, in general, individuals eligible for a minimum pension guarantee within the contributory system are not eligible for a social pension.[3]

There are, nonetheless, marked differences in the design of social pensions in low- and middle-income countries. The author of chapter 5 argues that few low-income countries have implemented social pensions. In part this is because the elderly account for a relatively low proportion of the population; multigenerational households are dominant; and government resources for poverty reduction are scarce. In countries that have implemented social pensions, poverty incidence is high, inequality among the poor is low, and political resistance to poverty reduction is significant. Social pensions then have a clear and transparent target group and provide widely supported life-cycle and sectoral redistribution. Middle-income countries, on the other hand, are more likely to implement social pensions, but the programs tend to be smaller, in part as a result of wider coverage of the contributory system.

Thus, two separate groups emerge when it comes to the coverage of social pensions. The first group includes countries where the coverage of the programs, expressed as the ratio between the number of beneficiaries and the population over age 65, is small—around or below 20 percent.[4] Examples include Algeria, Argentina, Chile, and Colombia. In general, these are countries with a prominent contributory system, albeit one that covers, in the majority of cases, less than 60 percent of the labor force. Social pensions in these cases are therefore targeted to low-income individuals not covered by the contributory system. In the second group are, for example, Bolivia, Kosovo, and South Africa, where the coverage of social pensions is universal or almost universal. In this group the contributory system does not exist or has only a marginal role. An exception is Mauritius, where the coverage of the contributory system is moderate, but the social pension was introduced when the contributory system was in its infancy. Brazil is another special case; in urban areas an income-tested social pension for those over age 67 covers around 7 percent of the elderly, but in rural areas there is an almost universal social pension. Although rural workers can make contributions to the national scheme and are eligible for contributory pensions, they are all also eligible for a nontested rural pension after age 55 (for females) or 60 (for males), and the majority follows this route.

The level of the benefit does not seem to be correlated with per capita gross domestic product (GDP) or with the region. Among the programs reviewed, there is a large range of variation; benefits can be as low as 3 percent of GDP per capita (Algeria) and as high as 45 percent (Kosovo). The average benefit across programs is close to 18 percent of per capita GDP (see figure 1.4).

Another difference between low- and middle-income countries is in policy priorities, as reflected in program design. As noted in chapter 5, in low-income countries particular attention is given to having in place some mechanism for controlling pension liabilities: late age of entitlement (Lesotho), cohort restrictions (Bolivia), or a cap on the number of pensions (Bangladesh). Issues related to the direct fiscal costs of the programs thus become more important than those related to incentives or better integration of contributory and noncontributory systems. Middle-income countries such as Brazil, Chile, and Mexico, by contrast, seem to be moving toward a more integrated type of social protection system. Although fiscal considerations remain important in the design of programs, emphasis is also placed on issues related to distortions in labor markets and saving decisions (see chapter 6). This is, in a way, to be expected because informal and formal labor markets tend to be more integrated and workers transit between the two. They thus go through periods when they are covered by the contributory system (formal sector) and periods when they are implicitly covered by the noncontributory system (informal sector).

IMPACT OF SOCIAL PENSIONS ON POVERTY

What has been the impact of these programs on the welfare of the elderly? In contrast to the debate about relative poverty rates among the elderly outlined in the previous section, there is a broad consensus that retirement income transfers, and in particular social pensions, have played an important role in reducing poverty. Chapter 3 shows that in OECD countries poverty rates among the elderly would be significantly higher without the transfers. In France, for instance, the poverty rate would be almost 90 percent in the absence of public pensions, rather than the present 6 percent. Clearly, this is not the proper counterfactual, given that in the absence of public pensions, individuals are very likely to save more on their own. Nonetheless, the figure shows the importance of public pensions as a source of income during old age.

FIGURE 1.4 **Benefits and coverage of social pensions in middle- and low-income economies**

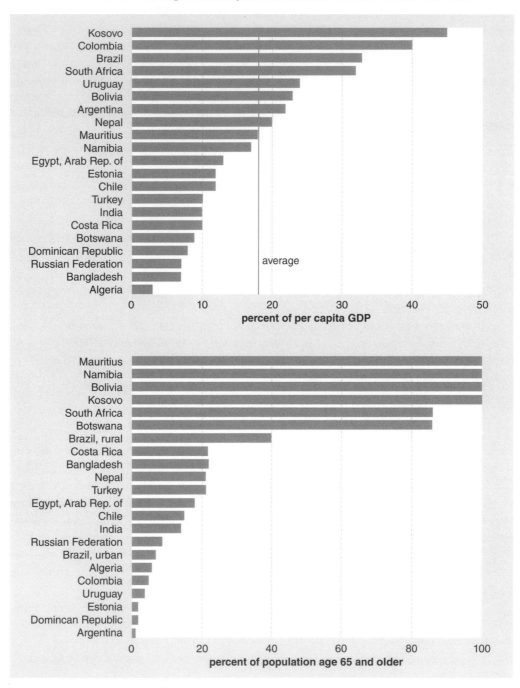

SOURCE: Palacios and Sluchynsky 2006.

NOTE: GDP, gross domestic product.

More rigorous studies for developing countries, reviewed in chapter 3, also show that social pensions have had positive effects on poverty rates. In Brazil 77 percent of older people benefit from a public pension. The old-age poverty rate in the absence of these pensions would be 47.9 percent, as against the actual rate of 3.7 percent (see Gasparini et al. 2007). In Mauritius, which has had a universal social pension since 1950, poverty rates for older people living with more than one younger person would be 30 percent without the universal pension, rather than the actual poverty rate of 6 percent (Kaniki 2007). In the case of the South African noncontributory social pension, Samson (2006) shows that among households that include older people, the almost universal pension reduces the poverty gap by 54 percent. For older people living alone, the poverty gap almost disappears.

There are, of course, exceptions, in part because of low benefit levels or narrow coverage. In Nepal, for example, the pension is just US$2 per month and is paid only to those over age 75. It is also quite clear that social pensions will generally have very limited effects on aggregate poverty rates. As discussed in chapter 5, in most countries in Sub-Saharan Africa a social pension would reach less than one-third of the poor. Social pensions could be a powerful instrument for poverty reduction for households affected by HIV/AIDS or migration and where adults of working age are missing, but these are a small fraction of households in poverty.

But even when social pensions are able to reduce poverty rates significantly, at least among the elderly, there are questions about expanding the programs or designing new ·ones. Lower poverty rates are indeed among the benefits of the programs, but there are costs that need to be taken into account.

Technical and Allocative Efficiency

As with any public program or investment decision, implementing a retirement income transfer involves an assessment of both technical and allocative efficiency. By technical efficiency, we mean that if a transfer program is going to be implemented, its design should ensure that it will reach its objectives at the least possible cost. The costs relate not only to the payment of the transfer itself but also to any economic distortion that is generated as a result of the program—for instance, reductions in labor supply and employment levels, an increase in the share of informal employment, or lower saving rates. Chapter 10 suggests some policy-relevant guidelines on design features that can minimize distortions while improving redistribution.

The existence of an efficient technical design, however, is not a sufficient condition for implementation. Governments have limited resources and face many competing demands—for instance, to invest in education, health, or infrastructure. Whether part of the budget should be assigned to retirement income transfers is a question of allocative efficiency, which is discussed in chapter 11.[5]

TECHNICAL EFFICIENCY

Chapter 10 develops a framework for analyzing the potential distortions or economic costs resulting from retirement income transfers, distinguishing between effects related to the transfer itself and those related to the financing mechanism. Regarding the effects of the transfer, the chapter looks at changes in labor supply, sector choice (formal or informal), retirement ages, and the saving rate. From the financing side, the focus is on the potential impacts of the program on the tax burden, which can affect investments, growth, employment levels, and the size of the informal sector.

Unfortunately, the economic literature is quite thin on these aspects. and the available results are difficult to compare and are sometimes contradictory. In Brazil, for instance, there is strong evidence that the rural pension reduced the labor supply in pre-retirement ages and induced retirement at early ages. By contrast, in South Africa the overall labor supply effect was positive: eligible individuals reduced their number of hours worked, but the transfer seems to have facilitated the employment of other members of the household.

On formal sector versus informal sector work, the evidence for Chile and Mexico suggests that badly designed noncontributory arrangements can increase informality. In essence, other things being equal, the transfers reduce the net wage premium in the formal sector and can induce more workers to turn to self-employment or become wage earners in informal firms. As for saving rates, evidence from the United States and Spain suggests that retirement transfers can indeed induce eligible individuals to save less.

But how important are these effects? The general message from the analysis in chapter 10, not surprisingly, is that it all depends. Behavioral changes are very sensitive to individual preferences (e.g., discount rates, risk aversion, and preferences for consumption over leisure), to the structure of the labor market (distortions are more relevant in countries with more integrated informal and formal labor markets), and, of course, to program design.

Four aspects seem to be fundamental in program design: the level of the benefit; restrictions on the eligibility age; the effective marginal tax rates (EMTRs) imposed by the transfer, which depend on the type of resource test; and the degree of integration between transfers within and outside the contributory system.

The level of the benefit is obviously important, as it determines not only the fiscal cost of the program but also the strength of the incentives for individuals to change behaviors. In general, with modest transfers, negative impacts on savings and labor supply would be contained, particularly if the transfers were limited to low-income individuals who are less productive and have lower saving rates. It is not easy to define what constitutes a "modest transfer," but one can spot transfers that are definitely too high—for instance, equal to the average earnings of low-skilled workers, as in Brazil. Chapter 10 shows through simulations that transfers representing 30 percent or more of an individual's earnings can have significant effects on his or her labor supply and saving decisions. As the transfer increases, more individuals become eligible, and economic distortions become more serious.

Chapter 10 also highlights the importance of the eligibility age. Empirical studies and simulations provide strong evidence that, most of the time, transfers generate large incentives to advance retirement by several years. Individuals who in the absence of the transfer would not retire at the minimum statutory age are more likely to do so in the presence of the transfer. The implication is that any social pension or minimum pension guarantee should be conditional on meeting a minimum retirement age—ideally, close to the upper tail of the observed distribution of retirement ages. If anything, the transfer would then bring the average retirement age up, not down. Individuals who retired from the contributory system before this retirement age (through early retirement provisions) would not be eligible for the transfer.

The other issue discussed in chapter 10 emphasizes the need to index the eligibility age to life expectancy in order to contain costs and so reduce the additional tax burden imposed by the program. Depending on the share of taxable earnings in GDP, financing a retirement income transfer of even 1 percent of GDP can have significant effects (see chapter 11). In fact, the authors argue that in middle- and, in particular, low-income countries, one of the main distortions related to retirement income transfers would stem from the cost of the program itself and how it expands as the population ages. The recommendation is therefore to increase the eligibility age by one year every five to seven years. Estimates for Egypt suggest that long-term savings from automatic indexation can be in the order of 1 percent of GDP per year.

The last issue regarding technical efficiency addressed in chapter 10 has to do with program design and effective marginal tax rates (EMTRs). EMTRs are generated by the transfer when its value is reduced as a result of an increase in earnings or assets (for instance, an increase in the value of the contributory pension). A universal or basic pension at age 65 with no strings attached imposes a zero EMTR; it is a pure transfer and has a pure *income effect*. The moment the transfer is tested, however, EMTRs become positive for at least some individuals and generate a *substitution effect* between consumption and leisure. The interplay between income and substitution effects can reduce labor supply, contribution densities, or both (see also Levy 2008; Valdés-Prieto 2008; World Bank, forthcoming).

The analysis thus shows that there is a fundamental trade-off between maintaining low EMTRs to reduce distortions and keeping program costs at affordable levels (thus containing the tax burden). This trade-off suggests that universal programs (where the EMTR is zero) are suboptimal, as their fiscal cost would be too high. Programs with an EMTR of 100 percent (i.e., a reduction of one unit in the transfer for each unit increase in earnings), however, would be too distortionary, particularly if the level of the transfer is high in relation to average earnings.

There are two practical implications. The first is that ex post retirement income transfers should ideally be targeted, preferably on the basis of broad means, but with a gradual withdrawal rate. The second is that transfers outside and inside the contributory system should be carefully coordinated to control EMTRs. As in Chile, and probably soon Egypt, one alternative is to integrate the two. In essence, individuals, whether within or outside the contributory system, would be eligible for the same type of transfer. In other words, minimum pension guarantees within the contributory system that in most cases take the form of top-ups (100 percent EMTR) could be eliminated. Individuals within the contributory system would be eligible for the same resource-tested pension (with a gradual withdrawal of benefits) as those outside the contributory system.

ALLOCATIVE EFFICIENCY

Even with an optimal design, the question of whether countries should implement retirement income transfers or expand current ones persists. The first problem identified in chapter 11 is the difficulty of creating fiscal space to finance the programs, particularly in low-income countries. This difficulty remains even if the expected cost of the programs is relatively low (in the order of 0.5 to 2 percent of GDP, according to the various cost estimates presented in this book). Ultimately, there are only two non–mutually exclusive alternatives that can be considered: increasing revenues, or optimizing and reducing other public expenditures.[6]

Excluding natural resources, the main source of revenue for most governments is taxes. Chapter 11 shows, however, that tax revenues in middle- and low-income countries have remained flat over the past 25 years, at around 12–15 percent of GDP, despite efforts by governments to increase collection rates and the tax base. In part, this stagnation is explained by a reduction in import duties—a trend that is likely to continue as a result of trade liberalization. Governments have turned to indirect taxation, in particular through value added taxes (VATs). One alternative for mobilizing additional revenues to finance retirement income transfers would be to increase revenues from these taxes—for example, by eliminating exemptions or increasing the tax rate. Some countries in Europe have proposed taxing product and service imports and earmarking the revenues to finance growing social protection expenditures. But the potential impacts of this policy on growth and employment levels remain unclear, both theoretically and empirically. In addition, increased reliance on earmarked tax financing affects the structural and conceptual integrity of the budgetary process, with its basic principles of unity and fungibility among different types of resources and expenditures.

Regarding expenditures, the standard recommendation would be to reduce waste (i.e., expenditures for projects or items with low or negative social rates of return) and to increase the productive efficiency of spending on worthwhile projects. Candidates for reduction are regressive commodity subsidies, subsidies to bankrupt state-owned enterprises (SOEs), military spending, or simply the wage bill of an oversized civil service. Productive measures include more efficient spending on health, education, and infrastructure. Such improvements in public spending allocation should take place in any case. But, as chapter 11 emphasizes, the necessary changes are not easy to implement.

Even if expenditures could be reduced and additional resources mobilized, retirement income transfers have to compete with other programs for the open fiscal space. In theory, a fixed public budget should be allocated so as to equate the marginal social benefits of all interventions and programs (assuming that there are decreasing marginal returns to additional expenditures). In countries with lagging human development indicators, particularly low-income countries, the highest social returns are likely to be related to investments in education, health, and infrastructure. Reallocating expenditures away from these investments into retirement income transfers could be welfare decreasing, unless the transfer raises overall household income and contributes toward reducing aggregate poverty rates and promoting greater private investments in education and health. But if this is the case, probably a more efficient strategy would be to include the elderly in the general safety net: transfers would focus on the poorest households, with or without elderly members. This is one of the issues addressed in chapter 12, and it is discussed in more detail in the next section.

The bottom line is that, given a fixed budget, when policy makers decide about the implementation of a retirement income transfer, careful attention has to be paid to the opportunity cost of the resources involved and the contribution of the program to poverty reduction and aggregate social welfare. This is, of course, not easy. But it is an issue that needs to be taken seriously, particularly in low-income countries that face overwhelming challenges in improving human development indicators. In these cases, social pensions may not constitute an efficient use of public resources, given that the elderly are a minority of the population and not necessarily the poorest of the poor.

Institutional Arrangements and Targeting Mechanisms

Chapter 12 is a critical part of the book and an important complement to the discussion initiated in chapters 10 and 11. The chapter addresses two policy issues. The first has to do with horizontal equity: why design specific programs for the elderly instead of including them in the general social assistance system? The second concerns the design of the targeting system, if a special program is in fact created. We have argued so far, based on first principles, that universal programs are likely to be suboptimal. Chapter 12 deepens the analysis and compares the cost-effectiveness of different targeting systems, using data for the Kyrgyz Republic, Niger, Panama, and the Republic of Yemen. It also explores some of the difficulties encountered when measuring poverty among the elderly.

SOCIAL PENSIONS VERSUS SOCIAL ASSISTANCE

On the question of specific programs for the elderly, one of the chapter's main conclusions is that under ideal conditions, the most efficient strategy for preventing poverty in old age would be to include the elderly within general social assistance programs. In fact, the authors show that the best-known transfer programs, in Brazil, Ecuador, Jamaica, and Mexico, are already doing that. Concerns that the elderly would not be appropriately reached or empowered by the general programs (see chapter 3) could be addressed by reviewing the targeting system or adding further conditionalities to current programs. The main argument in favor of this strategy is horizontal equity: in all countries there are many elderly who are poor, but there also many, and often more, poor children or poor individuals of working age.

There are, nonetheless, cases in which special institutional arrangements for the elderly would be needed: (a) when the elderly face a significantly higher risk of poverty than the rest of the population or represent a significant share of the poor; (b) when social assistance programs are not in place and considerations of political economy constrain their implementation (see also chapter 5); and (c) when informal institutions discriminate against the elderly and a direct transfer would constitute an important tool for empowering them (see chapter 3). These three cases are obviously not mutually exclusive and would need to be analyzed country by country. When they do not constitute a binding constraint, the rationale for specific transfer programs for the elderly would be considerably weakened.

TARGETING SYSTEMS

To analyze the design question, the authors of chapter 12 simulate the cost-effectiveness of a social pension paid at age 65 under different targeting arrangements and without any targeting. Five targeting systems are analyzed: a pure means test (or perfect targeting), and four types of proxy means test that differ only in their degree of accuracy in identifying the elderly poor. The analysis is conducted under the assumption that countries invest a fixed budget in the transfer program (0.5 percent of GDP in the Kyrgyz Republic, Niger, and the Republic of Yemen, and 0.1 percent in Panama). The total budget is divided by the total number of beneficiaries, and the level of the transfer therefore depends on the type of targeting.

Three of the results from the analysis are of particular importance. First, although a targeting system necessarily introduces exclusion errors, the elderly are not likely to be excluded more often than the rest of the population. Moreover, exclusion errors are more frequent around the eligibility line; in the bottom quintile only 10 percent of the poor elderly would be excluded.

Second, the most effective type of targeting system is the proxy means test. In particular, under a fixed budget, the proxy means test has a larger impact on poverty than a universal transfer. This is a very important result because it mimics a situation that is likely to be common across countries. Given fiscal constraints, the budget for social pensions is usually small, and if it is spread too thin (which is the case with a universal pension) it would fail to have a significant impact on poverty.

Finally, there are significant reductions in exclusion errors that can be achieved by estimating separate proxy means test formulas for the elderly and the rest of the population, or by introducing additional variables that are correlated with poverty among the elderly, or both. These improvements in the targeting system come at zero cost.

The overall message is that good analysis can help countries decide whether to choose universal or resource-tested pensions. Given fiscal constraints, universal pensions are unlikely to be the most efficient alternative. Countries can generate important savings by instead targeting limited public resources to those who need them the most. The classical argument against this claim is that targeting itself has a cost and that a good system requires considerable institutional capacity to be implemented. The reality, however, is that the costs of a targeting system have fallen considerably through learning-by-doing and that institutional capacity can be built gradually (see chapter 14). Countries therefore might want to consider up-front investments in proxy means tests, which will have a use beyond social pensions.

Preliminary Policy Guidance and Directions for Research

The findings of the book are briefly synthesized here.

Many of the problems behind low coverage rates in low- and middle-income countries are structural, cannot be resolved overnight, and fall outside the scope of social protection policy. A sustained expansion of the contributory system in the average low- or middle-income country would require fundamental changes in the productive structure of the economy and the functioning of its product and labor markets. To some extent, better design of the contributory system should improve incentives to enroll, thus contributing to increase coverage rates. Examples of interventions include better regulations and enhanced enforcement capacity, a stronger link between contributions and benefits, lower administrative charges, better quality of services, more transparency and accountability, and sound financial management. But these measures are unlikely to make a substantial difference, given the structural factors discussed above.

Against this background, social pensions and other retirement transfers emerge as an important instrument for bridging the coverage gap—at least for the time being—by focusing on individuals with no or limited saving capacity, who are more likely to be outside the contributory system. But the design and implementation issues are not straightforward. Take the case of social pensions. Although most countries that have introduced social pensions have been able to reduce poverty among the elderly, there are growing concerns that the programs themselves have contributed to institutionalizing the informal sector, at least in the case of middle-income countries such as Brazil, Chile, and Mexico. Other concerns relate to the opportunity cost of the resources invested, particularly in low-income countries, and the perhaps unnecessary fragmentation of the social assistance system.

SOME GUIDELINES

The purpose of this book is to analyze the main issues in the design of retirement income transfers and to offer preliminary guidelines that could help policy makers and practitioners strike a better balance between income protection and redistribution, on the one hand, and economic efficiency, on the other. Some features of an integrated strategy for expanding access to old-age income security emerge from the analysis

The first component of the strategy would be a general social assistance system that acts as a safety net for all the poor. This general system would also cover those who for various reasons, including long-term poverty, were not able to accumulate sufficient savings or contributory pensions to finance an adequate level of consumption during old age.

When this is not possible because of particular circumstances that affect the elderly, or because of the absence or malfunctioning of the social assistance system, social pensions that directly target the elderly would be introduced. A first decision is whether the social pension should be universal or targeted. We argue that much of the answer will come from the fiscal situation of the country and the extent of other social demands. When only a "small" budget can be efficiently mobilized, the country would be better off if the pension were means tested, allowing limited public resources to be concentrated on those who need them the most. As shown in chapter 12, not doing so could spread the transfers too thin without having a significant impact on poverty. Clearly, implementing a targeting system automatically introduces exclusion errors. To minimize these, proxy means tests with benefit formulas modified to more accurately identify the elderly would be adopted. Proxy means tests should also be considered for general social assistance systems that target all the poor.

The efficient design of a social pension would incorporate a few additional features. First is an eligibility age that is, ideally, higher than the statutory retirement age of the contributory system and is indexed to life expectancy in order to control program costs. Second, the level of the benefit would be low in relation to average earnings. Transfers that represent more than 15 or 20 percent of economywide average earnings are likely to start showing noticeable negative effects on labor supply and saving. Third, to reduce incentives to evade the contributory system, the social pension would incorporate a gradual withdrawal (claw-back) rate. Thus, low-income individuals who contribute to the mandatory system could, in principle, be eligible for part of the transfer, as well. This also implies that occupation or employment sector would not have any influence on eligibility for a social pension; the pension would be allocated only on the basis of age and the results of the resources test. As discussed in chapter 10, this feature seems particularly important for middle-income countries with more integrated formal and informal sectors.

The second component of the strategy would involve interventions that, by providing incentives for saving for individuals with some, but limited, capacity to save for the long term, could help reduce the cost of social assistance or social pensions. Matching contributions, discussed in chapter 13, could have a role here. These would target individuals unable to afford in full the mandatory contribution rates or to contribute continuously. Most such individuals would be operating in the informal sector in urban or rural areas. They would be low-income self-employed persons or salaried workers in small informal enterprises, sometimes earning less than the mandatory minimum wage. The transfer, by design, would be resource tested and would incorporate a cap (maximum accumulated capital). Cooperatives or community organizations could be used to mobilize the savings that would flow either to a national plan or to private pension providers, possibly including microfinance companies. Contribution rates could take the form of flat payments. As with the social pensions, individuals enrolled in the formal sector who met the resource test would also be eligible for the matching. Again, the matching would not be allocated on the basis of occupation or employment sector.[7]

The analysis suggests, however, that choosing the right matching level is important. A matching level that is too low could induce individuals to join the program, reduce saving, and still benefit from the conditional minimum pension. A matching level that is too high would be financially unsustainable and regressive. In general, there are still several questions surrounding the design of this type of program that require further analysis and thought.

PRIORITIES FOR FUTURE RESEARCH

We end this overview by suggesting a few general areas on which we believe future research should focus. A first challenge is to compile better data for policy analysis. There are three areas that we consider important. One is the measurement of poverty among the elderly. From our overview here, it is clear that more needs to be done to gain a better picture of the situation of the elderly around the world, based on common data sources and methods, and, in particular, a better understanding of the intrahousehold distribution of income. A second area is the measurement of the coverage gap. Outside Latin America and a few countries in Asia, we know little about how coverage rates vary by socioeconomic group and geographic area. Although the broad patterns discussed here are likely to hold, it is important to better understand and explain idiosyncratic variations across countries. A third, related, area is the study of labor market transitions. We have seen that coverage is not a continuous state; workers move into and out of the informal sector. It would be important to have a better understanding of the determinants of these transitions and to try to pin down the role played by social protection policies.

Turning to policy analysis, a priority is to build evidence about the potential role of matching contributions. This is an ambitious task that will require the design and implementation of well-monitored and well-evaluated pilots at the country level. A key question is what is the value of the take-up rate/matching elasticity. That is, the increase in the number of individuals who contribute during a given period of time as a function of the level of the matching. These pilots are also the only way to assess the main logistic, institutional, and administrative challenges related to implementation.

Finally, it is essential to start assessing the interactions of the pension system with other components of the social insurance system. Indeed, when workers decide to enroll in or evade social security, the decision is not solely based on the pension system. In most countries pension benefits are bundled with health insurance, unemployment insurance, and a series of transfer programs such as family allowances and child care. Ultimately, it is the cost and the perceived benefits of this bundle that matter, not only for workers but also for employers.

Notes

1. There exist other forms of ex post implicit or explicit intervention, such as programs to cover health expenditures, that share the objective of preventing poverty during old age, but these fall outside the scope of this book.

2. Chapter 2 also discusses some methodological challenges and data constraints that make it difficult to come up with precise estimates of coverage rates.

3. That there is overlap between systems does not mean that the two types of program should be analyzed separately, particularly in the case of middle- and high-income countries. As shown in chapter 10, differences in design between the two programs can influence choices about formal versus informal sector work. In other words, coverage rates are, in part, endogenously determined by the design of retirement income transfers.

4. Clearly, this indicator is problematic, since eligibility ages vary across countries. It is used here, however, to provide a common basis for comparison.

5. Notice that the allocation problem persists even if the government is able to mobilize additional resources to finance the program, since those resources also have an opportunity cost. One consideration is whether there are programs worth the distortion involved in mobilizing the additional resources. Another is whether, in comparison with all the programs that are worth the trouble, the retirement income transfer gives the biggest bang for the buck.

6. Countries could also rely on foreign grants, but we do not consider this a sustainable alternative. (See chapter 11 for a discussion of some of the issues.)

7. Some have argued that promoting formality has a positive externality that could justify higher expenditures in matching contributions, but this question is difficult to analyze and remains elusive.

References

Gasparini, Leonardo, Javier Alejo, Francisco Haimovich, Sergio Olivieri, and Leopoldo Tornarolli. 2007. "Poverty among the Elderly in Latin America and the Caribbean." Background paper for the *World Economic and Social Survey, 2007: The World Ageing Situation.* United Nations, New York. http://www.un.org/esa/policy/wess/wess2007files/backgroundpapers/lac.pdf.

Holzmann, Robert. 2003. "A Provocative Note on Coverage in Public Pension Schemes." In *The Three Pillars of Wisdom? A Reader on Globalization, World Bank Pension Models and Welfare Society,* ed. Arno Tausch, 85(99. New York: Nova Publishers.

Holzmann, Robert, and Ufuk Guven. 2009. *Adequacy of Retirement Income after Pension Reform in Central, Eastern, and Southern Europe: Eight Country Studies.* Washington, DC: World Bank.

Holzmann, Robert, and Richard Hinz. 2005. *Old Age Income Support in the 21st Century: An International Perspective on Pension Systems and Reform.* Washington, DC: World Bank.

Kakwani, Nanak, and Kalanidhi Subbarao. 2005. "Ageing and Poverty in Africa and the Role of Social Pensions." Working Paper 8, International Poverty Centre–United Nations Development Programme, Brasilia.

Kaniki, Sheshangai. 2007. "Mauritius Case Study." Economic Policy Research Institute, Cape Town, South Africa.

Levy, Santiago. 2008. *Good Intentions, Bad Outcomes: Social Policy, Informality, and Economic Growth in Mexico*. Washington, DC: Brookings Institution Press.

Palacios, Robert, and Oleksiy Sluchynsky. 2006. "Social Pensions Part I: Their Role in the Overall Pension System." Social Protection Discussion Paper 0601, World Bank, Washington, DC.

Poblete, Dante. 2005. "Grado de focalización óptimo de las pensiones no contributivas en el Tercer Mundo." Tesis de economía, Instituto de Economía, Pontificia Universidad Católica de Chile, Santiago.

Robalino, David, A. Mason, H. Ribe, and I. Walker. Forthcoming. "The Future of Social Protection in LAC: Adapting Programs to Labor Markets and Rethinking Redistribution." Human Development Department, Latin America and the Caribbean Region. World Bank, Washington, DC.

Robalino, David, Gudivada Venkateswara Rao, and Oleksiy Sluchynsky. 2007. "Preventing Poverty among the Elderly in MENA Countries: Role and Optimal Design of Old-Age Subsidies." Human Development Department, World Bank, Washington, DC.

Robalino, David, Edward Whitehouse, Anca Mataoanu, Alberto Musalem, and Oleksiy Sluchynsky. 2005. "Pensions in the Middle East and North Africa: Time for Change." Orientations in Development Series, Middle East and North Africa Region, World Bank, Washington, DC.

Samson, Michael. 2006. "Social Pensions and Poverty Reduction." Prepared for Social Pensions Symposium at the International Federation of Ageing, 8th Global Conference, "Global Ageing: The North-South Challenge," Copenhagen, May 30–June 3.

Valdés-Prieto, Salvador. 2008. "A Theory of Contribution Density and Implications for Pension Design." Social Protection Discussion Paper 0828, Pension Reform Primer Series, World Bank, Washington, DC.

CHAPTER 2

Measuring the Coverage Gap

Alvaro Forteza, Leonardo Lucchetti, and Montserrat Pallares-Miralles

The inability of most pension systems to reach significant swaths of the population in developing countries is currently recognized as one of their principal flaws. Measuring the coverage gap is the first step toward explaining and solving the problem. In this chapter, we review the main sources of information on the coverage gap, the methods that have been used to quantify it, and the main empirical findings. The available data show that less than 20 percent of the elderly are covered, and only about 25 percent of the labor force is contributing or accruing pension rights in the world. Coverage of the active population tends to decrease in direct proportion to the country's per capita GDP, and within individual countries it tends to be lower among the less educated, who typically earn less. Moreover, low income workers tend to have significant gaps in their contribution history. These workers often get raw deals from social security because they contribute for several years, but not long enough to receive full benefits. There are no clear signs of improvement in most countries, and there is some evidence of declining coverage in certain regions and population segments.

The inability of most pension systems to reach significant swaths of the population in developing countries is currently recognized as one of their principal flaws (Gill, Packard, and Yermo 2004; Holzmann and Hinz 2005). As a reflection of this concern, the World Bank has devoted considerable effort in recent years to measuring coverage worldwide—gathering data, checking their quality, and designing appropriate indicators (see, for example, Palacios and Pallares-Miralles 2000; Rofman and Lucchetti 2006). Measurement is important not only for raising awareness about the coverage issue but also for improving the diagnostics and the design of policy options. Building stronger information systems within pension schemes will not only help improve our understanding of the incomplete coverage but will also be part of the solution.

The literature has used a variety of data sources to measure coverage. Household surveys and information provided by social security administrations are the most common sources. Although most statistical institutes currently make available the microdata from the surveys (the information corresponding to each individual in the sample), administrative data are typically provided in the aggregate. Only in recent years have a few social security administrations begun to supply microdata from work history records. These longitudinal microdata open the door for the analysis of the accrual of pension rights by active workers. This is important because not only is coverage low, but those who are covered are not covered all the time.

The authors thank David Robalino and Landis MacKellar for useful comments on an earlier version.

Data can also be characterized by the number of times each individual is interviewed. The information is cross-sectional if there is one observation on each respondent and longitudinal if there are two or more observations. Most surveys interview persons only once and contain only contemporary information; some interview the same person more than once. Work history records kept by social security administrations are longitudinal data sets.

The literature has used various methods to measure the coverage of pension systems. The choice of methodology is often dictated by data availability. With aggregate data, the percentage of the population covered is a natural indicator. The notion of covered population requires some clarification because different concepts have been employed. For example, in the case of contributory systems, at least three different indicators of coverage of the active population are used, based on the numbers of affiliates, of contributors, or of active members of the program. Where cross-sectional microdata sets are used, coverage is generally measured using a binary variable that takes value one for those who are covered and zero for those who are not. This variable has been used to estimate the probability that an individual may have to contribute. Longitudinal data have allowed researchers to compute the percentage of time over the work course that each individual is covered—the contribution density. More recently, this type of data has been used to analyze the dynamics of coverage, looking at the transitions between being and not being a contributor.

In the next two sections we describe and assess alternative data sources and methods of measuring coverage. We then summarize the main empirical findings. These sections draw extensively on results in Rofman and Lucchetti (2006), Bucheli, Forteza, and Rossi (forthcoming), and Hinz and Pallares-Miralles (forthcoming). Although the chapter addresses coverage worldwide, we illustrate some points by referring to specific regions and countries for which we have more data. The final section offers an assessment of the main challenges.

Data Sources

There are two main sources of information that can be used to measure coverage: administrative data and household surveys. Both have their advantages and disadvantages. One of the main advantages of using administrative data to compute coverage is that it is the same information that administrations use to manage the system. Unlike survey data, administrative data do not rely on surveys, respondents' recall, or their understanding of their current status in the social security system but, rather, on their true status according to the administration. Some administrative (usually aggregate) data are easy to collect from annual reports or other institutional documents. For example, most pension agencies and social security institutions release annual data on membership that can be used to monitor coverage trends over time.

On the downside, administrative records usually do not provide detailed information about the population's sociodemographic characteristics, and the records may be plagued by issues of availability and quality. In countries with multiple pension systems, it is common for records to be readily available for the largest national schemes but less accessible for smaller programs. Where pension systems are very fragmented, accessing all the data is even more complicated. Once the data from several schemes have been collected, there may be problems of aggregation because of coverage overlap (the fact that some individuals are covered by more than one pension program). As for quality, many pension systems suffer from incorrect records or duplication.[1] Other problems include corruption, evasion, and abuse of the pension systems, all of which sometimes make the records unreliable.

Household surveys collect data that can be used to estimate coverage, along with some sociodemographic and economic characteristics of individuals. This additional information, usually absent in administrative records, is important for describing individuals who lack adequate coverage. Longitudinal and cross-national comparability are, however, affected by problems of consistency and definition, which arise from differences in coverage (some surveys are national, other are urban only) and in wording (some surveys ask about affiliation in pension schemes, others about actual contributions). In some cases individuals are asked whether they are pensioners, whereas in others they are asked about sources of income, including pensions. Finally, those interviewed may not be representative of all individuals.

The estimations of coverage presented in this document are based on a variety of data sources. Much of the information was provided by national agencies and social security institutions; other material was taken from household surveys. We also used data collected by several international organizations.[2]

Methods

Even where data are available and reliable, there are further challenges, conceptual and methodological in nature, in measuring coverage. Very often, when discussing pension coverage, reference is made to those individuals who are receiving a pension or retirement benefit. But in earnings-related pension systems, it is also important to look at the phase during which individuals accrue pension rights.[3] More generally, we are interested in knowing the extent to which people who have not yet reached pensionable age will be entitled to a pension when they do attain that age. The most serious conceptual and methodological problems arise when considering coverage among active workers, since the definition of this status is not always clear. Also, whereas most studies use snapshot indicators of coverage, in most social security systems accrual of pension rights depends on the individual's contribution history. Lack of longitudinal data has been an obstacle to analysis of the issue, but in recent years some social security administrations have begun to facilitate this type of information.

When trying to accurately gauge the coverage of the elderly, still other problems arise, as outlined next.

COVERAGE OF THE ACTIVE POPULATION

Indicators based on cross-sectional databases. The most common indicator of social security coverage before retirement is the percentage of the workforce that is contributing to a pension scheme. Several factors must be carefully considered in order to correctly measure coverage of the labor force, particularly when comparisons across countries and over time are made.

1. The labor force is not defined the same way in all countries. Rural areas may not be included; most (but not all) countries exclude "family workers" and unemployed persons not seeking work; and there are differences in the age limits used in measuring the economically active population, in the treatment of emigrants, and, certainly, in the definition of the informal labor force.[4]

2. The numerator in the coverage index may be the number of affiliates, of contributors, or of active members. Affiliates are those individuals who are enrolled in pension institutions, even if they are not currently contributing or accruing pension rights. Contributors are individuals who are actively contributing to the system. Active members are individuals who are accruing pension rights while they work, even if they do not contribute. The estimation of coverage varies widely, depending on the specific groupings used.

The main reason for using the number of affiliates to compute coverage of the labor force is that this information is usually readily available. Even those pension systems with the most deficient administrations are generally capable of estimating the number of workers enrolled. Yet this indicator poses serious problems, since many individuals enrolled in the systems are not actually eligible for benefits. Many, if not most, of the social security institutions in developing countries have "dormant accounts" of workers who at some point contributed to the system but who are not currently doing so because they are unemployed or inactive or have joined the informal sector. The records of pension institutions also tend to exaggerate the number of actual affiliates because erroneous or duplicate records are rarely corrected. A phenomenon very often observed, particularly in developing countries, is high mobility of individuals between unemployment, informal employment, and formal employment. In short, many social security institutions have in their records individuals who will never receive a pension. Using the number of affiliates to measure coverage may, consequently, be very misleading.

Several authors use the number of current contributors rather than affiliates, to avoid the overestimation that may arise when the latter number is used. But some pension schemes do not require contributions in order to recognize pension rights, and a measure of coverage based on contributors might underestimate the total number of workers protected by the scheme. The problem can be overcome by using the number of active members to compute coverage of the labor force. This definition includes both contributors and those who are noncontributors but are nevertheless accruing pension rights in an earnings-related pension scheme.

As an indicator of social protection of individuals who have not reached pensionable age, the rate of labor force coverage has the obvious limitation of not providing information about the population outside the labor force. This population may be covered by noncontributory programs, informal networks, or their own savings, but the standard indicator of labor force participation in the social security system gives no information about their status. The information that is available about coverage of the nonelderly population not in the labor force is very limited. For this reason, we will follow the usual practice of focusing on labor force coverage.

Indicators based on longitudinal databases. Useful as they are, snapshot indicators such as the rate of coverage of the labor force are insufficient for describing coverage of the active population because they do not capture the dynamics of coverage. Coverage is usually a temporary status among the active population. Individuals do not contribute throughout their adult lives; they may not be continuously active, or they may be unemployed, working in noncovered jobs, or evading contribution. Pension entitlements depend on contribution history rather than on the contribution's status at any given time.

Two approaches have been used in the literature to describe and analyze individual contribution histories. The first looks at the proportion of time that individuals spend contributing. This measure, contribution density, is a direct estimate of contribution probability.

Indirect estimates can be drawn from econometric models in which the probability of contributing can be computed from the observed patterns of contribution status.

The second approach examines the probability of transition between contributing and not contributing. The statistical literature known as survival analysis offers several methods for estimating these probabilities. One is to compute transition rates directly as a proportion of individuals in any given category making a transition during each period. (Kaplan-Meier estimation is an example of this nonparametric approach.) It is also possible to fit parametric statistical models of the probability of transition and use them to test hypotheses about factors that affect contribution history.

Contribution densities and transition probabilities have been used to project work histories. Bucheli, Forteza, and Rossi (forthcoming) used these projections to estimate the risk that several groups of contributors to Uruguay's main social security program incur of failing to accumulate the number of years of contribution required to access an ordinary pension. Berstein, Larrain, and Pino (2006) projected work histories to estimate the proportion of contributors to the Chilean pension system who would not be eligible for a minimum pension because of insufficient contributions.

The analysis of social security coverage on the basis of flows in and out of contribution parallels the flow approach to labor markets advocated by Blanchard and Diamond (1992), Davis and Haltiwanger (1992), Mortensen and Pissarides (1994), and Davis, Faberman, and Haltiwanger (2006), among others. This approach exploits the information content of gross flows. As Blanchard and Diamond (1992, 356) put it, "When data on gross flows are available, looking at them is clearly more instructive than looking at the stocks." Davis, Faberman, and Haltiwanger (2006, 3) begin their survey of the flow approach to labor markets by emphasizing that "more than 10 percent of U.S. workers separate from their employers each quarter." A similar observation can be made about social security coverage. Bucheli, Forteza, and Rossi (2007) report rates of transition between contributing and not contributing as high as 12 percent per *month* for some categories of workers and ages. In view of these considerations, a flow approach to social security coverage seems a promising route.

COVERAGE OF THE ELDERLY

As mentioned above, measuring coverage of the elderly poses fewer difficulties than measuring coverage of the economically active population since, instead of measuring the accrual of rights to a potential benefit, the indicators are based on the number of individuals actually receiving benefits. Yet this criterion also has its limitations. For instance, some elderly individuals may qualify for retirement benefits but prefer to continue working. Others may not want to apply for the retirement benefits due to them because they have enough alternative resources. Some analysts might argue that spouses or dependent relatives of benefit recipients should be included as covered; others might count only the recipients.

The following main concepts should be carefully considered when measuring coverage of the elderly, particularly when drawing comparisons across countries and over time. First, it is important to note that there are different types of beneficiary. Most of the mandatory pension programs in the world provide not only old-age pensions but also pensions for disability, survivorship, and other circumstances.[5]

Second, under some systems individuals have the right to receive several pensions. In some cases the pensions are provided by the same institution; in others, the individual can receive pensions from various institutions, which complicates the task of measuring coverage through the use of administrative records.

Third, some countries have noncontributory pension schemes, usually geared to the needs of the elderly, in which benefits are assigned either to the entire elderly population (universal models) or only to those who require some sort of assistance (means-tested targeted models). Recipients of noncontributory pensions should be included as covered, but in a number of countries such information is either unavailable or unclear.

Finally, there exist pension systems that provide only lump-sum payments. Some argue that beneficiaries of these payments should be regarded as covered, while others maintain that only recipients of regular payments should be considered covered. Our preferred definition of elderly coverage includes those individuals who are regularly receiving a pension; lump-sum payments do not exactly provide old-age income security because individuals tend to spend those transfers too rapidly.

We are concerned with the percentage of the population above a certain age that receives pensions. This indicator can usually be computed from household surveys. Administrative data are often less useful because the number of beneficiaries is not usually grouped by age. It is always possible to measure coverage of the elderly by dividing the total number of beneficiaries by the number of people above a certain age, but this could be misleading because many beneficiaries are not, in fact, elderly. Indeed, the age variation among the disabled and survivors is considerable. Even old-age pensions could include significant numbers of relatively young beneficiaries because of early retirement.

When using administrative data as the main source for measuring coverage of the elderly, careful consideration should be given to various factors that might lead to overestimation of the coverage rates. In some cases, for instance, pensions are being paid to people who have left the country and thus are not included in the population base. Some social security administrations do not receive automatic notification when a pensioner dies. Fraud, whether intentional or unwitting, may contribute to overestimation of elderly coverage.

Patterns Observed

In this section we look at the empirical evidence on each coverage issue in turn.

COVERAGE OF THE LABOR FORCE

Figure 2.1 shows coverage of the labor force by country. The structure of coverage frequently depends on the age of the system. Historically, coverage was often provided first to government employees and to members of the armed forces, and there are still a few countries that only have pension schemes for public employees. Coverage was eventually extended to workers in industry and commerce and finally to all wage earners and salaried employees. In many countries this evolution is reflected in fragmentation into various special schemes, the most common being for public employees, military personnel and civil servants, teachers, and employees of public utilities.

About 25 percent of the global labor force is currently accruing pension rights. This average hides the great variation that exists both among and within countries. Countries with higher per capita gross domestic product (GDP) tend to have higher coverage of the labor force (figure 2.2).[6] The correlation probably encompasses several factors, including

FIGURE 2.1 **Coverage as measured by active members of mandatory pension systems as share of labor force, worldwide, early 2000s**

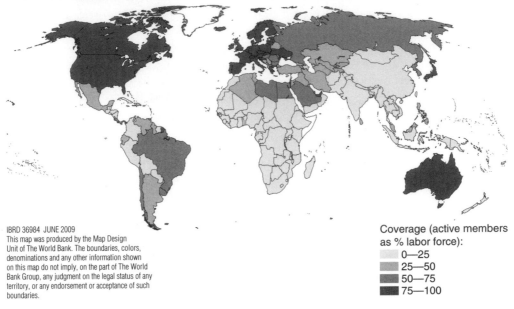

IBRD 36984 JUNE 2009
This map was produced by the Map Design
Unit of The World Bank. The boundaries, colors,
denominations and any other information shown
on this map do not imply, on the part of The World
Bank Group, any judgment on the legal status of any
territory, or any endorsement or acceptance of such
boundaries.

Coverage (active members
as % labor force):
0—25
25—50
50—75
75—100

SOURCE: Hinz and Pallares-Miralles, forthcoming.

FIGURE 2.2 **Relationship between coverage of the active population and GDP per capita, selected countries, early 2000s**

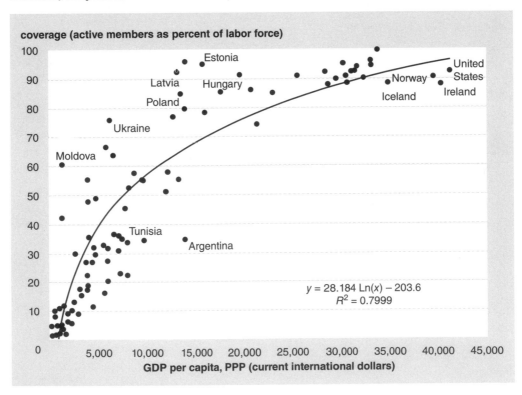

coverage (active members as percent of labor force)

$$y = 28.184 \, Ln(x) - 203.6$$
$$R^2 = 0.7999$$

GDP per capita, PPP (current international dollars)

SOURCE: Hinz and Pallares-Miralles, forthcoming.

NOTE: GDP, gross domestic product; PPP, purchasing power parity.

better enforcement capacity in high-income countries and greater capacity to contribute. Deviations from the line show the importance of country idiosyncrasies stemming from history and from political choices. For example, former socialist countries have higher coverage than one would expect from their per capita GDPs.

Workers tend to have lower coverage rates in agriculture than in other sectors of the economy, and countries with large agriculture sectors accordingly tend to have lower coverage (table 2.1). By contrast, services tend to show comparatively high coverage rates, and countries with large service sectors often have higher coverage rates. The impact of services on coverage is, however, smaller and less robust than that of agriculture.

High-income countries. When looking at the patterns by region, we observe that in most of the high-income countries of the Organisation for Economic Co-operation and Development (OECD), coverage is estimated to be above 90 percent.[7] Coverage of the labor force might, however, be overestimated in some OECD countries that do not count informal sector workers as part of the labor force. The uncovered population may include special exempt groups (for example, certain self-employed individuals, part-time workers, and so on) and the unemployed.

TABLE 2.1 **Coverage of the labor force worldwide, by sector and region**

	1	2	3	4
GDP per capita (U.S. dollars)	1.93*** (13.14)	1.41*** (8.74)	1.10*** (6.86)	1.08*** (6.54)
Sector				
Agriculture as percent of GDP		−0.63*** (−2.91)	−0.68*** (−3.46)	−0.62*** (−3.05)
Services as percent of GDP		0.53*** (3.11)	0.35** (2.17)	0.17 (1.02)
Region				
Europe			19.00*** (4.70)	27.45*** (4.69)
Asia				12.67 (0.26)
North America				88.57 (0.85)
Central America and the Caribbean				17.63*** (3.02)
South America				21.86 (0.36)
Oceania				252.20 (1.57)
Intercept	24.45*** (8.94)	82.17 (0.70)	175.48 (1.62)	21.38* (1.82)
N	108	104	104	104
R²	0.62	0.74	0.79	0.82

SOURCE: Authors' computations based on World Bank data.

NOTE: GDP, gross domestic product. Figures in parentheses are t-statistics.

*Significant at 10 percent **Significant at 5 percent ***Significant at 1 percent

Eastern Europe and the former Soviet Union. The countries of Eastern Europe and the former Soviet Union have had much higher coverage rates than would have been predicted by their income per capita, particularly at the beginning of the last decade. This outcome was a function of high public sector employment and collectivized agriculture, which made tax collection a matter of transfers within the state apparatus. The transition led to the emergence of small private firms, which are much more difficult to monitor. Along with early retirement, unemployment, and migration, the growth of the informal sector is shifting coverage rates in the region back to levels found in market economies with similar income levels.

Middle East and North Africa. The coverage of mandatory pension systems in the Middle East and North Africa is low to moderate. The Arab Republic of Egypt has one of the highest rates in the region, followed by Jordan and Tunisia; the Republic of Yemen has the lowest.

Sub-Saharan Africa. Coverage in Sub-Saharan African countries has always been low, and it declined even further during the economic crisis that hit the region in the 1980s. Some countries still lack a pension system beyond that covering public employees or other special professions. Mauritius has the highest coverage rate—about 50 percent of its labor force; Cape Verde has a coverage rate of around 27 percent. The remaining countries have coverage rates lower than 20 percent—some fall between 5 and 10 percent, and most countries cover less than 5 percent of their labor force.

Asia and the Pacific. Pension systems in Asia and the Pacific commonly have a low coverage rate. As in most developing countries, coverage is usually limited to public sector workers and to some private sector employees working in the formal sector. As we have seen, the extent of coverage of private sector employees is strongly related to the structure of the labor market. In countries with large agriculture and urban informal sectors, coverage tends to be lower than in countries with a more organized private sector. In India, for instance, less than 10 percent of the working population is protected in old age, and in China coverage is around 20 percent. Only in more industrialized countries, such as the Republic of Korea, Malaysia, and Singapore, does coverage exceed 60 percent.

Latin America and the Caribbean. Latin America is a region in which a great deal of effort has been devoted to measuring and modeling coverage (Rofman and Lucchetti 2006)—albeit coverage of the workforce is not very different from what would be expected from the region's income per capita. This means, however, that the labor force is only partially protected: nearly half of the countries have coverage rates below 30 percent (figure 2.3). The long tradition of several of the region's social security institutions and the profound reforms that several countries have implemented since the 1980s have not been enough to overcome this situation. Furthermore, there are no general signs of improvement in recent years, and some countries are actually experiencing declining coverage.

Coverage is naturally higher among the employed than among the active population as a whole, but significant segments of those employed remain unprotected in Latin America. Salaried workers have much higher coverage rates than the self-employed, and salaried workers in small firms exhibit much lower coverage rates than those in large firms. Recent trends show no improvement—and even some decline—in coverage among the unemployed, the self-employed, and salaried workers in small firms.

FIGURE 2.3 **Coverage rates of the economically active population, Latin America, 1990s and early 2000s**

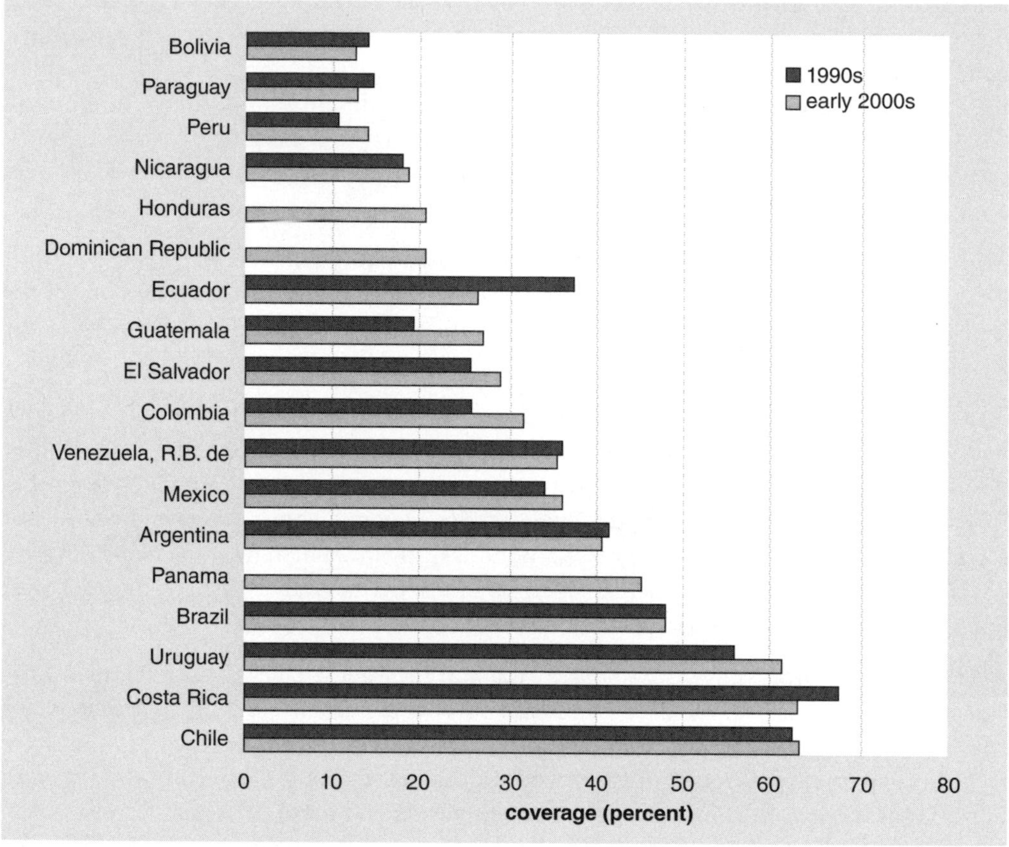

SOURCE: Rofman, Lucchetti, and Ourens 2008.

NOTE: Data periods are as follows: Argentina, 1995–2006; Bolivia, 1999–2005; Brazil, 1995–2006; Chile, 1996–2006; Colombia, 1996–2006; Costa Rica, 1995–2006; Dominican Republic, 2006; Ecuador, 1995–2006; El Salvador, 1995–2005; Guatemala, 1998–2006; Honduras, 2006; Mexico, 1998–2006; Nicaragua, 1998–2005; Paraguay, 1999–2006; Peru, 1999–2006; Uruguay, 1995–2006; República Bolivariana de Venezuela, 1995–2006.

Coverage of the labor force varies widely by sector of activity. Agriculture and construction often exhibit comparatively low coverage rates in Latin America. Although manufacturing traditionally had comparatively high coverage rates, steady declines have taken place in recent years in most countries. Not surprisingly, the public sector shows higher rates of coverage than the private sector. Yet in Argentina, Bolivia, and Peru less than 80 percent of public sector workers are covered by social security.

Particularly worrisome is the fact that coverage in Latin America is especially low among the less educated and among low-income workers. These coverage gaps tend to be larger in countries with lower average coverage.

Incomplete coverage seems to be associated with highly fragmented contribution histories. Because of this discontinuity, a significant proportion of workers may not accumulate the required number of contribution years to access benefits. Berstein, Larrain, and Pino (2006) estimate that most of the contributors to the Chilean pension system who do not accumulate funds sufficient to self-finance a pension above the minimum pension guarantee will not attain the 20 years of contribution required to access benefits. Indeed, about half of the retirees will not get a pension above the minimum, and only about 2 percent will be eligible for the guarantee. The study challenges the previously dominant view that many workers would be receiving the minimum pension guarantee because of insufficient accumulation in their savings accounts. This important result was a contributing factor in the design of the reform that was passed by the Chilean parliament in January 2008 and that, among other things, eliminated the 20-years requirement.

Bucheli, Forteza, and Rossi (forthcoming) report some distinctive patterns in the transitions between contributing and not contributing to the main social security program in Uruguay. First, and for both categories, transition rates decline over time. In other words, the chances of remaining a contributor rise as individuals put in more time contributing, but, conversely, the chances of staying out of the system rise as individuals spend time not contributing. History and luck early in the work life seem to be crucial in determining a person's working career. Second, low-income workers face a higher risk of ceasing to be contributors and have lower chances of beginning to contribute than high-income workers. This is consistent with the lower density of contributions observed among low-income workers. Third, young workers are more mobile than mature workers. They therefore face a higher risk of leaving the category of contributors but also of leaving the category of noncontributors. Finally, economic downturns raise the probability that private workers who are contributing will stop doing so and reduce the probability that private workers who are not contributing will start doing so.

Using the estimated transition rates, Bucheli, Forteza, and Rossi (forthcoming) project that only 25 percent of contributors in Uruguay will have accumulated the requisite 35 years of contributions to access an ordinary pension at the normal retirement age. The risk of not satisfying the years requirement rises with lower incomes. For example, a man working in the private sector has an almost 68 percent chance of accumulating 35 years of contributions by age 60 if he belongs to the richest quintile but less than a 1 percent chance if he belongs to the poorest quintile. These somber projections seem to be at odds with the currently high proportion of older persons receiving pensions in Uruguay, until one takes into account the limited ability of the administration to enforce the eligibility conditions. Lacking work history records, the social security administration is in a weak position to enforce the 35-years rule. That requirement, however, is likely to become increasingly binding in coming years because in 1996 the social security administration began to keep records of contributions. The results of the study had much to contribute to the social security dialogue that the government launched in 2007 to assess options for reform and to the reform law passed by parliament in 2008.

COVERAGE OF THE ELDERLY

Less than 20 percent of the elderly in the world are covered by pensions. Coverage varies widely across countries, and there is a positive correlation between the percentage of elderly covered by social security and the level of development as measured by income per capita (figure 2.4). But elderly coverage is not only determined by the level of development; political options make a big difference. The experience of the former socialist countries is particularly telling. On average, the rates of elderly coverage in these countries

FIGURE 2.4 **Relationship between elderly coverage and GDP per capita, selected countries, early 2000s**

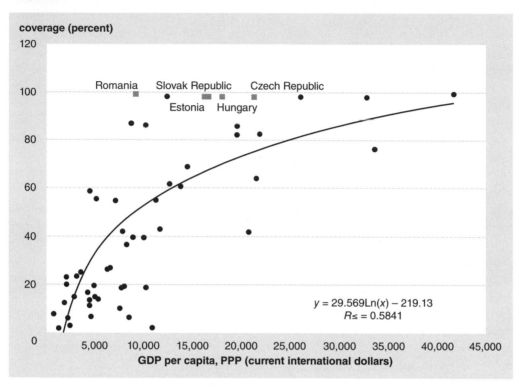

SOURCE: Authors' computations based on World Bank data.

NOTE: GDP, gross domestic product; PPP, purchasing power parity. Elderly coverage is the proportion of the population age 65 and above that is receiving a benefit from social security.

currently surpass the expected values based on GDP per capita by as much as 26 percentage points.

In most developing countries pension coverage of the elderly remains low, leaving the majority of the elderly to the care of their families. With growing workforce mobility, this support is diminishing, leaving more elderly people in a vulnerable situation.

High informality in labor markets and the small size of social pensions in most developing countries help explain the coverage gap. Contributory programs are by far the largest pension programs in the majority of developing countries. Although this pattern is not a peculiarity of these countries, contributory programs are less effective in providing social protection in old age in developing than in developed countries because of the high incidence of labor informality in the former. In addition, many developing countries have no or only small social pension programs (figure 2.5).

The percentage of elderly covered in high-income OECD countries is more than 80 percent, on average. In Eastern Europe and the former Soviet Union, privatization and enterprise restructuring in the 1990s led to open unemployment. One important reaction to this development was to ease early retirement conditions, either through explicit programs designed to absorb redundant labor via the pension system or through an informal policy of loosening eligibility requirements, often through the disability pension program.

FIGURE 2.5 **Social pensions as share of per capita GDP, early 2000s**

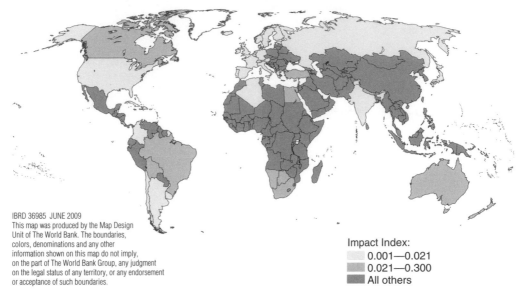

IBRD 36985 JUNE 2009
This map was produced by the Map Design
Unit of The World Bank. The boundaries,
colors, denominations and any other
information shown on this map do not imply,
on the part of The World Bank Group, any judgment
on the legal status of any territory, or any endorsement
or acceptance of such boundaries.

Impact Index:
 0.001—0.021
 0.021—0.300
 All others

SOURCE: Palacios and Sluchynsky 2006.

NOTE: The impact index is derived by multiplying recipients as a percent of the population age 65 and over by benefits as percent of income per capita. The category "All others" consists of economies with no social pensions or for which no data are available.

Currently, around 18 percent of the region's population is receiving some type of pension, and more than 90 percent of the elderly receive benefits. Coverage among actives has decreased, however, and coverage among the elderly is likely to fall in the future.

In the Middle East and North Africa, around 40 percent of the elderly receive some type of pension. Survivors' benefits are often awarded liberally to relatives beyond the immediate family. Around 80 percent of the elderly in Malta are receiving pensions. The figure is about 60 percent in Tunisia, 50 percent in Egypt, and more than 40 percent in Jordan.

In South Asia, on average, less than 20 percent—and in most countries, less than 10 percent—of the elderly currently receive pensions. In East Asia around 25 percent of the elderly receive some type of pension benefit. Korea has the highest coverage rate in the region.

In Sub-Saharan Africa less than 20 percent of the elderly are covered, and in most countries coverage is less than 10 percent. The countries where social pensions are important, such as Botswana, Namibia, and South Africa, are exceptions.

About 55 percent of the population aged 65 and above in Latin America receives a pension. There is much heterogeneity in the region, with rates of elderly coverage ranging from about 15 percent in Guatemala to more than 80 percent in Brazil and Uruguay (figure 2.6). Rofman, Lucchetti, and Ourens (2008) categorize countries in three groups according to the protection they afford to income in old age: (a) those that offer low protection to everyone (the Dominican Republic, Ecuador, El Salvador, Guatemala, Mexico, and Paraguay); (b) those that protect mainly the rich (Colombia, Panama, Peru, and the

FIGURE 2.6 **Coverage rates of the elderly, Latin America and the Caribbean, 1990s and early 2000s**

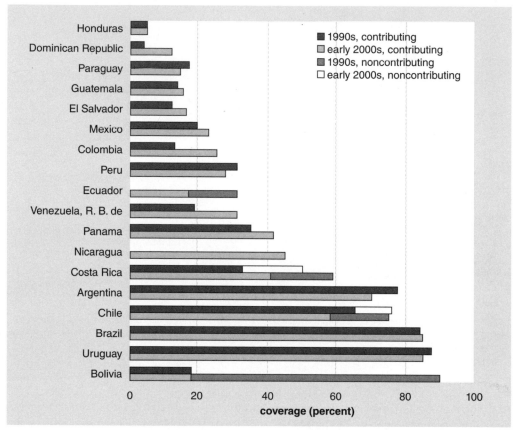

SOURCE: Rofman, Lucchetti, and Ourens 2008.

NOTE: Data periods are as follows: Argentina, 1995–2006; Bolivia, 1999–2005; Brazil, 1995–2006; Chile, 1996–2006; Colombia, 1996–2006; Costa Rica, 1995–2006; Dominican Republic, 1996–2006; Ecuador, 2006; El Salvador, 1997–2005; Guatemala, 1998–2006; Honduras, 1995–2006; Mexico, 1998–2006; Nicaragua, 2005; Panama, 1995–2006; Paraguay, 1999–2006; Peru, 1999–2006; Uruguay, 1995–2006; República Bolivariana de Venezuela, 1995–2006.

República Bolivariana de Venezuela); and (c) those that give adequate protection to everyone (Argentina, Bolivia, Brazil, Chile, Costa Rica, and Uruguay).

In most countries in Latin America, elderly coverage tends to increase with income per capita and level of education. The most vulnerable groups are often barely covered. Furthermore, recent years have witnessed a decline in coverage among the most impoverished groups. As a result, some of the countries that currently protect most of the population seem to be moving to protect only the rich. Coverage rates tend to increase with age, and the gap in coverage between age groups is steadily increasing in countries with higher coverage. As expected, most beneficiaries are urban residents, and coverage is much lower in rural than in urban areas. Women tend to have lower coverage rates; in many countries coverage rates for elderly men are twice those for their female counterparts.

Over the last decade there have been no clear signs of improvement in most developing countries, and a few countries have witnessed a decline in the proportion of older persons covered. There are, however, some remarkable exceptions, as described in box 2.1.

BOX 2.1 **Expansion of social security coverage for the elderly in the Philippines, the Republic of Korea, and Bolivia**

The Asia and Pacific Region is going through a particularly speedy demographic transition from high to low rates of fertility and mortality. An evolution that spanned a century or two in Europe is being compressed into a few generations. Asia's population is aging rapidly. Given that the coverage of pension systems is still very low and that informal support is crumbling, the need for some kind of old-age support to keep the elderly out of poverty is becoming increasingly apparent.

Some countries are already very aware of the problem and, particularly after the return of economic stability to the region, have put substantial effort into expanding coverage of their pension systems. Two countries that managed to increase coverage during the last few years are the Philippines and the Republic of Korea. Member registrations in their social security institutions have increased considerably. The compliance level, operational enhancements, and prudent investments have been key factors in expanding coverage.

The Philippines has initiated an expansion aimed at covering not only employed people but also the self-employed and voluntary members. It recently launched a campaign to make members aware that even in difficult times, it is prudent to continue active membership. Even if participants become unemployed, they are encouraged to continue paying as voluntary members at a salary bracket they can afford so that there are no gaps in their contribution records and they can obtain larger benefits, especially when contingencies arise. In only six years, 5 million members have been added to the rolls of the Philippine Social Security System.

Bolivia and Korea also managed to expand social security coverage in recent years. For a detailed discussion of these experiences, see chapters 5 and 8.

Conclusions

Pension systems are not currently reaching most of the world's vulnerable people. Less than 20 percent of the elderly are covered, and only about 25 percent of the labor force is contributing or accruing pension rights. Moreover, coverage of the active population tends to decrease in direct proportion to the country's per capita GDP, and within individual countries it tends to be lower among the less educated, who typically earn less. Coverage of mandatory pension systems is particularly low in South Asia and Sub-Saharan Africa, where less than 10 percent of the workforce is protected.

In addition, many active workers who participate in contributory programs have significant gaps in their contribution histories. These workers often get raw deals from social security because they contribute for several years, but not long enough to receive full benefits. The situation is especially worrisome because highly fragmented contribution histories seem to predominate among low-income workers.

There are no clear signs of improvement in most countries, and there is some evidence of declining coverage in certain regions and population segments. The former socialist countries are the clearest example; even though they still provide comparatively wide social protection, coverage has been steadily decreasing in recent years. In the 1990s some Latin American countries experienced reductions in coverage that went hand in hand with the partial deregulation of labor markets and the expansion of self-employment. It is also possible that in some countries, particularly those that have only recently organized their work history records, the increasing ability of administrations to enforce the fulfillment of the contribution requirements will leave many contributors with a diminished pension or with none at all.

Contributory systems link pensions to labor markets. Countries that have highly informal labor markets also have low contributory pension coverage, and economic activities that are less amenable to formalization are harder to cover. Self-employment and agriculture usually exhibit low coverage in developing countries, and therefore social security coverage tends to be low in countries in which these sectors represent an important part of economic activity. Conversely, coverage is usually high in the public sector, and so the participation of the public sector in the economy is positively correlated with social security coverage across countries.

Many pension schemes currently offer poor incentives to participate. The incentives to evade a mandatory pension system are likely to be stronger, the higher is the tax wedge and the lower is the return that workers expect to get from the system. The loose links between contributions and benefits that prevail in many schemes do not seem to provide good incentives to contribute. Yet, surprisingly, systematic empirical evidence to support this "common-sense" view is fairly weak. The failure of Latin American pension systems to expand coverage in the aftermath of the reforms that introduced savings accounts contributed to skepticism about this perspective. More empirical analysis seems to be necessary to clarify this important point.

Low coverage is also indicative of significant institutional weaknesses. In most developing countries legal coverage is almost universal, but effective coverage is a far cry from this ideal. The large gap between legal and effective coverage highlights the low capacity of the administrations to enforce social security laws. Under such circumstances, the pension system itself becomes informal, and the rule of law gives way in part to discretionary decisions. Weak information systems are usually key ingredients of such informal pension systems.

One of the most significant and frequent information flaws in contributory pension schemes is lack of contribution records. With no records, administrations cannot verify that eligibility conditions are fulfilled or compute the accrued benefit. This shortcoming has macro and micro implications. At the macro level the estimate of the pension system's contingent liabilities becomes highly uncertain. The government loses the capacity to adjust parameters in due time, and the pension system generates macro instability. At the micro level participants in the pension system do not know what benefit they will receive, and the system becomes unreliable. As the recent literature on tax morale shows, citizens are less willing to contribute when they feel that the system is unreliable and unfair. Weak information systems are therefore likely to compound the low coverage problem.

Notes

1. Too often, the information provided in pension systems' annual bulletins is not consistent with the individual records kept by statistical or actuarial departments in the same institution.

2. The organizations from which data were drawn are the Asian Development Bank (ADB); EUROSTAT; the International Labour Organization (ILO); the International Social Security Association (ISSA); the U.S. Social Security Administration (SSA); the Organisation for Economic Co-operation and Development (OECD); the International Monetary Fund (IMF); and the World Health Organization (WHO).

3. We prefer the term "earnings-related pension systems" to "contributory pension systems" because of the existence of noncontributory schemes in which workers accrue rights depending on past earnings. This pattern is relatively common among civil servants and in some specific professions.

4. In countries with high percentages of emigrant workers, the coverage rate (defined as a percentage of the labor force) varies enormously depending on whether emigrants are included in the labor force.

5. In many countries other pensions are provided by the same pension scheme to parents, siblings, unmarried daughters, and so on.

6. A simple regression of coverage on GDP per capita, as is presented in figure 2.2, explains as much as 80 percent of total variation in coverage across countries.

7. Because New Zealand has a social pension system, the country has zero coverage under this definition of active members as a share of the labor force.

References

Berstein, Solange, Guillermo Larraín, and Francisco Pino. 2006. "Chilean Pension Reform: Coverage Facts and Policy Alternatives." *Economía* 6 (2): 227–79.

Blanchard, Olivier, and Peter Diamond. 1992. "The Flow Approach to Labor Markets." *American Economic Review* 82 (2): 354–59.

Bucheli, Marisa, Alvaro Forteza, and Ianina Rossi. 2007. "Work Histories and the Access to Contributory Pensions in Uruguay: Some Facts and Policy Options." Working Paper, Departamento de Economía, Facultad de Ciencias Sociales, Universidad de la República (FCS–UdelaR); Pension Reform Primer, World Bank, Washington, DC.

———. Forthcoming. "Work Histories and the Access to Contributory Pensions: The Case of Uruguay." *Journal of Pension Economics and Finance*.

Davis, Steven, and John Haltiwanger. 1992. "Gross Job Creation, Gross Job Destruction, and Employment Reallocation." *Quarterly Journal of Economics* 107 (3): 819–63.

Davis, Steven J., R. Jason Faberman, and John Haltiwanger. 2006. "The Flow Approach to Labor Markets: New Data Sources and Micro-Macro Links." *Journal of Economic Perspectives* 20 (3): 3–26.

Gill, Indermit S., Truman G. Packard, and Juan Yermo. 2004. *Keeping the Promise of Social Security in Latin America.* Palo Alto, CA: Stanford Economics and Finance, Stanford University Press; Washington, DC: World Bank.

Hinz, Richard, and Montserrat Pallares-Miralles. Forthcoming. "International Patterns of Pension Provision II." Social Protection Discussion Paper, World Bank, Washington, DC.

Holzmann, Robert, and Richard Hinz. 2005. *Old Age Income Support in the 21st Century: An International Perspective on Pension Systems and Reform.* Washington, DC: World Bank.

Mortensen, Dale, and Christopher Pissarides. 1994. "Job Creation and Job Destruction in the Theory of Unemployment." *Review of Economic Studies* 61: 397–415.

Palacios, Robert, and Montserrat Pallares-Miralles. 2000. "International Patterns of Pension Provision." Social Protection Discussion Paper 0009, World Bank, Washington, DC.

Palacios, Robert J., and Oleksiy Sluchynsky. 2006. "Social Pensions Part I: Their Role in the Overall Pension System." Social Protection Discussion Paper 0601, World Bank, Washington, DC.

Rofman, Rafael. 2005. "El sistema de pensiones." Bolivia Policy Notes, World Bank, Washington, DC.

Rofman, Rafael, and Leonardo Lucchetti. 2006. "Pension Systems in Latin America: Concepts and Measurements of Coverage." Social Protection Discussion Paper 0616, World Bank, Washington, DC.

Rofman, Rafael, Leonardo Lucchetti, and Guzmán Ourens. 2008. "Social Security in Latin America: Concepts and Measurements of Coverage." Social Protection Discussion Paper 0616. updated October 2008, World Bank, Washington, DC.

CHAPTER 3

Pensions and Old-Age Poverty

Stephen Kidd and Edward Whitehouse

Over half of older people worldwide lack income security, and the number could grow to 1.2 billion by 2050. A number of recent studies have argued that in many countries households containing older people are better off than the general population. These studies, however, do not take into account intrahousehold distribution of wealth and income in favor of children and those of working age.

Aggregate measures also hide the fact that poverty levels are often higher among subgroups of older people. For example, elderly-headed households with children tend to be among the poorest households, and poverty among older women is higher than among older men. Indeed, older women make up the majority of older people. Furthermore, older people are particularly vulnerable to sickness or disability. As they age, they are likely to become even poorer.

Public pensions have had a major impact on old-age poverty in some developing countries, as well as in developed countries. Among other benefits, they give older people more choice about whether to work. If the international community is serious about tackling old-age poverty, a social pension is the best answer we have.

The twenty-first century is the century of aging. Worldwide, there are more than 670 million people over age 60, representing 10.4 percent of the global population. This number will increase to almost 2 billion by 2050, or 21.7 percent of the total. By 2015 more than 67 percent of older people will live in developing countries, and by 2050 this proportion is estimated to rise to nearly 80 percent, or almost 1.6 billion people. Currently, over half of older people worldwide, 342 million, lack income security. Unless action is taken to improve the situation, it is estimated that by 2050 more than 1.2 billion older people will be without access to secure incomes (UNDESA 2007).

In 1948 the Universal Declaration of Human Rights recognized income security in old age as a fundamental human right. Since then, the world has broadly taken two diverging paths. Rich countries have invested heavily in providing income security for older people, with average spending on public pensions of 7.0 percent of gross domestic product (GDP), according to the social expenditure database of the Organisation for Economic Co-operation and Development (OECD). In poor countries the opposite has happened. Coverage of formal pension schemes has remained low, restricted to contributory pension schemes for those in formal sector jobs, who often constitute less than 10 percent of the working-age population. Some middle-income countries—for example, Bolivia, Botswana, Brazil, Chile, Namibia, and South Africa—are providing retirement benefits to the vast majority of older people, regardless of whether they have contributed to formal pension systems.

In this chapter we examine the nature of poverty among older people. We begin by considering a number of studies that compare the poverty of households containing older people with that of the general population. It is often assumed that such studies show rates of old-age poverty that are the same as or less than those for the population as a whole. Our analysis questions whether this is so. We go on to examine the impact that public pension schemes have on old-age poverty and note that in the absence of pensions, older people are often obliged to work. We further argue that studies of average old-age poverty rates can gloss over large differences between groups of older people, such as those who live with children, those who live alone or with their spouses only, and older women. Finally, we demonstrate that older people become increasingly vulnerable to illness and disability as they age, which heightens their risk of falling into poverty. The conclusion is that tackling old-age poverty must be an important part of achieving the United Nations Millennium Development Goals and that ensuring access to pensions for older people is the best contribution that pension policy can make to these objectives.

Old Age and Poverty: Are They Correlated?

An important question is whether older people are poorer than the population as a whole. Some researchers have argued that they are not, while others report that old age and poverty are correlated. This section reviews some of the empirical evidence.

Figure 3.1 compares poverty rates among older people and the general population in 27 OECD countries. The picture is mixed. In 12 countries old-age poverty rates are lower than the national rate. In nine countries national and old-age poverty rates are broadly comparable, but in six, old-age poverty is clearly more pronounced than national poverty as a whole, despite substantial retirement income programs.

Turning to lower-income countries, Kakwani and Subbarao (2005) compared national poverty rates with those of households containing older people in 15 Sub-Saharan African countries. None of these countries has a social pension scheme. The authors found statistically significant differences in poverty rates in nine countries. In all of them, households with older people were poorer than those without older people (figure 3.2). In the other six countries, the differences were not statistically significant. On this evidence, the most likely conclusion is that in Sub-Saharan Africa households with older people tend to be poorer than the general population.

In Latin America and the Caribbean, Gasparini et al. (2007) found that in only 6 out of 18 countries studied were poverty rates among older people higher than in the nonelderly population. Public pension programs were identified as a key explanation for lower poverty rates among older people. When putative poverty rates were calculated as if pensions did not exist, old-age poverty rates were higher than non-elderly poverty rates in 14 countries and were lower in only 4 (see figure 3.3).

Turning to Asia, Pal and Palacios (2008) examined 1995–96 Indian National Sample Survey household data from 16 states and found that in 6, poverty rates for households with older people were lower than those for the population at large. In Kerala the opposite was found, with elderly households significantly more likely to be poor. In Vietnam Evans et al. (2007) found that those over age 60 have slightly higher average incomes, at

FIGURE 3.1 **Comparison of poverty rates for national population and elderly population, OECD countries, various years (2003–06)**

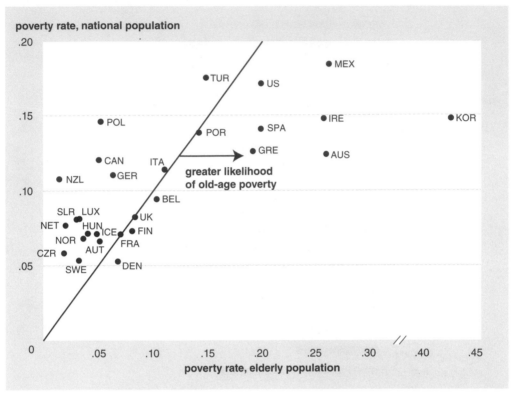

SOURCE: OECD income distribution database.

NOTE: Data is from 2004 except as shown. AUS, Australia; AUT, Austria; BEL, Belgium; CAN, Canada (2005); CZR, Czech Republic; DEN, Denmark (2005); FIN, Finland; FRA, France; GER, Germany (2005); GRE, Greece; HUN, Hungary (2005); ICE, Iceland; IRE, Ireland (2005); ITA, Italy; JAP, Japan; KOR, Korea, Rep. of (2006); LUX, Luxembourg; MEX, Mexico; NET, Netherlands (2003); NZL, New Zealand; NOR, Norway; POL, Poland; POR, Portugal; SLR, Slovak Republic; SPA, Spain; SWE, Sweden; SWZ, Switzerland; TUR, Turkey; UK, United Kingdom; USA, United States;

FIGURE 3.2 **Poverty rates, nonelderly households and households with older people, selected Sub-Saharan African countries, 1998–2001.**

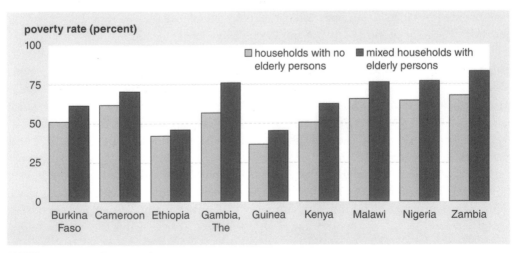

SOURCE: Kakwani and Subbarao 2005.

FIGURE 3.3 **Old-age poverty rates and nonelderly poverty rates, controlling for the effect of pensions, Latin America and the Caribbean (2001–2005)**

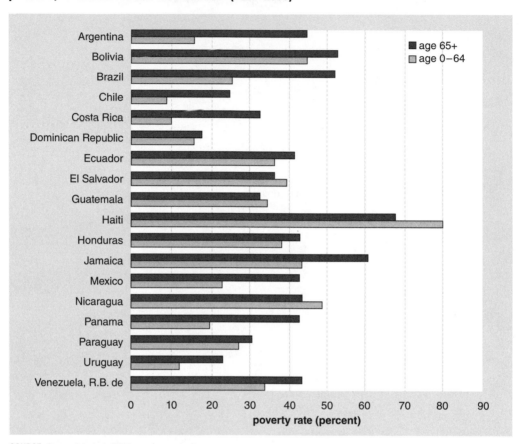

SOURCE: Gasparini et al. 2007.

NOTE: Poverty rates for the nonelderly population, as well as for the elderly population, have been adjusted to take into account the impact of the pension. The poverty line is US$2 per day.

6.4 million Vietnamese dong (D), than those under age 60 (D 6.0 million). If social security income is removed from both categories, older people are poorer, with D 5.7 million for the over-60 age group and D 5.8 million for those under age 60.

For the Middle East and North Africa, Robalino, Rao, and Sluchynsky (2008) calculated that in the five countries they studied—Djibouti, the Arab Republic of Egypt, Jordan, Morocco, and the Republic of Yemen—poverty rates for households with older people are lower than for households without older people. In Djibouti the difference is smallest, with a 43.5 percent poverty rate in households with older people, as against 45.1 percent in other households. In Morocco, by contrast, the figures are 13.2 and 9.0 percent, respectively.

It is important to recognize that studies of income distribution are based on household survey data, which aggregate all the income sources of the household. Living standards are then assessed by dividing household income equally among the members. Despite assertions to the contrary by some researchers, results using this methodology cannot claim to have calculated levels of poverty among older people. Rather, they can only show the poverty rate of those households in which older people live—a significant difference. Depending on the intrahousehold distribution of income, older people could potentially be richer or poorer than other members of their households.

A key question, therefore, is whether the income of older people living in multigenerational households is higher or lower than average. The answer is particularly significant in low- and middle-income countries, where multigenerational households are common. For instance, in rural India 89 percent of older people live in three-generation households (Rajan and Mathew 2008). Kakwani and Subbarao (2005) report similar proportions for Sub-Saharan Africa.

Despite the common belief in a golden age when older people were taken care of and held in great respect by their families, there is little empirical evidence that this state of affairs ever prevailed. Research in recent years has demonstrated a very different picture—one in which households, especially poor households, give preference to those of working age and to children. Van der Geerst (2002) and Aboderin (2006) have described how in Ghana adult children decide how well to care for their parents on the basis of their perceptions of the quality of care they received during childhood. Even if older people are judged to be deserving of care, in times of economic scarcity support will not be forthcoming. Women are particularly vulnerable because they live longer and are a burden to their families for more years; when times are difficult, this can lead to accusations of witchcraft by their children—a phenomenon observed elsewhere in Africa by Miguel (2005). Similarly, UNFPA (2007a) reports that in China, "the tradition for family to provide older persons with basic life assurance is being continuously weakened, and the proportion of older persons receiving economic support from their children is declining." Even when older people bring in significant income themselves, it is distributed within the household; in Namibia, for instance, 70 percent of pension income is shared among household members (Palacios and Sluchynsky 2006).

It is likely, therefore, that in most cases older people, especially those in a more dependent situation, receive a smaller than average share of income in multigenerational households. If this is correct, it is probable that studies comparing old-age poverty with overall poverty underestimate poverty rates among older people. Claims that older people are better off than the population at large should be treated with caution.

Effect of Pension Systems on Old-Age Poverty

Public pension programs have had a major impact on old-age poverty. Figure 3.4 compares putative old-age poverty rates in selected OECD countries, supposing that public pension schemes did not exist, with actual poverty rates. This analysis does not imply that such poverty rates would be observed in the absence of public retirement income programs; it is simply a device to show the current role of the public sector in providing incomes in old age for lower-income groups.

In almost all cases poverty would be significantly higher in the absence of public pensions. France, for example, would have the highest poverty rate, at almost 90 percent, compared with its present rate of around 6 percent. This achievement comes at a cost in public pension spending of 12.4 percent of GDP, the third-highest share after Italy

FIGURE 3.4 **Old-age poverty rates and putative poverty rates in the absence of public pensions, OECD countries**

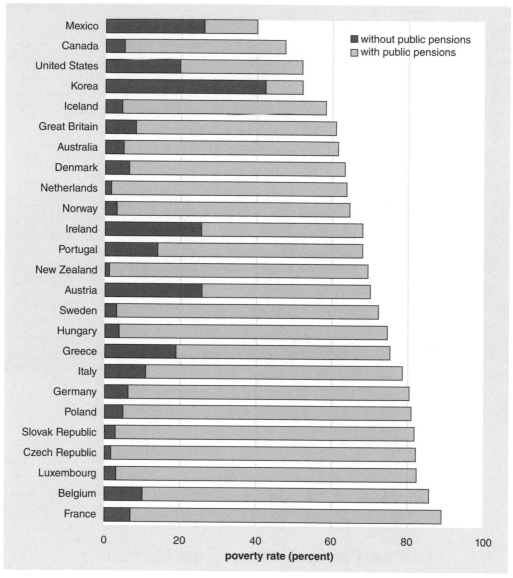

SOURCE: OECD income distribution database.

and Austria, according to the OECD social expenditure database. In countries such as the Czech Republic, the Netherlands, and New Zealand, public pensions have been so effective that income poverty in old age has been almost eliminated. The countries where impacts are smallest are those in which public pensions are less developed or less extensive, such as the Republic of Korea and Mexico.

The effectiveness of pensions in reducing old-age poverty is not restricted to developed countries; similar situations can be found in some middle-income countries. In

Brazil 77 percent of older people benefit from a public pension. The old-age poverty rate in the absence of these pensions would be 47.9 percent, compared with the actual rate of 3.7 percent (Gasparini et al. 2007). Mauritius has had a universal social pension since 1950. The scheme, which costs 1.7 percent of GDP (Willmore 2007) has had an extensive effect on old-age poverty. For example, poverty rates for older people living with more than one younger person would be 30 percent without the universal pension, compared with an actual poverty rate of 6 percent (Kaniki 2007). South Africa's noncontributory pension reaches about 68 percent of those over age 65 (Samson et al. 2007). It provides up to US$75 per month and costs 1.4 percent of GDP. Samson (2006) has examined the impact of this program on the poverty gap—the amount by which household incomes fall below the poverty line. Among households that include older people, the poverty gap drops by 54 percent. The effect is naturally much more significant for older people living alone, with a 96 percent reduction in the poverty gap.

Of course, retirement income programs do not always have a significant impact on poverty, because of low benefit values or narrow coverage. In Nepal, for example, prior to its 2008 expansion the pension was only US$2 per month and paid only to those over age 75. In Bangladesh and India noncontributory pensions are targeted on a very small group of the most vulnerable. Many eligible older people are unable to make successful claims for the grants, and there are myriad accounts of corruption. A survey by HelpAge India found that only one in 10 eligible older people was receiving the pension (Kumar 2008).

Work in Old Age

In countries without comprehensive public pensions, most older people need to work, whereas in developed countries, pensions provide people with much more choice, and older persons are able to retire. As figure 3.5 indicates, in the world's poorest countries just over 70 percent of men and 35 percent of women over age 60 are engaged in work outside the home, compared with around 20 percent of men and 10 percent of women in developed countries. The impact of pensions in providing older people with choices on whether to work can be observed in Morocco; work participation rates among older people are higher in rural areas, where there is no pension coverage, than in urban areas (World Bank 2008).

Although for many older people the option of continuing to work is important for leading active lives, older workers in developing countries are usually in the informal

FIGURE 3.5 **Labor force participation rates for people over 60, by country group**

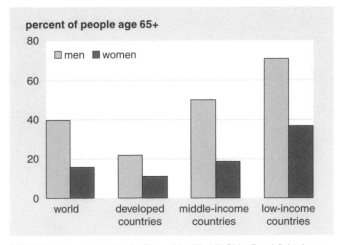

SOURCE: HelpAge International, "State of the World's Older People" database.

sector, in less attractive jobs, with lower pay than people of prime age. In Latin America, for example, older people work fewer hours and receive lower wages than younger workers (Gasparini et al. 2007). As older people age, they are able to work less because of poor health and disability. In Vietnam weekly hours worked by men decline from 36 hours at age 60 to around 18 at age 85 (Evans et al. 2007). In India 56 percent of those over age 60 are employed, but for those over age 80 the figure is only 16 percent (Rajan and Mathew 2008).

Differences in Poverty Rates among Older People

Measures of old-age poverty that rely on aggregate data give only a partial picture; hidden within the averages are pockets of old-age poverty that affect particular groups. This section examines the situation of three kinds of household: elderly-headed households with children; households consisting entirely of older people; and older women.

HOUSEHOLDS WITH CHILDREN HEADED BY OLDER PEOPLE

Older people often assume the role of caregiver to children at a time in their lives when they may have expected to be taken care of by their own children. There are two main reasons: HIV/AIDS and migration. Kakwani and Subbarao (2005) find that in Africa elderly-headed households range from 12 percent of the total in Madagascar to 27 percent in The Gambia.

In countries with a high prevalence of HIV/AIDS, older people have to care for orphans. For example, more than 60 percent of orphans in Namibia, South Africa, and Zimbabwe, and 50 percent in Botswana, Malawi, and Tanzania, live with their grandparents (UNDESA 2007). And the situation has been worsening; in Namibia the proportion rose from 44 percent in 1992 to 61 percent in 2000. Similar figures can be found elsewhere. In Thailand half of all orphans live with their grandparents. According to Kakwani and Subbarao (2005), poverty rates among households in Africa headed by older people are higher than national poverty rates in 11 of 15 countries surveyed. In those countries where poverty rates were lower, the results were not statistically significant.

Many older people in HIV-affected households also have to look after their own adult children who are ill with AIDS. A study by HelpAge International of 12 communities in Africa shows that in some communities even more adults with HIV/AIDS (PLWHA) than orphans (OVC) are cared for by older people (figure 3.6).

In addition, migration can place a burden on older people who care for their grandchildren while their own children seek work elsewhere. In Thailand, for example, 28 percent of those age 60–64 and 18 percent of those age 70–79 are looking after a grandchild whose parents have migrated (UNFPA 2007b). Migration can lead to a rapid aging of rural communities. The Russian Federation, for example, has over 34,000 villages with fewer than 10 inhabitants, typically older women (Harding 2008).

The evidence indicates that in many countries households consisting only of older people and children are even poorer than three-generation households. In 10 of 15 Sub-Saharan African countries studied by Kakwani and Subbarao (2005), the poverty gap for households made up only of older people and children was higher than that for three-generation households. Such households, however, represent less than 1.5 percent of total households in all the countries studied.

FIGURE 3.6 **Percentage of orphans and people living with HIV/AIDS being cared for by older people, 12 communities across Africa, 2006**

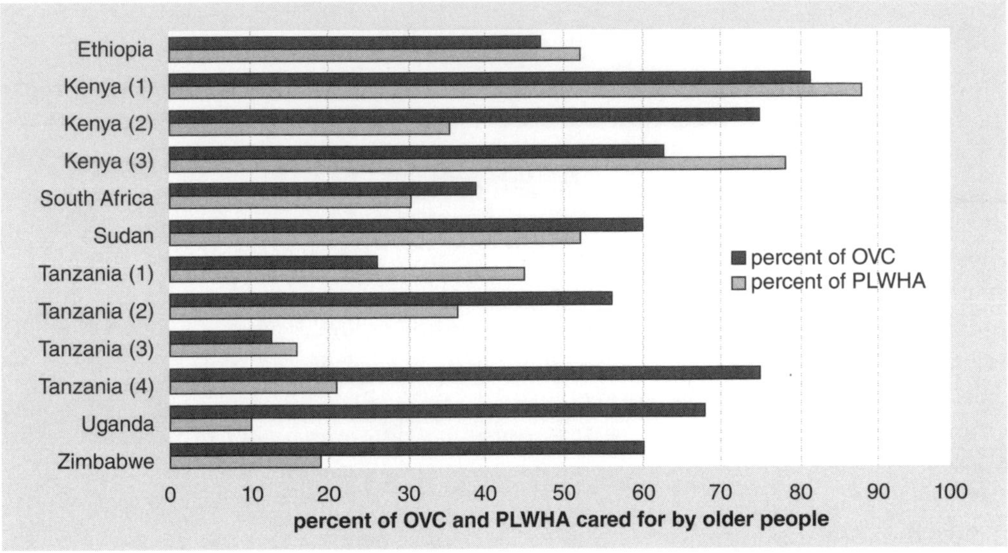

SOURCE: HelpAge International.

NOTE: Specific communities were sampled in each country, and multiple communities were surveyed in Kenya and Tanzania, as indicated by the numerals in parentheses.

Further evidence of the poverty of households consisting of only older people and children can be found in other regions. In the Republic of Yemen, for example, 63 percent of those households live in poverty, compared with 43 percent of three-generation households (Robalino, Rao, and Sluchynsky 2008). In Vietnam families containing only older people and children have incomes of just D 4.4 million, as against D 5.6 million for three-generation households (Evans et al. 2007). Yet households made up only of older people and children are not always poorer, on average. In Egypt, Jordan, and Morocco these families have lower poverty rates than three-generation households. As in Sub-Saharan Africa, such households are a small proportion of the total—less than 0.2 percent of all households in the five Middle East and North African countries studied by Robalino, Rao, and Sluchynsky (2008).[1]

Migration can have varying impacts on poverty. Remittances can reduce poverty significantly, but not all migrants remit their earnings to those looking after their children, and in some cases they are unable to send enough to cover costs. In Thailand, for example, among those age 60–64 who are responsible for caring for the children of migrants, 41 percent pay half or more of the expenses of raising the grandchild, and the figure is 32 percent for those age 70–79 (UNFPA 2007b). Older people in this situation could find themselves becoming increasingly poor.

Overall, therefore, households that include both older people and children—and, in particular, those without other adults present—are likely to be among the poorest households in any country, as indicated by evidence from Sub-Saharan Africa and Vietnam. The situation is likely to be particularly severe for households caring for orphans because the death of the children's parents means the loss of key breadwinners. The situation of people caring for the children of migrants may not be as clear-cut because they may or may not benefit from remittances.

HOUSEHOLDS CONSISTING ONLY OF OLDER PEOPLE

In developing countries only a modest proportion of older people lives alone or in households made up only of older people (usually a married couple). The figures are 17 percent in Africa, 23 percent in Asia, and 25 percent in Latin America and the Caribbean (UNDESA 2007). Studies are inconclusive as to whether such households are poorer than the average. Kakwani and Subbarao (2005) compared the incidence of poverty among single older people with the average for all persons in Sub-Saharan Africa. In only two countries—Uganda and Zambia—were there significantly statistical results, and in both, single older people had higher poverty rates than the national average. The authors note that when the depth rather than the rate of poverty is compared, poverty seems greater among single older people in most countries.

A study of Vietnam revealed that average income was higher in households with only older people: D 6.8 million compared with D 6.0 million for households in which all members were under 60 (Evans et al. 2007). The higher income in elderly households, however, was mainly a result of social security benefits and remittances. Without these, households containing only older people would be much poorer, with D 2.7 million income, as against D 5.2 million for the under-60 group. Households made up only of older people not receiving pensions or remittances are likely to live in deep poverty.

Robalino, Rao, and Sluchynsky (2008) found that in Djibouti, Egypt, Jordan, Morocco, and the Republic of Yemen households containing only older people were less poor than the average older person. Although the authors did not take into account the proportion of income provided by social security benefits, they did point out that the results may reflect the fact that better-off older people may well choose to live alone. This may also be true elsewhere, and it is likely to partly explain why in developed countries 68 percent of older people live alone or with their partners (UNDESA 2007). Some studies may have exaggerated the wealth of households made up only of older people by not taking into account higher expenses per capita compared with large households, since elderly households do not enjoy the same advantages of economies of scale.

POVERTY AMONG OLDER WOMEN

Women are more likely to reach old age than men. In developed countries there are 76 men age 60 and older for every 100 women in that age group, and in developing countries there are 88 (UNDESA 2007). The discrepancy becomes wider as people age: among those over 80, there are 49 men to 100 women in developed countries and 67 men to 100 women in developing countries.

Older women tend to be poorer than men, as illustrated by figure 3.7, which covers 10 European countries. The difference between the sexes is largest in the United Kingdom, where 18.1 percent of older women but only 11.7 percent of men live in poverty. In developed countries this outcome is in large measure the result of pension arrangements. Women have shorter working lives than men and earn less, so they tend to receive lower pensions. Women are also more likely to live alone, and poverty rates for older women living by themselves are usually higher than for men who are alone (UNDESA 2007). In

FIGURE 3.7 **Poverty rates for men and women age 65 and older, selected European countries (1996)**

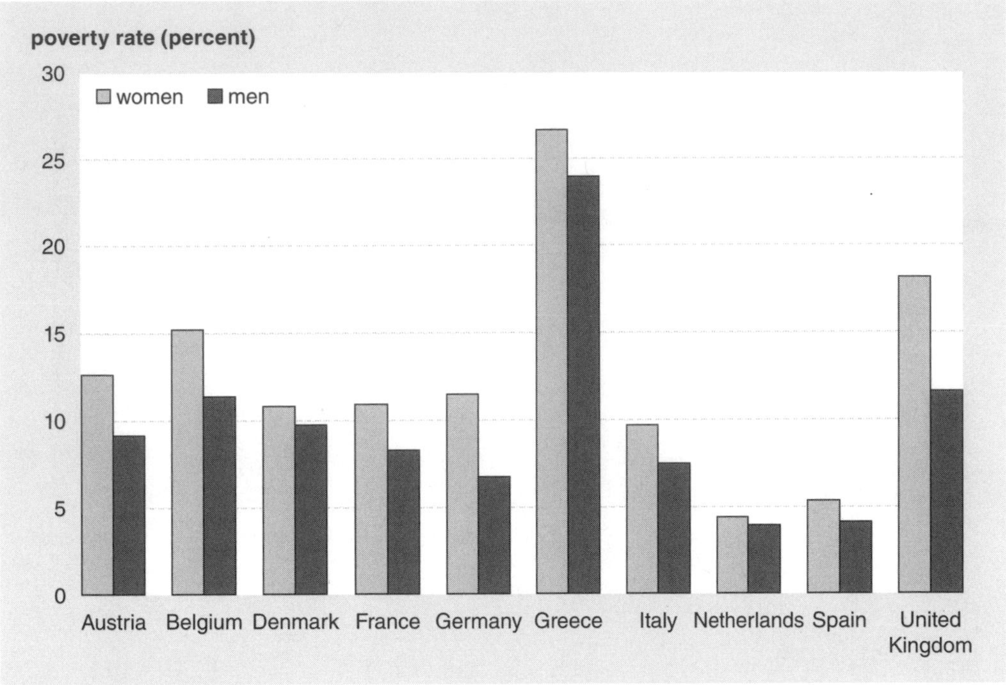

SOURCE: UNDESA (2007, 95)

NOTE: The poverty line is set at 50 percent of median per capita income.

part, this is because women who have not participated in the labor market often have to live on survivors' benefits, which are lower than normal old-age pensions.

In developing countries it is likely that a similar situation of greater poverty among older women exists, but more work is needed to differentiate poverty by age and sex. Women tend to have lower rates of labor market participation than men, often engaging in domestic labor in their own households for which they receive no remuneration. There are, however, exceptions: Rajan and Mathew (2008) found that in India rural work participation rates were 59 percent for older men and 66 percent for older women, and in urban areas the rates were 57 and 62 percent, respectively. As is true of younger women, it is likely that older women earn less than men of similar age.

In developing as in developed countries, older women are more likely to live alone than are older men (figure 3.8). The differences are greatest in Asia and Africa, with about 10 percent of older women in Africa living alone. This pattern is likely to exacerbate differences in the incidence of poverty between older men and women. Moreover, there are differences in wealth; in India, for example, around 60 percent of women but just 30 percent of men have no valuable assets in their own names (Rajan and Mathew 2008). Those living alone are often in a particularly precarious position.

Older women in developing countries almost certainly live in greater poverty than their male counterparts. In urban China, for example, poverty rates are three to four times higher among older women than among older men (UNFPA 2007a).

FIGURE 3.8 **Proportions of older women and older men living alone, 1996**

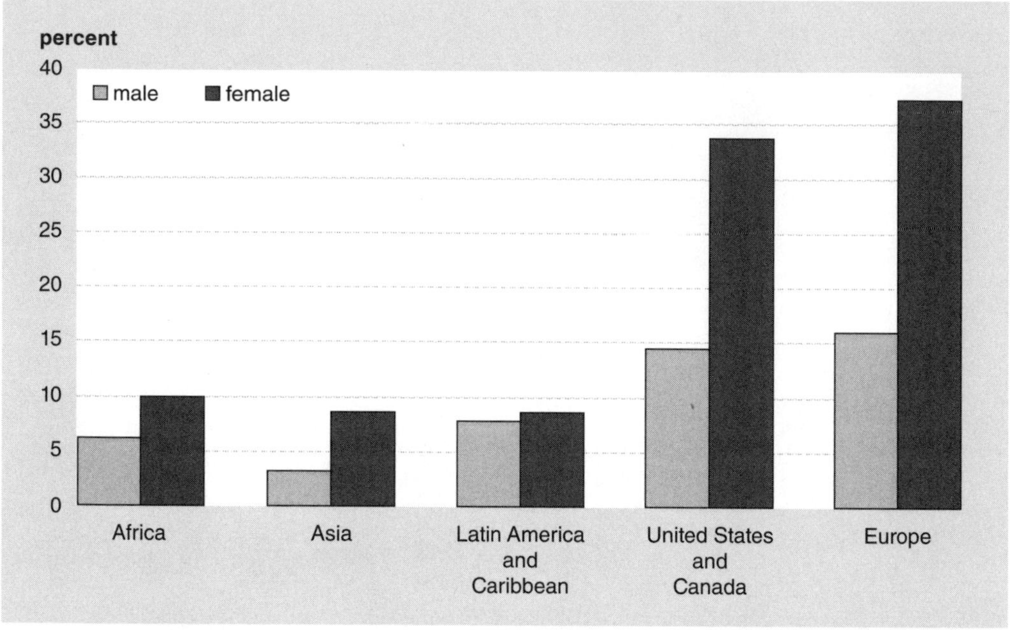

SOURCE: UNDESA (2007:34).

Old Age and Vulnerability

Studies of old-age poverty that rely on poverty rates or poverty gaps present a static picture. They do not take into account the fact that older people are a vulnerable group and that as they age, they become increasingly vulnerable. They are open to risks that could at any time cause them to fall into poverty or make their existing poverty worse. In particular, as people age, they are more likely to become sick or disabled. This can reduce their chances of gaining income through work and can increase their expenditures substantially.

A number of studies have demonstrated that the frequency of illness is higher among older people. For instance, Kakwani, Son, and Hinz (2006) have calculated that in Kenya the incidence of sickness is 26 percent among people over 60 but 16 percent for the total population. In India half of all older people suffer from at least one chronic disease that requires lifelong medication (Rajan and Mathew 2008). In interviews for the 52nd National Sample Survey (1995–96), 10 percent of older people in India reported being ill the day before the interview.

Vulnerability to poor health increases as people age. Evans et al. (2007) show that in Vietnam the number of days people spend incapacitated in bed increases significantly as they get older, from around 15 percent at age 60 to nearly 55 percent at age 95.

Older people are not just more likely to be ill; they are increasingly likely to be disabled. In India 38 percent of older people have at least one disability, and 15 percent suffer from two or more (Rajan and Mathew 2008). A separate study in urban areas of Gujarat in 1993 found that two-thirds of older people had deteriorating physical conditions such as poor vision, hearing impairment, arthritis, and loss of memory (Shah 1993, cited in Rajan and Mathew 2008). In Africa about 9 percent of those over age 50 are blind, while for younger people the figure is much less than 1 percent.[2] Functional blindness among older people caused by lack of spectacles is likely to be much higher.

Increasing poor health and disability among older people have economic consequences. In countries where older people cannot access a pension, these problems have ramifications for their income—and for their families. For example, Rajan and Mathew (2008) report that in India 33 percent of households with a hospitalized older person have suffered loss of income as a result of caregivers' absence from work. Sick older people have to find cash for the costs of seeking treatment and medicine; 40 percent of families in India use savings to meet hospital charges, while another 27 percent fall into debt by borrowing money (Rajan and Mathew 2008).

The impact of deteriorating health and disability as people age almost certainly leads to greater poverty among the elderly. In China, for example, the percentage of older urban residents in poverty increases with age; UNFPA (2007a) reports a poverty rate among those age 60–64 of 11.3 percent, rising to 30.1 percent for those age 85 and older.

Thus, studies of average income and poverty rates among older people paint only a partial picture. As older people age, the risk of falling into poverty can increase substantially, not only because of reduced capacity to work and to secure income but also because poor health and disability can result in much higher expenditure levels. Pension policy therefore not only has to tackle existing poverty but also has to provide security for older people who are in danger of falling into poverty.

Conclusion

There is strong evidence that in many developing countries older people as a whole are likely to be one of the poorest categories of the population, in particular, in the absence of comprehensive public pension schemes. Studies claiming to demonstrate that older people are wealthier than the general population need to be treated with caution, in part because of the assumptions they make about intrahousehold distribution of wealth but also because they do not take into account a range of other factors, including the increasing risk that older people will fall into poverty as they age. Furthermore, subcategories of older people, such as women and those living only with children, tend to be much poorer than the average.

There is strong evidence that public pensions, in particular those that reach the vast majority of older people, constitute a key means of reducing poverty among older people in both developed and developing countries. In developing countries there is good evidence that noncontributory pensions with very broad coverage among the older population—in other words, social pensions—can have significant impacts on old-age poverty. In countries where most older people live in poverty, as in much of Sub-Saharan Africa, the role of social pensions as part of a broad-based antipoverty strategy needs to be recognized.

The need for social pensions will increase as populations age. Pal and Palacios (2008) point out that as countries develop, more poor people will reach old age. Older populations, in turn, are likely to grow increasingly poor. Putting comprehensive social pensions in place now will enable countries to prepare for the future.

Of course, poverty reduction is not the only reason for countries to decide to implement a social pension for all older people. Pensions that benefit the vast majority of older people are likely to be politically popular and are therefore more likely to be sustainable than poverty-targeted safety nets. Moreover, there are strong arguments that after a lifetime of working and caring for families, as well as contributing to national finances, older people deserve to have the state step in. Social pensions could make a change for the better in the lives of millions of older people who currently live in poverty in poor countries, just as they have for older people in many developed countries. They could imbue the lives of poor older people and their families with a measure of predictability, replacing the uncertainty in which they currently live and transforming their behavior, encouraging them to plan for and invest in the future. If the international community is serious about tackling old-age poverty, a social pension is the best answer we have.

Notes

1. It is possible that the low numbers of households consisting of only older people and children affect the sample size and lead to less accurate assessments of their relative poverty.

2. HelpAge International, "State of the World's Older People," http://www.helpage.org/Researchandpolicy/Stateoftheworldsolderpeople/Accesstoservices.

References

Aboderin, Isabella. 2006. *Intergenerational Support and Old Age in Africa.* New Brunswick, NJ, and London: Transaction Publishers.

Evans, M., I. Gough, S. Harkness, A. McKay, H. Dao Thanh, and N. Do Le Thu. 2007. "The Relationship between Old Age and Poverty in Viet Nam." United Nations Development Programme Vietnam, Hanoi.

Gasparini, Leonardo, Javier Alejo, Francisco Haimovich, Sergio Olivieri, and Leopoldo Tornarolli. 2007. "Poverty among the Elderly in Latin America and the Caribbean." Background paper for the *World Economic and Social Survey, 2007: The World Ageing Situation.* New York: United Nations. http://www.un.org/esa/policy/wess/wess2007files/backgroundpapers/lac.pdf.

Harding, L. 2008. "No Country for Old Men." *Guardian,* February 11, G2.

Jensen, Robert T., and Kaspar Richter. 2003. "The Health Implications of Social Security Failure: Evidence from the Russian Pension Crisis." *Journal of Public Economics* 88 (1–2, January): 209–36.

Kakwani, Nanak, and Kalanidhi Subbarao. 2005. "Aging and Poverty in Africa and the Role of Social Pensions." Social Protection Discussion Paper 0521, World Bank, Washington, DC.

Kakwani, Nanak, Hyun H. Son, and Richard Hinz. 2006. "Poverty, Old-Age and Social Pensions in Kenya." Working Paper 24, International Poverty Centre–United Nations Development Programme, Brasilia.

Kaniki, Sheshi. 2007. "Mauritius Case Study." Economic Policy Research Institute, Cape Town, South Africa.

Kumar, Avijeet. 2008. "Challenging Officials in India." *Ageways* 71: 13.

Miguel, Edward. 2005. "Poverty and Witch Killing." *Review of Economic Studies* 72 (4): 1153–72.

Pal, Sarmistha, and Robert J. Palacios. 2008. "Understanding Poverty among the Elderly in India: Implications for Social Pension Policy." IZA Working Paper 3431, Institute for the Study of Labor (IZA), Bonn.

Palacios, Robert, and Oleksiy Sluchynsky. 2006. "Social Pensions Part 1: Their Role in the Overall Pension System." Social Protection Discussion Paper 0601, World Bank, Washington, DC.

Rajan, S. Irudaya, and E. T. Mathew. 2008. "India." In *Social Security for the Elderly: Experiences from South Asia,* ed. S. Irudaya Rajan. New Delhi: Routledge.

Robalino, David A., Gudivada Venkateswara Rao, and Okeksiy Sluchynsky. 2008. "Preventing Poverty among the Elderly in MENA Countries: Role and Optimal Design of Old-Age Subsidies." Human Development Department, World Bank, Washington, DC.

Samson, Michael. 2006. "Social Pensions and Poverty Reduction." Prepared for Social Pensions Symposium at the International Federation of Ageing, 8th Global Conference, "Global Ageing: The North-South Challenge," Copenhagen, May 30–June 3.

Samson, Michael, Kenneth MacQuene, Ingrid van Niekerk, Sheshi Kaniki, Karen Kallmann, and Martin Williams. 2007. "Review of Targeting Mechanisms, Means Tests and Values for South Africa's Social Grants." Economic Policy Research Institute, Cape Town, South Africa.

Shah, V. P. 1993. "The Elderly in Gujarat." Department of Sociology, Gujarat University, Ahmedabad.

UNDESA (United Nations Department of Economic and Social Affairs). 2007. "Development in an Ageing World." *World Economic and Social Survey 2007: The World Ageing Situation.* New York: United Nations.

UNFPA (United Nations Population Fund). 2007a. "Demographic Change in China: Ageing of the World's Largest Population." Papers in Population Ageing 4, UNFPA, Bangkok.

———. 2007b. "Migration and Intergenerational Solidarity: Evidence from Rural Thailand." Papers in Population Ageing 2, UNFPA, Bangkok.

Van der Geerst, Sjaak. 2002. "Respect and Reciprocity: Care of Elderly People in Rural Ghana." *Journal of Cross-Cultural Gerontology* 17 (1): 3–31.

Willmore, Larry. 2007. "Universal Pensions for Developing Countries." *World Development* 35 (1): 24–51.

World Bank. 2008. "Morocco: Skills Development, Social Insurance and Employment." Human Development Department, Middle East and North Africa Region, World Bank, Washington, DC.

CHAPTER 4

Rights-Based Approach to Social Security Coverage Expansion

Krzysztof Hagemejer

This chapter presents the vision, originating from International Labour Organization (ILO) conventions and recommendations, of the universalization of affordable retirement as part of a wider objective of guaranteeing a basic social security package to all. Both the principles that sustain the vision and issues related to design and implementation are outlined, as are the minimum requirements, derived from international labor standards, that are applicable to social security and, in particular, to pensions. To meet these requirements—that is, to provide at least minimum income security in old age to all—it will be necessary to go beyond purely earnings-related contributory pensions and to introduce various noncontributory interventions, within and outside contributory schemes. Adequacy and cost concerns have to be balanced carefully to arrive at affordable and viable pension polices. The analysis shows that the magnitude of the existing coverage gap is closely linked to labor market patterns, which are shaped in many countries by prevailing self-employment, with noncash and nonregular incomes, and by informality. To close the gap, greater reliance has to be placed on noncontributory provisions because contributory systems cannot effectively cover many of those groups, or those individuals with shorter, broken careers and low lifetime incomes. A noncontributory basic pension—combined, if applicable, with noncontributory interventions within social insurance schemes—is a possible strategy for filling the gap and gradually realizing income security in old age for all people everywhere.

This chapter presents the vision, originating from conventions and recommendations of the International Labour Organization, regarding the universalization of affordable retirement as part of the basic social security package. The discussion encompasses both the principles that sustain the vision and issues related to design and implementation.

The section that follows introduces the "rights approach" to social security promoted by the ILO and describes the minimum requirements, derived from international labor standards, that pension systems should meet (see ILO 2008c). The second section shows that to meet these requirements—that is, to provide at least minimum income security in old age to all—it will be necessary to go beyond purely earnings-related contributory pensions and to introduce various noncontributory interventions. The need for carefully balancing adequacy and cost concerns in order to arrive at affordable and viable pension polices is discussed. The third section, which complements chapter 2 in this volume, examines the magnitude of the coverage gap that is closely linked to prevailing labor market patterns. The final section outlines a possible strategy for filling the gap and for gradually providing income security in old age to all, as part of a broader objective of guaranteeing access to basic social security.

The Right to Social Security: The ILO View

The Declaration of Philadelphia, which in 1944 became part of the constitution of the International Labour Organization, obliged the ILO "to further among the nations of the world programmes which will achieve . . . the extension of social security measures to provide a basic income to all in need of such protection and comprehensive medical care."[1]

Also in 1944, members of the ILO adopted Income Security Recommendation No. 67and Medical Care Recommendation No. 69. The former recommends that members progressively apply a number of general guiding principles "as rapidly as national conditions allow, in developing their income security schemes."[2] It specifies that "income security schemes should relieve want and prevent destitution by restoring, up to a reasonable level, income which is lost by reason of inability to work (including old age) or to obtain remunerative work or by reason of the death of a breadwinner."

Social security was confirmed as a human right in article 22 of the 1948 Universal Declaration of Human Rights. Article 25 of the declaration states more specifically, "Everyone has the right to a standard of living adequate for the health and well-being of himself and of his family, including food, clothing, housing and medical care and necessary social services, and the right to security in the event of unemployment, sickness, disability, widowhood, old age or other lack of livelihood in circumstances beyond his control."

The right to comprehensive social security received its precise formulation in 1952 through the Social Security Minimum Standards Convention No. 102.[3] Convention 102 defines nine branches of social security: medical care, sickness, unemployment, old age, employment injury, family, maternity, invalidity, and survivors' benefits. For each of these branches, the convention sets specific standards with respect to the scope and nature of benefits, eligibility conditions, coverage, and benefit levels. It also outlines overall standards with respect to social security financing and governance.

The intention of Convention 102 was to specify the scope of social security provisions that should be accessible to everybody at minimum levels. The idea was that after attaining the minimum levels, countries should progress toward higher levels of protection. Those higher standards were set up in conventions adopted in subsequent years: the Employment Injury Benefits Convention, no. 121 (1964); the Invalidity, Old-Age and Survivors' Benefits Convention, no. 128 (1967); the Medical Care and Sickness Benefits Convention, no. 131 (1969); the Employment Promotion and Protection against Unemployment Convention, no. 168 (1988); and the Maternity Protection Convention, no. 183 (2000).

The important policy message emerging from the ILO social security standards is that social security should be seen as a comprehensive and consistent set of complementary policies and measures providing income security and affordable access to medical care. To conform to international labor standards, national policies should build a basic set of provisions and then, as economic and social development advance, progressively expand coverage and increase the protection level.

Social security pensions designed to provide income security in old age or in case of disability or the loss of a breadwinner are inseparable aspects of that minimum social security package. Parts V, IX, and X of ILO Convention 102, along with ILO

Convention 128, specify rights to social security benefits at retirement (old-age pensions), in case of disability (disability pensions), and in case of loss of the breadwinner (survivors' pensions).[4]

RIGHT TO AFFORDABLE RETIREMENT

Conventions 102 and 128 both stipulate that old-age pensions are to be paid in the form of life annuities ("periodical payments" paid "throughout the contingency") to persons reaching the age prescribed by national legislation. In general, this age should not be higher than 65. The conventions do allow a higher retirement age, if justified. Selection of a retirement age above 65 should give "due regard to the working ability of elderly persons" (Convention 102) and to "demographic, economic and social criteria, which shall be demonstrated statistically" (Convention 128).[5]

RIGHT TO INCOME SECURITY ON THE LOSS OF A BREADWINNER OR DISABILITY

Conventions 102 and 128 stipulate, in identical language, that a survivors' pension should be awarded on "the loss of support . . . as the result of the death of the breadwinner" and incapacity for self-support. Disability pensions are to be paid in case of "inability to engage in any gainful activity, to an extent prescribed, which inability is likely to be permanent or persists after the exhaustion of sickness benefit." Disability and survivors' pensions are to be periodic payments paid "throughout the contingency" (or, in case of disability pensions, "until an old-age benefit becomes payable").

MINIMUM PENSION LEVELS

The conventions give wide freedom of choice as to the mechanism (or combination of mechanisms) for delivering old-age, disability, and survivors' pensions: earnings related or flat rate, contributory or noncontributory, means tested or not.[6] What is important is the outcome, as seen in benefit levels.

If basic income security is to be provided mainly by earnings-related pensions, the minimum replacement rate should be guaranteed, at least for those with earnings lower than prevailing, typical, or average levels. For old-age earnings-related pensions going to such lower-income beneficiaries, Convention 102 requires the minimum replacement rate to be at least 40 percent of previous earnings after 30 years of contributions (if the scheme is contributory).[7] Survivors' and disability earnings-related pensions, as well, should also not be lower than 40 percent of the previous earnings of the beneficiary. In case disability and survivors' pensions are contributory, the full amount of the pension should be paid at least to those with 15 years of contributions. Reduced pensions should be provided for those with shorter contribution periods.

If pensions are paid at a flat rate, the amount should not be lower than 40 percent of the prevailing levels of earnings of unskilled manual workers. This applies as well to pensions provided as means-tested benefits. The level of such pensions should also meet an additional criterion: they "shall be sufficient to maintain the family of the beneficiary in health and decency." Amounts of all kinds of pensions awarded originally to the beneficiaries should be reviewed regularly and adjusted accordingly, following any "substantial changes" in the general level of earnings or costs of living.

Above-threshold replacement rates were set up in 1952 on the basis of a review of actual policies in ILO member countries and ILO tripartite constituents' policy preferences with respect to minimum benefit setting. Table 4.1 presents these thresholds (calculated in two variants, as 40 percent of average gross earnings and 40 percent of the minimum wage) for selected European countries in 2002–04 in comparison with a relative poverty line of 60 percent of median income in each country. Whereas at an average earnings level a 40 percent replacement rate would, except in Bulgaria, yield a pension well above the relative poverty line, pensions based on the minimum wage level would be well below the line. Of course, in many countries the actual poverty lines adopted for social assistance purposes are lower than 60 percent of the median income, but it seems that achievement of a minimum pension "sufficient to maintain the family of the beneficiary in health and decency" requires, in many countries and circumstances, total benefits (from contributory and noncontributory programs) higher than 40 percent of the lowest earnings (European Union 2006b).

TABLE 4.1 **Minimum pension requirements of ILO Convention 102, at 40 percent of average earnings and of the minimum wage, compared with a national poverty line of 60 percent of median income**
(poverty line = 100)

Country	2002		2003		2004	
	Average earnings variant	Minimum wage variant	Average earnings variant	Minimum wage variant	Average earnings variant	Minimum wage variant
Belgium			146	61	149	61
Bulgaria	85	32	82	32	85	34
Cyprus			106			
Czech Republic			113	40		
Denmark			142			
Estonia	140	43	138	45		
Finland	123		122		124	
France	129	63	126	62		62
Germany	165		162		164	
Greece			153	61		57
Hungary	121	49	126	43		
Ireland			103	49	101	50
Latvia	116	41	123	46		
Lithuania	136	50	131	47		
Luxembourg			108	45		
Netherlands	137	56	141	57		
Norway			110		110	
Poland	180	59	181	61		
Portugal					148	50
Romania	194	61	185	69		
Slovak Republic			117	40	116	39
Slovenia	100	45	97	45		
Spain	131	44	131	43	127	42
Sweden	123				130	
Turkey				85		
United Kingdom	144	49	147	49		

SOURCE: ILO calculations based on EUROSTAT database.

Meeting the Challenge: Approaches and Strategies

Several points about the ILO conventions have to be borne in mind.

1. The conventions are concerned with setting a minimum necessary level of protection (in the case of pensions, minimum necessary income security), but extending it to *all* those in need of such protection.[8]

2. Affordability and sustainability have always been concerns alongside those about adequacy of coverage and benefit levels; achievement of minimum standards was to happen "as soon as possible" but "as rapidly as national conditions allow."[9] Actually, it is quite clear that financial affordability and sustainability, on the one hand, and adequacy of benefit provision (as measured by amounts paid and people effectively reached and protected), on the other, are two sides of the same coin. Only meaningful benefits that effectively cover those in need can create the political will among contributors and taxpayers to finance the policies. As too many examples in the history of social security show, inadequacy, as well as bad governance, undermines sustainability because willingness to finance such programs quickly erodes. Generous benefit promises will never become realities if they are not supported by sustainable financing. There should be a long-run collective equivalence between the total amount of contributions and taxes paid to finance the pension scheme and the total amount of benefit paid (Cichon et al. 2004, 226).

3. The financing, by whatever means, should be equitable and should be affordable for all protected persons. In particular, the need to pay taxes or contributions to finance future benefits should not be a source of hardship for those with low incomes.

4. Adequate benefits should be guaranteed in the first place to those with lower incomes, and when contribution or residency periods are taken into account to establish the right to benefits, the required periods should not be set too high. At least reduced benefit amounts should be guaranteed even to those with working careers or residency shorter than the generally prescribed periods.

It is clear that any pension system which is solely based on lifetime contributions and pays "actuarially fair" or "actuarially neutral" pensions will not be able to deliver the commitments set forth above to many individuals. There is a need to create or provide pension entitlements outside the pure earnings-and contribution-related system. This is usually achieved only by subsidizing contributions, or subsidizing benefits for some individuals, or both. The subsidies can be financed through redistribution of contributions paid within the social insurance system or with general tax revenues.

Historically, social insurance pensions have been based on the solidarity principle. They do not just pool risk; they also introduce at least some degree of redistribution among contributors to protect those with lower contributory capacity, shorter careers, and lower lifetime earnings.[10] A range of strategies has typically been applied. One is the institution of a minimum pension. Another is the use of a redistributive benefit formula (in a defined benefit system); this formula has to be well designed to ensure the desired pattern of redistribution. A third option, often employed with the redistributive benefit formula, is, when calculating benefits, to treat as contributory specified noncontributory periods of certain categories of contributors; examples include maternity leave or military service. A fourth method is outright subsidization, within the scheme, of the contributions of certain categories of members.

The type of redistribution described above may be seen by members of the scheme as unacceptable, or by policy makers as undesirable because of possible disincentive effects. Some countries have addressed the problem by allocating general revenue resources from outside the scheme for the benefit of selected members. The practice of topping up pensions from the contributory scheme to a guaranteed minimum using state budget funds (but only for those beneficiaries who have contributed a required minimum number of years, as in Chile or Poland) is one example. Another is the payment, from general fiscal revenues, of contributions on behalf of certain categories of members during specified periods such as maternity or parental leave, as in Sweden and to a certain degree in Poland. Still another group of measures would include subsidization from the general revenues of employees' or employers' contributions for low-income earners (or other specific categories of contributors), with the aim of enhancing these earners' membership and accumulation of pension entitlements.

In general, there are two types of interventions of the kind described above: ex ante (matching contributions) and ex post (topping up benefits on retirement). Both types usually set minimum eligibility conditions (age, contributory periods, or residency). Eligibility may be subject to a narrow (pension income) or broad (all income or all means) test.

Depending on the circumstances, it may be advantageous to carry out the necessary redistribution within the social insurance scheme or to do it from outside with general revenues. Subsidies from outside the scheme to its members can, to some extent, have positive effects on membership and contribution incentives, but there are important equity questions if membership in the scheme is not universal, if subsidies are not directed to the worst-off members, or if the worst-off members are still much better off than those not covered by the scheme. For example, why should all taxpayers—as in Chile and Poland—subsidize the pensions of those with low incomes and with more than 20 or 25 years of contributions more generously than the pensions of persons who had no chance to contribute for so long? Although such a policy for securing minimum pensions while avoiding moral hazard can be justified if redistribution takes place within the contributor group, it is more difficult when all taxpayers are involved and members of the scheme in question are better off than nonmember taxpayers. General revenues should subsidize the contributory system only if coverage is large, and only to the extent that individuals outside the system also benefit from at least equivalent support.

The extent to which redistribution among members of the contributory pension scheme has or has not negative effects on membership and incentives to contribute depends on many factors and always needs to be tested empirically. Members' understanding and acceptance of the redistribution matter (in some cases the system may be overcomplicated and not transparent). Also important are the actual contributory behavior of members and the readiness of potential new members to join the scheme.

Another way to deliver minimum income security is to do it outside the pension insurance scheme, through a universal pension paid to all residents who meet specified age or other criteria, or through an income- or means-tested pension guaranteed to all those below a specified income threshold. These pensions are sometimes called "social pensions," and they are seen as the most effective way of reaching in a relatively short time all those who for some reason cannot be members of a contributory scheme. (Reasons for nonparticipation may include very low incomes or irregular incomes that make regular contributions to a contributory scheme unaffordable or infeasible.) In short, such noncontributory pensions are seen as a quick way of achieving universal coverage.

ILO standards allow both universal and means-tested pensions as a way of providing minimum income security. For many, the universal pension solution has an advantage over the means-tested approach because it is much simpler and less costly to administer and deliver and because it is the most equitable way of providing everybody with minimum income security at retirement, avoiding the stigma and exclusion often associated with means testing. Budgetary constraints, however, often lead to solutions that involve narrower or broader means testing. The actual approach taken will always depend on prevailing societal attitudes toward equity and redistribution and on overall cost concerns.

Providing a pension to everyone in need of support requires a concerted effort through a pension system composed of a mix of policy measures: contributory and noncontributory (specifying the means of building entitlements to pensions); earnings related and flat rate (determining pension amounts); and contributory and tax financed (referring to financing sources). The different kinds of policy measure can be applied through separate schemes forming discrete tiers or pillars of the pension system, but often multiple measures are present within a single scheme. To a large extent it is the presence of the noncontributory and non-earnings-related components that makes social security pension schemes and systems "social."

The Right to Affordable Retirement: For Most, Still a Dream

It is commonplace knowledge that although social security has been declared a human right, most of the world's population is deprived of adequate social security benefits and services. These specifically include the right to affordable retirement and income security in case of old age, disability, or loss of a breadwinner.

Probably there is no country in the world that does not have at least one pension scheme for a specific group of employees, but in many parts of the world the groups covered are few (see chapter 2 in this volume). Most schemes are contributory, and coverage is in practice limited to those who have a formal employment contract as an employee. The pattern of coverage indicators measured in relation to the labor force (percentage of employed covered) across the world is thus quite similar to the pattern of indicators reflecting the percentage of employees in total employment. Taking into account that women in developing countries, if employed at all, less often have wage or salary employment and that both economic activity rates and employment rates are usually significantly lower for women than for men, women are much less likely to be covered than men.[11]

Table 4.2 shows the percentage of those with wage or salary employment among all employed and among the working-age population. Globally, slightly less than half (47 percent) of those employed are wage and salary workers, and among all those of working age, only one-third of men and one-fifth of women have regular employee status. The regions with the lowest shares of employees among those on the labor market are South Asia and Sub-Saharan Africa; about 20 percent of those employed are employees in this sense. Only 15 percent of employed women and only 4 to 7 percent of women in the working-age group are regular employees. In these regions, actual coverage by contributory schemes is even lower than the above rates. For example, the ILO's recent analysis of the coverage situation in Tanzania and Zambia shows that only about half of those with employee status actively contribute to existing contributory pension schemes, either because employers in smaller establishments are not obliged to register their employees and contribute, or because, overall, these workers' wage employment is of a highly informal character (see ILO 2008d, 2008e). There is thus still considerable scope in these countries for existing contributory schemes to increase effective coverage among employees,

Implementation of contributory schemes that effectively cover larger proportions of the self-employed has until now proved possible only in very highly formalized economies such as those in Europe and in some other countries of the Organisation for Economic Co-operation and Development (OECD). In countries with large proportions of mostly rural self-employed and in highly informal economies, noncontributory pension schemes (universal or income tested) able to provide income security to the elderly, the disabled, orphans, and widows are limited in number, although more countries are embarking on or considering the road successfully chosen earlier by countries such as Brazil, Namibia, and South Africa.

Coverage measured by beneficiaries of contributory pensions (based on the percentage of the population older than retirement age or any other age threshold identifying the elderly) is, in many countries of Africa or Asia, or anywhere else where such schemes are relatively recent, even lower than coverage measured with respect to the labor force. Members of many of these schemes are still building entitlements to their future pensions; the number that has already acquired and is exercising this right is low. The great majority

TABLE 4.2 **Persons with wage or salary employment status on the labor market, circa 2008** (percent)

	Total		Men		Women	
	Share of employed	**Share of working-age population**	**Share of employed**	**Share of working-age population**	**Share of employed**	**Share of working-age population**
South Asia	20.8	9.7	23.4	15.6	14.6	3.5
Sub-Saharan Africa	22.9	13.8	29.2	20.5	14.4	7.4
Southeast Asia and Pacific	38.8	21.9	41.5	28.6	35.0	15.1
East Asia	42.6	23.3	46.0	28.9	38.3	17.6
North Africa	58.3	24.4	58.8	38.5	56.7	10.5
Middle East	61.5	29.0	64.4	41.6	53.5	15.0
Latin America and the Caribbean	62.7	38.6	60.6	46.1	65.8	31.8
Central and Southeastern Europe and CIS[a]	76.6	41.5	75.4	48.0	78.0	35.7
Developed economies	84.3	46.6	81.7	51.8	87.5	41.6
World	46.9	26.5	47.4	33.0	46.0	20.1

SOURCE: Author's calculations based on ILO (2008b), using 2006 estimates for status of employment for ratio of employment to population.

NOTE: The country classification is that used in ILO (2008b).

a. Does not include members of the European Union. CIS, Commonwealth of Independent States.

of elderly persons in the world has no right to retire or to any form of pension, and these people have to continue working as long as they are still physically able to do so. The economic activity rates of the elderly and the extent to which economic activity declines with advancing age can thus be treated as indicators of how many people are actually retiring, although we still do not know how many of them are forced into retirement through inability to work or failure to find employment. We do not have data detailed enough to calculate average ages of exit from the labor market in all countries.

These limitations aside, table 4.3 compares labor force participation rates of those age 65 and older with average economic activity rates for all those over age 14. Here again, it is evident that retirement from economic activity in old age, although widespread in developed parts of the world, is rare in developing countries. In Sub-Saharan Africa men are able to reduce their economic activity rates only slightly, by up to 20 percent, in old age. Strikingly, in Africa, in contrast to other regions, the situation in this respect did not change between 1980 and 2005. In South Asia and East Asia, too, exit from economic activity in old age is less common than elsewhere. Women nearly everywhere reduce their economic activity more than men do when they reach old age, but it is obvious that very often they simply switch to occupations that are not classified by labor force surveys as "employment"—that is, caregiving and unpaid household labor.

In most developing countries only a minority of older persons has any pension. Yet even in the poorest countries, people who reach age 65 will live for more than another 10 years, on average (see table 4.3). The question is, how dignified their lives will be and what form of income security a society can give them.

Men and women age 65 and older now constitute 8 percent of the world's population, but by 2050 they will make up 16 percent. Most of the elderly live in countries in which only small minorities are covered by any form of pension scheme and where social security in general, including affordable access to essential health care services, is a luxury. More than 60 percent of the elderly now live in countries classified by the United Nations as less developed, and by 2050 the elderly in these countries will account for nearly 80 percent of the world's elderly population.

The consequence is that these developing and aging societies will have to do something urgently to ensure their elderly members the right to retire in dignity and social security. Particularly dramatic is the situation of older women, who constitute the majority among this growing number of elderly. In many countries women are excluded to a large extent from the labor market when they are still able to work. Thus, even where contributory pension schemes exist, these women have no chance to contribute and build their pension entitlements. Furthermore, very often neither prevailing traditional societal rules nor more formal pension arrangements provide women with even minimum security when they are left by their male partners or are widowed.

Before suggesting a proper strategy for meeting these challenges and starting to fill the existing coverage gap, it is important to understand why, several decades after social security was declared a human right and accepted as a standard for decent employment and living, only a minority is able to claim these rights.

The answer has many dimensions. It lies in the specific approach to development that at some point saw countries at early stages of development fail to adopt the redistributive policies that worked well and played an enormous role in the past development of now-industrialized OECD countries. But it also lies in a misjudgment of future developments

TABLE 4.3 **Participation in the labor market by the elderly (age 65+) and life expectancy at age 65**

| | Labor force participation at age 65+ as percent of labor force participation of population age 15+ (percent) | | | | Life expectancy at age 65, 2000–2005 (additional life years) | |
| | Men | | Women | | | |
	1980	2005	1980	2005	Men	Women
Middle Africa	84.4	85.0	55.1	56.5	10.96	12.38
Western Africa	81.4	82.3	58.7	56.3	11.36	12.50
Eastern Africa	82.7	81.5	62.5	59.1	11.31	13.00
South-Central Asia	68.5	60.2	39.3	43.8	13.36	14.58
Southeastern Asia	62.0	57.9	38.4	32.7	13.36	15.33
Central America	73.6	56.6	53.4	34.0	16.24	18.16
South America	43.5	44.5	22.2	25.4	15.35	17.98
Northern Africa	59.9	42.9	61.5	22.3	12.81	14.58
Western Asia	46.2	42.7	35.7	40.5	13.16	15.14
Caribbean	47.3	38.2	29.1	17.0	15.30	17.67
Eastern Asia	38.3	33.5	10.8	16.9	14.81	17.53
Southern Africa	33.0	32.9	20.6	12.5	10.69	14.18
Australia and Oceania	19.1	19.9	10.4	9.9	16.49	19.86
Eastern Europe	20.2	15.4	8.7	10.7	11.56	15.27
Northern Europe	17.0	13.7	8.9	7.5	15.76	19.05
Southern Europe	20.3	12.8	15.7	9.7	16.12	19.75
Western Europe	10.1	5.7	7.3	3.2	16.06	20.01
World	40.6	38.2	18.4	21.5	14.39	16.95
More developed regions	21.9	19.3	12.2	12.2	15.47	18.92
Less developed regions	54.2	48.5	24.9	27.8	13.80	15.64

SOURCE: For labor force participation, author's calculations based on ILO, "Economically Active Population Estimates and Projections," version 5, 1980–2020, http://laborsta.ilo.org/; for life expectancy, United Nations *World Population Prospects, 2006 Revision,* CD-ROM edition.

NOTE: Country groupings are those used in United Nations, *World Population Prospects,* http://esa.un.org/unpp/index.asp?panel=5.

by those who were actually supporting the buildup of social security provisions all over the world.

The ILO Recommendations of 1944 saw contributory social insurance as a main vehicle for gradually expanding social security coverage to all in need, This view was based on the belief that urbanization and industrialization would progressively expand and that wage and salary employment would gradually become the dominant form of employment. Coverage of social insurance schemes, which in developing countries originally applied only to relatively narrow groups, would thus incrementally but automatically spread to the majority of the working population. Noncontributory, residual social assistance would take care of minorities that for some reason were excluded from social insurance coverage.

Actual developments, as we know well, were and are dramatically different; the shares of wage employment and of the formal economy have not been increasing as expected, and they even shrank in some parts of the world in the 1980s and 1990s. The same applies to social insurance coverage, which is stagnating in many parts of the world. Underfunded social assistance programs designed to provide cash transfers or other benefits and services to relatively small groups of the most vulnerable minorities are more and more often expected to bring relief to those affected by widespread, large-scale poverty.

Implementing a Universal Pension within the Basic Social Security Package

The new ILO social security policy development vision focuses on building country-specific, effective, efficient national social security systems that are affordable for countries at different levels of development (ILO 2009).

The principal objectives of the social security development approach are the fastest possible achievement of universal access to basic benefits, to combat poverty, and the reduction of income insecurity to the extent possible and compatible with economic performance. As countries mature economically, higher levels of protection can gradually be achieved.

The key objective is universality. That is the core mandate of the ILO global campaign for social security and coverage for all. Universality does not mean uniformity—it is not realistic to believe that all societies can, left to their own devices, achieve the same level of social protection irrespective of their level of economic development. National social security systems inevitably have to grow with the fiscal space that is made available through growing economies. What is critical is that systems are progressive in a rational way; that is, they address priority needs in a logical order and are so designed that the level of security can be increased as economic development progresses. Within an overall national resource envelope, at different stages of development, contributions and taxes allocated to social security priority expenditures have to be defined. In developing countries, social expenditures should be prioritized according to their contribution to achievement of an acceptable level of health, poverty reduction, and the reduction of social insecurity.

"Universality" may refer to the various dimensions of social security. In this discussion, the main emphasis is on universality of access of individuals to formal systems of social protection. The notion of a universal benefit, payable without distinction to all qualified members of a scheme, fits well into the concept of a rights-based scheme but may in practice have to be tempered by some form of targeting of resources, when these are limited.

Social security in the poorest countries can start gradually, with a basic package consisting of a fundamental and modest set of social security guarantees implemented through social transfers in cash and in kind for all citizens. This will ensure that, ultimately, all residents have affordable access to essential health care; that all children enjoy income security at least at the poverty level through various family and child benefits aimed at facilitating access to nutrition, education, and care; that employment guarantees and targeted income support to the working poor and the unemployed exist; and that all residents in old age or with disabilities enjoy income security, at least at the poverty level, through old-age, disability, and survivors' pensions.

The basic package is a guaranteed set of social transfers, in cash or in kind, to all in need. It is formulated as a set of guarantees rather than a set of defined benefits. This leaves the option open for individual countries to realize these guarantees by way of means-tested, conditional, or universal transfers. The essential fact is that everybody in a given society can access these essential transfers when in need. Although conceptually these are a part of the country's social security architecture, in most countries the benefits provided are likely to have the characteristics of noncontributory universal or social assistance benefits rather than social insurance benefits. It is also assumed here that the basic benefits will probably be financed from general taxation. The transfers of the social floor are granted to all residents as a right; thus, their financing is generally a responsibility of the society as a whole.

The ILO has studied the costs of a basic social protection package in 12 low-income countries now and over the coming decades.[12] The benefit package costed includes (a) universal basic old-age and disability pensions; (b) basic child benefits; (c) universal access to essential health care; and (d) social assistance in the form of a 100-day employment guarantee scheme. In all 12 countries considered, the initial annual cost of the whole basic social protection package is projected, if introduced all at once, to be in the range of 3.7 to 10.6 percent of gross domestic product (GDP) in 2010. Six countries—Burkina Faso, Ethiopia, Kenya, Nepal, Senegal, and Tanzania—would spend more than 6 percent of GDP.

The basic pension was assumed to be set at the level of 30 percent of GDP per capita and would be paid to all men and women age 65 and older and to persons of working age with serious disabilities. Given these assumptions, the annual cost of providing a universal basic old-age and disability pension is estimated at between 0.6 and 1.5 percent of annual GDP in 2010 in the countries analyzed. The projected costs for 2010 remain at or below 1.0 per cent of GDP in Bangladesh, Cameroon, Guinea, India, Pakistan, and Vietnam; in Burkina Faso, Ethiopia, Kenya, Nepal, Senegal, and Tanzania costs are between 1.1 and 1.5 percent of GDP.

The projections show that introducing a complete package of basic social security benefits requires a level of resources that is higher than current social security spending in most low-income countries, which rarely spend more than 3 percent of GDP on health care or more than 1 percent of GDP on nonhealth social security measures. The package therefore has to be introduced gradually. It is up to a national debate to decide whether basic pensions will be implemented as a priority, and in what form. The discussions in this chapter and in chapters 2 and 3 show that, taking into account the situation of the elderly, the prevailing lack of coverage, and the aging process, provision of basic income security to older persons may be a priority in many countries. Recent experience with modest universal pension systems in a number of developing countries has shown positive poverty-reducing effects for whole families. These programs not only provide benefits for the old and disabled but also use this disadvantaged group, whose status in families is greatly enhanced through the cash income they thus receive, as effective agents of social transfers for families. Pension recipients redistribute cash income within the household, finance school fees and medication, and so on (see HAI 2004). Strong evidence of positive experience comes from countries such as Brazil, Mauritius, Namibia, Nepal, South Africa, and Zambia.[13] Another ILO simulation exercise shows that even a very modest universal pension, costing about 1 percent of GDP, would reduce the poverty gap in Senegal and Tanzania by more than 20 percent (Gassmann and Behrendt 2006).

Basic noncontributory pensions are the quickest mechanism for providing at least minimum income security in old age to the uncovered majority. In countries where coverage is predominantly based on contributory earnings-related pensions (defined contribution or defined benefit), there is still a need for noncontributory guarantees provided outside the schemes, in the form of basic pensions, or built into the contributory schemes. Many countries have moved recently on reforms to strengthen the link between contributions paid and benefits received, and replacement rates are expected to fall significantly for those with shorter, broken careers and low lifetime incomes (see OECD 2005; European Union 2006a). Noncontributory interventions represent the only way to secure minimum income security for those who are covered by such schemes but have not been fortunate enough to have accumulated sufficient contribution periods and contribution amounts to avoid poverty at retirement.

Notes

1. For the ILO Constitution, see http://www.ilo.org/ilolex/english/constq.htm.

2. For the full texts of ILO conventions and recommendations cited, see the ILOLEX database, http://www.ilo.org/ilolex/english/. Both of the 1944 recommendations refer directly to the Atlantic Charter, the document signed on August 14, 1941, by U.S. President Franklin Delano Roosevelt and British Prime Minister Winston Churchill and endorsed by the International Labour Conference the same year. In particular, the recommendations are based on the Atlantic Charter's fifth principle, proclaiming "the fullest collaboration between all nations in the economic field with the object of securing, for all, improved labor standards, economic advancement and social security."

3. Throughout its history, the ILO had adopted conventions related to various branches of social insurance, starting as early as 1919 with the Maternity Protection Convention (no. 3). Convention 102, however, was the first, and so far the only, agreement to look at all branches of social security in a comprehensive way, and the first to go beyond what is clearly social insurance when defining an array of policies for providing social security.

4. Specific types of disability and survivors' pension are also required in cases related to employment accident, injury, or sickness, as provided for by part VI of Convention 102 and by Convention 121.

5. Convention 128 also states, "If the prescribed age is 65 years or higher, the age shall be lowered, under prescribed conditions, in respect of persons who have been engaged in occupations that are deemed by national legislation, for the purpose of old-age benefit, to be arduous or unhealthy."

6. The mechanisms would include voluntary insurance that is administered by public authorities or jointly by workers and employers; that covers a substantial proportion of lower-income workers; and that meets other provisions of the convention.

7. Convention 128 requires higher benefit levels: 45 percent for old-age and survivors' pensions, and 50 percent for disability pensions.

8. Although countries can ratify conventions while initially providing protection only to a specified percentage of the population, it is expected that all those needing protection will eventually be covered. This expectation is explicitly expressed in the 1944 Income Security Recommendation (no. 67) stating that even countries that already have necessary social security provisions in place should "take further steps towards the attainment of income security by the unification or co-ordination of social insurance schemes, the extension of such schemes to all workers and their families, including rural populations and the self-employed, and the elimination of inequitable anomalies."

9. This provision should not be used as a justification for doing nothing. The phrases cited should be interpreted in a similar way as is article 2 of the International Covenant on Economic, Social, and Cultural Rights (1966). According to that article, "Each State Party to the present Covenant undertakes to take steps, individually and through international assistance and co-operation, especially economic and technical, to the maximum of its available resources, with a view to achieving progressively the full realisation of the rights . . . by all appropriate means. As Committee on Economic, Social and Cultural Rights explains: while the full realisation of the relevant rights may be achieved progressively, steps towards that goal must be taken within a reasonably short time . . . Such steps should be deliberate, concrete and targeted as clearly as possible towards meeting the obligations." The comment quoted may be found at Committee on Economic, Social and Cultural Rights, General Comment 3, 1990, "The Nature of States Parties Obligations," http://www.unhchr.ch/tbs/doc.nsf/(Symbol)/94bdbaf59b43a424c1256 3ed0052b664?Opendocument. For an interesting paper discussing the relationship between the rights-based approach and economic analysis, see Seymour and Pincus (2008).

10. Even strictly defined contribution pension systems allow a certain degree of redistribution from male to female contributors when unisex life tables are used to calculate pensions.

11. In addition, many of the existing pension schemes in Africa or Asia do not provide survivors' pensions, so women, most of whom are not in the formal economy, are not entitled to anything when they become widows, even if their deceased husbands were covered by a pension scheme.

12. For details on the assumptions and results of the costing study, as well as on other studies concerned with the potential poverty reduction impact of the universal pension and some other cash benefits, see ILO (2008a).

13. See Bertranou and Grushka (2002); Durán-Valverde (2002); Schleberger (2002); Schwarzer and Querino (2002); Barrientos and Lloyd-Sherlock (2003); Bertranou, van Ginneken, and Solorio (2004).

References

Barrientos, Armando, and Peter Lloyd-Sherlock. 2003. "Non-Contributory Pensions and Social Protection." Issues in Social Protection Series, Discussion Paper 12, Social Protection Sector, International Labour Office, Geneva.

Bertranou, Fabio, and Carlos O. Grushka. 2002. "The Non-Contributory Pension Programme in Argentina: Assessing the Impact on Poverty Reduction." Extension of Social Security (ESS) Paper 5, International Labour Office, Geneva.

Bertranou, Fabio M., Wouter van Ginneken, and Carmen Solorio. 2004. "The Impact of Tax-Financed Pensions on Poverty Reduction in Latin America: Evidence from Argentina, Brazil, Chile, Costa Rica and Uruguay." International Social Security Review 57 (4): 3–18.

Cichon, Michael, Wolfgang Scholz, Arthur van de Meerendonk, Krzysztof Hagemejer, Fabio Bertranou, and Pierre Plamondon. 2004. Financing Social Protection. Quantitative Methods in Social Protection Series. Geneva: International Labour Office.

Durán-Valverde, Fabio. 2002. "Anti-Poverty Programmes in Costa Rica: The Non-Contributory Pension Scheme." Extension of Social Security (ESS) Paper 8, International Labour Office, Geneva.

European Union. 2006a. "Current and Prospective Theoretical Pension Replacement Rates." Report by the Indicators Sub-Group (ISG) of the Social Protection Committee, European Union, Brussels.

———. 2006b. "Minimum Income Provision for Older People and Their Contribution to Adequacy in Retirement." Social Protection Committee, European Union, Brussels.

Gassmann, Franziska, and Christina Behrendt. 2006. "Cash Benefits in Low-Income Countries: Simulating the Effects on Poverty Reduction for Senegal and Tanzania." Issues in Social Protection Series, Discussion Paper 15, Social Security Department, International Labour Office, Geneva.

HAI (HelpAge International). 2004. "Age and Security: How Social Pensions Can Deliver Effective Aid to Poor Older People and Their Families." HAI, London.

ILO (International Labour Office). 2006. "Social Security for All: Investing in Global Social and Economic Development. A Consultation." Issues in Social Protection, Discussion Paper 16, Social Security Department, ILO, Geneva.

———. 2008a. "Can Low-Income Countries Afford Basic Social Security?" Social Security Policy Briefings, Paper 3, Social Security Department, ILO, Geneva.

———. 2008b. "Key Indicators of the Labour Market," 5th ed, ILO, Geneva. http://www.ilo.org/public/english/employment/strat/kilm/.

———. 2008c. "Setting Social Security Standards in a Global Society: An Analysis of Present State and Practice and of Future Options for Global Social Security Standard Setting in the International Labour Organization." Social Security Policy Briefings, Paper 2, Social Security Department, ILO, Geneva.

———. 2008d. "Tanzania: Social Protection Expenditure and Performance Review and Social Budget." Social Security Department, ILO, Geneva.

———. 2008e. "Zambia: Social Protection Expenditure and Performance Review and Social Budget." Social Security Department, ILO, Geneva.

———. 2009. "Social Security for All: Investing in Social Justice and Economic Development." Social Security Department, Social Security Policy Briefings, Paper 7. ILO, Geneva.

OECD (Organisation for Economic Co-operation and Development). 2005. *Pensions at a Glance: Public Policies across OECD Countries.* Paris: OECD.

Schleberger, Eckard. 2002. "Namibia's Universal Pension Scheme: Trends and Challenges." Extension of Social Security (ESS) Paper 6, International Labour Office, Geneva.

Schwarzer, Helmut, and Ana Carolina Querino. 2002. "Non-Contributory Pensions in Brazil: The Impact on Poverty Reduction." Extension of Social Security (ESS) Paper 11, International Labour Office, Geneva.

Seymour, Dan, and Jonathan Pincus. 2008. "Human Rights and Economics: The Conceptual Basis for Their Complementarity." *Development Policy Review* 26 (4): 387–405.

CHAPTER 5

Social Pensions in Low-Income Countries

Armando Barrientos

This chapter throws light on the specific challenges and opportunities confronting social pensions in low-income countries. Following a thematic discussion of design, coverage, finance, and politics, social pension schemes in Bangladesh, Bolivia, and Lesotho are examined. A brief comparative analysis identifies key issues and features of social pensions in low-income countries.

Theoretically, comprehensive social assistance programs that do not exclude the elderly living in poor households might have the best chance of reducing aggregate poverty. In practice, many social assistance programs in developing countries contain exclusions that operate against the elderly and their households. Priority should be given to eliminating these exclusions and ensuring that older people are incorporated into existing social assistance programs. Nevertheless, social pension schemes can be effective as a complement to existing social assistance schemes wherever age-related exclusions are in place.

In low-income countries with scant social assistance provisions, social pension schemes might be a strong policy option where poverty incidence is high, inequality among the poor is low, and resistance to poverty reduction policies is significant. Social pensions have a number of advantages in such cases: they have a clear and transparent target group, they help manage future liabilities, and they provide generational and sectoral redistribution that enjoys broad political support. Moreover, the likelihood of adverse labor supply and saving responses to the income transfer is weaker where the elderly are involved.

This chapter seeks to analyze the challenges and opportunities associated with social pension schemes in low-income countries by examining social pension schemes in Bolivia, Lesotho, and Bangladesh.[1] The main justification for this choice is that experience in these countries, with their distinct approaches to social pensions, provides valuable insights into the spectrum of policy options in low-income countries. Indeed, one of the main findings of the paper underlines the uniqueness of the policy processes shaping each of the schemes.

The next section contains an overview of social pension systems. Following that is a survey of the three countries' social pension schemes and a thematic discussion on design and coverage, financing, and politics. The final sections draw some conclusions on the role of social pensions in low-income countries.

Overview of Social Pensions

In discussing social pensions, it is helpful to begin with a brief comparison of the role of these schemes in developed and developing countries.

Some features of social pensions are common to both country groups. Social pensions are income transfers to older people that are designed to prevent or reduce old-age poverty. These transfers come in different forms, including old-age grants, old-age allowances, and cash transfers. They are mostly tax financed. In many developing countries social pensions have additional features that help define a different role for them; for instance, they may be core antipoverty programs. By contrast, in most developed countries social pensions constitute a residual safety net intended to catch those who are unable to access mandatory pension schemes.

In both developed and developing countries social pensions are paid to the elderly, but in developing countries social pensions address household, not individual, poverty. In developed countries social pensions are expected to raise beneficiaries above the poverty line, but in developing countries they provide fixed-level income supplements that are often insufficient to lift beneficiaries and their households out of poverty.

Most important, social pensions in developing countries are ad hoc and highly country specific. Global studies on pensions find that their most common characteristic is that they facilitate retirement from the labor force (Mulligan and Sala-i-Martin 1999). Interestingly, in developing countries social pensions seldom enforce or facilitate retirement and generally lack inactivity tests. These distinguishing features of social pensions in developing countries apply with greater force in low-income countries.

Social pensions are in place in most developed countries and exist in a good proportion of middle-income countries, but only a handful of low-income countries have them (Barrientos 2006). Perhaps this is to be expected. In the main, low-income countries are characterized by younger populations, a high incidence of multigenerational households, high poverty incidence, and limited public resources and delivery capacity; furthermore, they have other pressing needs in, for example, education and health. In this policy environment, old-age poverty and social pensions are less likely to become policy priorities. Explaining why some low-income countries have chosen to introduce social pensions is therefore important, and it is one of the main questions addressed in this chapter.

There are large knowledge gaps regarding social pensions in low-income countries. Information on their design is readily available, but little is known about their incidence and impact. Moreover, the considerable heterogeneity in policy environment and design makes it difficult to generalize across low-income countries.

Taking social pension schemes in developing countries as a whole, it is possible to observe three main clusters. In Latin America social pensions are concentrated in the more developed countries of the Southern Cone, including Argentina, Bolivia, Brazil, Chile, and Uruguay. In southern Africa social pensions are found in Botswana, Lesotho, Namibia, South Africa, and Swaziland. In South Asia they have been introduced in Bangladesh, India, and Nepal. As noted above, this chapter focuses on Bolivia, Lesotho, and Bangladesh—one country from each of the three clusters. The three systems reflect different approaches to social pensions and are only loosely representative of their respective clusters.

Social Pensions in Bolivia, Lesotho, and Bangladesh

We examine the main features of the social pension schemes in the three countries, focusing on issues related to design and coverage, politics, and finance. Table 5.1 summarizes the main features of the programs in the three sample countries.

Bolivia's BONOSOL (Solidarity Bond) emerged from a complex privatization process in the 1990s. To secure popular support for privatization of utilities, the government promised to distribute shares of the proceeds to the adult population. Subsequently, studies revealed the complexities associated with implementation, and BONOSOL was eventually introduced as an alternative. It is a guarantee to all citizens who were age 21 in 1995 that on reaching age 65, they will be provided with a lifelong annual pension transfer. The transfers

TABLE 5.1 **Summary of social pension schemes, Bolivia, Lesotho, and Bangladesh**

Feature	Bolivia	Lesotho	Bangladesh
Scheme and year established	BONOSOL, 1996 (succeeded by BONO DIGNIDAD, 2008)	Old-age pension, 2004	Old-age allowance, 1998
Gross national income per capita (PPP 2006 U.S. dollars)	3,810	1,810	1,230
Population	9,400,000	2,000,000	156,000,000
Share of population over age 60 (percent)	6.9	7.6	5.8
Life expectancy at birth (years)	65.2	42.9	63.7
Target group	Persons older than age 21 in 1995, on reaching age 65	Age 70 and older	Persons older than age 57; 20 oldest and poorer in ward
Percent receiving pension (approximate)	80	93	16
Selection	Cohort universal	Universal	Community committee
Transfer (U.S. dollars)	230/year (under BONO DIGNIDAD, 320 if no other pension; 160 otherwise)	25/month	2.30/month
Beneficiaries	450,000 (700,000 expected)	70,000	1.3
Budget (percent of GDP)	1.3	2.4	0.03
Finance	Privatization fund (plus 30 percent of energy tax under BONO DIGNIDAD)	Tax revenues	Tax revenues
Politics (at inception)	Facilitated privatization (scheme extended in 2008 by new government committed to renationalization)	Presidential initiative	Five-year plan

SOURCE: Barrientos and Holmes 2006; Bolivia, SPVS 2007a, 2007b; Pelham 2007; World Bank, *World Development Indicators 2007*; United Nations, *World Population Ageing 2007*.

NOTE: GDP, gross domestic product; PPP, purchasing power parity.

are financed from the proceeds of a privatization fund consisting of half of the shares of the privatized utilities. BONOSOL paid out in 1996 for the first time, and it currently provides an annual transfer of US$230.[2] The transfers represent around 24 percent of per capita gross domestic product (GDP), or about 11 percent of average earnings.

Lesotho introduced a social pension in 2004, following a presidential initiative that was subsequently approved by parliament. In introducing a social pension scheme, Lesotho followed the example of neighboring countries in southern Africa. Lesotho, however, is a low-income country, without the natural resources and fiscal capacity of South Africa or Botswana. Entitlement to the social pension covers all citizens from age 70 on and involves a monthly transfer of US$25. This amounts to about 28 percent of per capita GDP and is equivalent to the poverty line. The program represents a significant fiscal commitment, absorbing more than 2 percent of GDP and constituting by far the largest component of social expenditure.

Bangladesh introduced an old-age allowance scheme in 1998, following commitments in the preceding five-year plan. The old-age allowance scheme is managed together with a program aimed at widows and destitute women, but this chapter focuses exclusively on the former. The program provides a transfer of US$2.30 a month to the oldest and poorest persons in each ward (the lowest administrative unit in Bangladesh.) The transfer represents about 1.7 percent of per capita GDP. The government allocates a fixed number of 20 social pensions to each ward, to be allocated by a community committee. Since its introduction, the old-age allowance has been rapidly scaled up and now reaches around 1.3 million beneficiaries.

DESIGN AND COVERAGE

All three schemes provide a fixed-level transfer, the level of which is decided by policy makers on the basis of available resources. BONOSOL and the social pension in Lesotho guarantee a transfer to all individuals who have reached the age of entitlement (age 65 in Bolivia and age 70 in Lesotho). In Bangladesh entitlement to the old-age allowance is restricted to one elderly person per household. The social pensions in Bangladesh and Lesotho disqualify potential beneficiaries who receive other public assistance benefits. Bolivia has both social pension transfers and contributory pension benefits, and in 2007, 12 percent of BONOSOL recipients reported receiving a contributory pension.

The fact that the level of the transfers is fixed suggests that social pensions lack insurance components beyond those provided by the additional income. For example, the level of the pension does not vary in response to financial crises or other hazards affecting the household. The additional income provided by the social pension affords a measure of protection against risks and it has been observed that beneficiaries sometimes save a portion of their pension benefit to meet health costs. The lack of insurance components is most obvious when a pensioner dies. Only Bolivia's BONOSOL includes a fixed payment in that event—a provision intended to cover funeral expenses. Transfers are paid annually in Bolivia, quarterly in Bangladesh, and monthly in Lesotho. In all three schemes initial implementation was delayed by problems with registration and by difficulties in transferring funds to cover payments. There is very little information on the costs of administering schemes and delivering benefits.

The schemes differ with respect to age of entitlement. In Bolivia 65 is the standard retirement age for contributory pensions—a provision common to many pension schemes in the region. Lesotho's age of entitlement was the outcome of policy trade-offs, within a fixed budget, between the level of the benefit and the size of the target group. Policy makers had to make a choice between setting a lower age of entitlement and correspondingly lowering the level of benefits, or setting a higher eligibility age, thus reducing the beneficiary group and enabling a higher benefit level. They opted for the latter, setting the age at 70. This choice has implications for the likely progressivity of the social pension scheme, given the current relationship between life expectancy and wealth. In Bangladesh the age of entitlement is 57, but the fixed number of transfers available at the local level and the requirement that older and poorer persons be given priority imply that, in practice, the beneficiary groups are considerably older than that.

In Lesotho and Bolivia the fact that social pension entitlements are universal ensures a high rate of coverage. The coverage gaps affect mainly two distinct groups: the self-excluding wealthy, and those living in very remote rural areas where collecting the transfer is difficult and costly. In Bangladesh the low level of coverage is a direct consequence of the fixed number of pensions available to the community selection committees.

Selection of beneficiaries in Bangladesh is conducted at the community level by a committee of local elites who then advise a government official. In low-income countries the selection of beneficiaries can be costly because of the high incidence of poverty and low differentiation among the poor. Community selection is one in a very limited range of selection instruments available. It can make effective use of local knowledge of those in poverty but can also provide opportunities for patronage and clientelism and increase the power of local elites. Studies of the incidence of the old-age allowance scheme in Bangladesh find that community selection does a good job in distinguishing between poor and nonpoor older persons but that it is much less accurate in selecting the poorest among the poor. Table 5.2 presents some indicators of the incidence of the social pension in Bangladesh across wealth index quintiles in 2000, in the early stages of the scheme's implementation.

FINANCING

Financing social pensions is a significant challenge for low-income countries, and this is perhaps the main reason why more low-income countries have not instituted these programs. A recent macrosimulation exercise by the Social Security Department of the International Labour Organization (ILO) for a number of low-income countries in Africa and Asia suggests that the introduction of a universal old-age pension in these countries would absorb around 1 percent of GDP. Social pensions are thus affordable in most countries. Many low-income countries,

TABLE 5.2 **Incidence of the old-age allowance by wealth quintile Bangladesh, 2000**
(percent)

Wealth quintile	Quintile share of all households with a pension beneficiary	Share of households in each quintile with a pension beneficiary
1 (lowest)	39.6	6.4
2	37.6	6.0
3	15.8	2.5
4	5.9	0.8
5 (highest)	1.0	0.2

SOURCE: Author's calculations from Bangladesh Demographic and Health Survey, 2000 data.

NOTE: A weighted sample of households with at least one member age 57 or older is used.

however, have only limited capacity for collecting revenues through taxation and lack contributory pension programs that cover most of the labor force. In countries where tax revenues collected are below 15 percent of GDP, allocation of 1 percent of GDP to social pensions would involve significant budgetary reform (see also the discussion in chapter 11 in this volume). Bolivia and Lesotho manage to spend 1.3 and 2.4 percent of GDP on their social pension programs. Bolivia's BONOSOL was financed off budget, and the shift to tax financing for its successor plan, BONO DIGNIDAD, has proved controversial. In Lesotho the social pension is a flagship program and absorbs a significant share of public social spending. In Bangladesh the limited coverage of the social pension explains its small share of GDP.

The approach adopted in the three countries under examination has been to try to manage the liabilities arising from social pensions by restricting the number of beneficiaries, or the extent of benefits, or both. Bolivia's BONOSOL is cohort restricted; it is available only to those who were 21 or older in 1995. On paper, entitlements will gradually fall until 2085, when the cohort will disappear. The rationale for this arrangement had to do with the fact that entitlements are tied to the collective privatization fund. A number of studies have concluded that the fund's current benefit levels are unsustainable, in part because the assumptions made at the start of the scheme regarding profitability turned out to be unduly ambitious. Governments have suspended the payment of the benefit and reduced its size in response to these findings, but political pressure has led to the reinstatement of benefits at their original level. The dividends from the privatization fund have proved insufficient to cover BONOSOL transfers, and new sources of finance are needed.[3] The approach adopted in Bolivia for managing liabilities has had limited success to date.

In Bangladesh managing the liabilities from the social pension has taken the form of capping the number of beneficiaries at the ward level and setting a low transfer amount. The cap on the number of allowances available to the ward committee has risen over time, suggesting that it is a policy lever for the government. In 2007 the scheme was extended to cover urban areas. As the total number of beneficiaries rises, so does the visibility of the scheme. Grassroots organizations and nongovernmental organizations (NGOs) have been formed to advocate for the program and monitor its operations. The establishment of the old-age allowance scheme in Bangladesh is important because it is a publicly financed and managed social assistance program in a country where the main poverty reduction interventions are managed by NGOs and focus on microcredit and microfinance.

In Lesotho the main mechanism for managing the liabilities of the social pension is the late age of entitlement. In comparison with its immediate neighbors, Lesotho begins with smaller benefits and sets a much higher eligibility age, 70 years. (In South Africa, for example, the age of entitlement to a social pension is 60 for women and 65 for men, and the level of the benefit is about US$75.) Entitlement is subject to a means test that excludes the wealthy elderly. Nonetheless, for being a low-income country, the financial cost of the pension is large; it absorbs 1.43 percent of GDP, the same share as the more generous social pension in South Africa.

This discussion brings several points to the fore:

1. In low-income countries, financing the introduction of social pensions requires creative thinking. The schemes reviewed provide few pointers. Bolivia's innovation in financing BONOSOL from the proceeds of privatization does not appear to offer a successful

example. The assumptions made at the start of the scheme apparently resulted in a transfer level that seems unsustainable but that is politically difficult to adjust. The privatization fund has not generated the resources needed to finance the transfers, implying that maintenance of the level of the social pension has required sales of the shares in the fund. The new BONO DIGNIDAD will be financed mainly through energy taxes, but this route has proved controversial because it will divert resources from local authorities.

2. It is important to give joint consideration to financing the scheme and managing the liabilities from the scheme. Relying on a late age of entitlement to manage liabilities in countries such as Lesotho has implications for the effectiveness of the social pension in reducing poverty, as well as for income inequality.

3. There is a large knowledge gap surrounding the trajectory of liabilities in the future, and especially in the medium term. This is particularly true with regard to low-income countries affected by HIV/AIDS and migration.

POLITICS

No explanation of the introduction and sustainability of the social pension schemes would be complete without taking into account the political environment in the three countries under study. Only in Bangladesh was the introduction of the social pension scheme the outcome of established policy processes—specifically, the five-year plans; the old-age allowance scheme was the result of a gradual strengthening of the plans' proposals. The political factors leading to the introduction of social pensions in Bolivia and Lesotho were highly country specific. The main driving force for the introduction of BONOSOL in Bolivia was the need to obtain political support for the privatization program. The social pension scheme was instrumental in securing that support by providing a mechanism for distributing the projected gains from privatization to the adult population. In Lesotho the social pension scheme was wholly a presidential initiative. It appears that the proposal was being discussed by parliament at the same time as the beneficiaries were being registered (Pelham 2007). There is little evidence indicating latent demand for a social pension scheme, suggesting that the initiative owed more to a regional domino effect. It is likely that the presence of social pension schemes as the dominant form of welfare provision in neighboring countries exerted an influence on Lesotho. It is hard to see the examples of Bolivia and Lesotho as indicative of more general trends in low-income countries.

It is a feature of social pensions that, once established, they are able to generate sufficient political support to ensure their sustainability. Several explanatory factors are relevant here. Across developing countries, well-designed social pensions have the advantage of combining life-cycle, vertical, and sectoral redistribution. There is a widely shared perception that children and the elderly are more vulnerable than other people and are therefore more likely to rely on the support of others in society at some point in their lives. There is also a rather well-founded perception that in the absence of effective pension programs or strong family support, old age is associated with poverty in developing countries, so that redistribution to older people implies a redistribution from the nonpoor to the poor (Barrientos, Gorman, and Heslop 2003). In fact, the link between old age and poverty is somewhat blurred in low-income countries because of the high incidence of multigenerational households, household asset accumulation, and the extant correlation between wealth and life expectancy.

Social pensions are also perceived to affect redistribution from urban to rural areas, especially since labor migration leaves a high proportion of older people in rural areas. In low-income countries in Sub-Saharan Africa, Lesotho included, social pensions are also seen to be effective in addressing the adverse impacts of migration and HIV/AIDS on households, and especially children. Rural-urban sectoral factors have contributed to ensuring support for the schemes in Bolivia and Bangladesh.

Social Pensions for Poverty Reduction in Low-Income Countries

Assuming that poverty reduction is the main policy priority, it is advisable to consider the circumstances under which a low-income country would be justified in introducing a social pension scheme.

It is important to acknowledge that social pension schemes have limited scope in low-income countries, simply because the share of poor households with pensioner members is low in countries with younger populations. Figure 5.1 indicates the proportion of the population predicted to be in poverty and living with an elderly person for selected countries in Sub-Saharan Africa. The figure illustrates the scope of a perfectly targeted, or universal, social pension in the countries represented. In only one country, The Gambia, would a social pension cover half the poor, and in two other countries a social pension would extend to over 40 percent of the poor population. In most of the countries studied, however, a social pension would reach less than one-third of the poor. Social pensions might be a powerful instrument for poverty reduction for households affected by HIV/AIDS or migration and from which adults of working age are missing, but these are a small fraction of households in poverty. A social pension by itself would be of limited use in reducing poverty in the majority of countries in Sub-Saharan Africa, most of which are in the low-income category. Social pensions are more likely to be effective in combination with interventions targeting other impoverished groups, such as children.

The limited scope of a social pension in low-income countries suggests that a stronger impact on

FIGURE 5.1 **Share of the poor population living with a person age 60 and older, Sub-Saharan Africa, late 1990s and early 2000s**

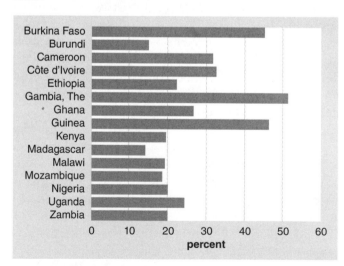

SOURCE: Kakwani and Subbarao 2005.

NOTE: The Kakwani and Subbarao study used national poverty lines computed from nutritional requirements and domestic prices. Data years are as follows: Burkina Faso, 1998; Burundi, 1998; Cameroon, 1996; Côte d'Ivoire, 1998; Ethiopia, 2000; The Gambia, 1998; Ghana, 1998; Guinea, 1994; Kenya, 1997; Madagascar, 2001; Malawi, 1997; Mozambique, 1996; Nigeria, 1996; Uganda, 1999; Zambia, 1998.

poverty could be achieved by focusing on the creation of social assistance programs to cover those in poverty, instead of emphasizing pensions (see also the discussion in chapter 12).[4] On paper, this would be a preferable option. In practice, however, many social assistance interventions have built-in design features that exclude older people and sometimes their households, too. Over the last decade and a half there has been a rapid expansion in developing countries of large-scale social assistance programs based on income transfers; among the many examples are Mexico's Oportunidades, Brazil's Bolsa Familia, Ethiopia's Productive Safety Nets Program (PSNP), India's National Rural Employment Guarantee Scheme (NREGS), and Indonesia's Safety Net Program. Many social assistance programs do not cover older people and their households. For example, work requirements in India's NREGS and Ethiopia's PSNP largely exclude older people, especially where labor-intensive public works are involved. A focus on human capital in Mexico's Progresa and Brazil's Bolsa Escola, which preceded the current programs, also excluded older people living in households without children. It is worth noting, however, that the recent expansion of these programs has reduced the exclusion of older people. Bolsa Familia in Brazil has extended support to all poor households regardless of household composition, and Mexico's Oportunidades now includes supplementary transfers to older people along with an old-age savings scheme.

Research on microcredit and related asset accumulation programs has often found that these schemes leave out older people. Even membership-based microfinance programs such as the Self-Employed Women's Association (SEWA) in India exclude women over age 55. Interestingly, programs focused on the poorest are less likely to exclude older people and their households; an example is Zambia's Kalomo Pilot Social Transfer Scheme (Barrientos and Holmes 2006).

The establishment of comprehensive social assistance programs that do not exclude older people and their households should be a priority in low-income countries. Social pensions can be most effective as a component of these programs.

Social pensions can be a policy priority in low-income countries in one or more of the following circumstances:

1. Where social assistance programs contain exclusions that work to the disadvantage of older people (for example, public works focused on infrastructure, asset accumulation programs that exclude older people as a poor risk, and human development programs that focus only on children), social pensions can be an effective means of incorporating excluded groups.

2. Where the incidence of poverty is high, inequality among the poor is low, and political resistance to poverty reduction policies is significant, social pensions have proved an attractive option for policy makers. Social pensions have a clear and transparent target group, help manage future liabilities, and provide widely supported life-cycle and sectoral redistribution. The pensions can help establish a support constituency for extending social protection under adverse political and economic conditions.

3. Social pensions can be effective in addressing new forms of poverty that have a direct impact on household composition and vulnerability, particularly poverty arising from labor migration and HIV/AIDS.

In adverse political environments, social pensions can minimize concerns about the incentive compatibility of social assistance programs, as the likelihood of adverse labor supply and saving responses to the income transfer is weaker for elderly groups.

Conclusions

Few low-income countries have social pension schemes. This is hardly surprising, given that in those countries the elderly account for a relatively low proportion of the population, poverty incidence is high, multigenerational households are dominant, and government resources for poverty reduction are scarce. Old-age poverty and social pensions are less likely to be policy priorities in these circumstances. It is therefore interesting to explore why some low-income countries have introduced social pensions, difficult though it is to generalize from the existing handful of examples. The case studies of Bolivia, Lesotho, and Bangladesh underlined the highly country-specific factors leading to the adoption of social pensions.

Comparative analysis of the social pension schemes confirmed that the fixed level of transfers supplements household income. The schemes lack any insurance component beyond the income supplement, except for BONOSOL, which includes a transfer to cover the beneficiary's funeral. In Bolivia and Lesotho the entitlements are universal and coverage is high, but in Bangladesh a cap on the number of transfers available at the local level means that only a fraction of eligible beneficiaries, around 16 percent, is reached. The old-age allowance scheme in Bangladesh has a community-level selection and management process that appears to work reasonably well in screening out the nonpoor but is less successful in distinguishing between the different causes of poverty. In all three schemes, design features were included to manage pension liabilities, such as the late age of entitlement in Lesotho, cohort restrictions in Bolivia, and the cap on the number of pensions in Bangladesh.

Should low-income countries adopt social pension schemes? The current analysis suggests that on paper, comprehensive social assistance programs that do not exclude the elderly living in poor households might have the best chance of reducing aggregate poverty. In practice, a high proportion of social assistance programs in developing countries contains exclusions that operate against the elderly and their households. Priority should be given to eliminating these exclusions and ensuring that older people are incorporated into existing social assistance programs. The extension of human development transfer schemes in Mexico and Brazil to older people and their households through supplements linked to older persons provides a good example. Nevertheless, social pension schemes can be effective as a complement to existing social assistance schemes where age-related exclusions prevail. In low-income countries with scant social assistance provisions, social pension schemes might be a strong policy option where poverty incidence is high, inequality among the poor is low, and resistance to poverty reduction policies is significant. Under such circumstances, social pensions have a number of advantages. They have a clear and transparent target group, they help manage future liabilities, and they allow for generational and sectoral redistribution that enjoys broad political support. Moreover, social pensions minimize policy makers' concerns about the incentive compatibility of social assistance transfers, as the likelihood of adverse labor supply and saving responses to the income transfer is weaker for elderly groups. In the specific context of southern Africa, social pension schemes have proved effective in dealing with new forms of poverty arising from the impact of migration and HIV/AIDS on household composition and vulnerability.

Notes

1. Bolivia is not strictly a low-income country according to the World Bank classification, but it is one of the poorest countries in the Latin America and Caribbean Region, just above the low-income threshold.

2. In the wake of the election of President Evo Morales and the partial renationalization of previously privatized utilities, BONOSOL is being replaced by BONO DIGNIDAD. Implementation began in February 2008, after the completion of this study. The new scheme constitutes an extension of BONOSOL, but with some differences. It is paid beginning at age 60 and at a higher level (US$320 a year). Furthermore, it is means tested and is paid at a reduced rate to beneficiaries of social insurance pensions. Most important, revenues from energy taxes will complement existing financing from the privatization fund. In this chapter, reference is made to the implications of these new design features where appropriate.

3. BONO DIGNIDAD will supplement the contribution from the privatization fund with revenues from energy taxes; these amounts for 2008 are estimated at US$25 million and US$165 million, respectively.

4. The term "social assistance" is used in this chapter to describe tax-financed public programs that explicitly address poverty and vulnerability through regular, reliable transfers. This definition includes programs financed from international assistance, where taxes are collected in a different jurisdiction; it also excludes humanitarian programs.

References

Barrientos, Armando. 2006. "Pensions for Development and Poverty Reduction." In *Oxford Handbook of Pensions and Retirement Income*, ed. G. L. Clark, A. H. Munnell, and M. Orszag, 781–98. Oxford: Oxford University Press.

Barrientos, Armando, and R. Holmes. 2006. "Social Assistance in Developing Countries Database." Institute of Development Studies, University of Sussex, Brighton, U.K.

Barrientos, Armando, Mark Gorman, and Amanda Heslop. 2003. "Old Age Poverty in Developing Countries: Contributions and Dependence in Later Life." *World Development* 31 (3): 555–70.

Bolivia, SPVS (Superintendencia de Pensiones, Valores y Seguros). 2007a. "Estudio de impacto BONOSOL." SPVS, La Paz.

———. 2007b. "Programa BONOSOL." PowerPoint presentation, SPVS, La Paz.

Kakwani, Nanak, and Kalanidhi Subbarao. 2005. "Ageing and Poverty in Africa and the Role of Social Pensions." Working Paper 8, International Poverty Centre–United Nations Development Programme, Brasilia.

Mulligan, Casey B., and Xavier Sala-i-Martin. 1999. "Social Security in Theory and Practice (I): Facts and Political Theories." NBER Working Paper 7118, National Bureau of Economic Research, Cambridge, MA.

Pelham, Lissa. 2007. "The Politics behind the Non-Contributory Old Age Social Pensions in Lesotho, Namibia and South Africa." CPRC Working Paper 83, Chronic Poverty Research Centre, Manchester, U.K.

United Nations. 2007. *World Population Ageing 2007*. Department of Economic and Social Affairs, United Nations, New York.

World Bank. 2007. *World Development Indicators 2007*. Washington, DC: World Bank.

CHAPTER 6

Social Pensions in Four Middle-Income Countries

Mukul G. Asher

Policy makers are increasingly recognizing that social pensions can play an important role in expanding the coverage and achieving the poverty mitigation objectives of the social security system. Contributory formal employment-related schemes are leaving significant segments of the population uncovered or inadequately covered. There has also been greater acceptance of the right of the elderly to a basic minimum income, particularly in middle- and high-income countries. This chapter examines the role of social pensions in closing the coverage gap in four middle-income counties—Brazil, Chile, Mauritius, and South Africa—that have instituted fairly extensive social pension systems. These programs, it is argued, have been effective in reducing both the coverage gap and poverty among the elderly. Nonetheless, there is room to improve the design of the schemes in order to minimize economic distortions, improve equity, and make the plans sustainable. A common challenge is to better integrate noncontributory and contributory arrangements and prevent adverse incentives that could reduce labor supply, bring down employment levels, or encourage informality.

Provision of adequate retirement security, which includes mitigation of poverty among the aged, is a major challenge in all countries of the world. Not only is the proportion of the elderly population expected to rise, but each elderly individual will have to be supported by fewer working individuals and for a longer period of time, assuming that rising longevity is not matched by increases in the retirement age.[1] Compounding the need for income security is the fact that the elderly are major consumers of health care.

The World Bank (Holzmann and Hinz 2005) a few years ago proposed a multitier framework under which an elderly individual would obtain income from multiple sources with differing risk and other characteristics. The original formulation had three pillars:

- *Pillar 1.* a reformed version of the current mandatory pay-as-you-go (PAYG) defined benefit pension system that is in place in almost all countries
- *Pillar 2.* a mandatory defined contribution retirement saving scheme
- *Pillar 3.* voluntary individual retirement saving accounts or occupational pension plans.

But these three pillars are not the end of the story, as they leave substantial coverage gaps. Most workers no longer spend their careers in a stable long-term relationship with a single employer, or even in a single economic sector. It is thus unlikely that they will benefit from a voluntary occupational pension. Rising informality has reduced the share of the labor force that contributes steadily to pillar 1 over an entire working life (see chapter 2 in this volume), and the lifetime poor are unlikely to accumulate savings in any of the pillars. At the same time, certain socioeconomic changes complicate the situation. Women, although they have benefited from greater freedom to participate in the labor force, no longer enjoy the social protection that was implicit in the traditional male-breadwinner family. And informal family or community arrangements for taking care of the elderly are becoming less effective as a result of urbanization and migration.

Confronted with the inadequacy of the three-pillar approach, policy makers across the world have increasingly recognized that non-earnings-related, noncontributory schemes ("pillar 0") can help reach a large segment of the population that is unable to make sufficient contributions to the three pillars. Women—who, on average, live longer than men, spend fewer years in the labor force, and receive lower earnings when they do work—may benefit disproportionately from these programs. Noncontributory programs can also insure workers who participate in pillars 2 and 3 against adverse macroeconomic developments, such as stock market crashes or low interest rates at the time of retirement, which would lead to low annuity income streams.[2]

Noncontributory schemes have existed for some time, but they have not been subjected to as much rigorous research, or even description, as contributory schemes. Exceptions include studies by Schwartz (2003), Palacios and Sluchynsky (2006), Robalino, Rao, and Sluchynsky (2007), and Willmore (2007). This chapter contributes to the current literature by looking at the principal features of social pensions in middle-income countries.[3] The goal is to understand the main constraints related to design and implementation and the need for additional reforms.

The analysis is based on studies of four countries: Brazil, Chile, Mauritius, and South Africa. All cluster around a per capita income of US$10,000–US$15,000, but they differ greatly demographically. Populations range from 1.3 million in Mauritius to almost 192 million in Brazil; the share of population above 65 varies from 4.5 percent in South Africa to 8.5 percent in Chile; the total fertility rate is 2.0 in Chile but 2.7 in South Africa; and life expectancy at birth ranges between 51 years in South Africa and 78 years in Chile (table 6.1).

The chapter begins with a description of the four social pension systems. It then raises several policy issues regarding the adequacy and affordability of the programs,

TABLE 6.1 **Macroeconomic and demographic indicators, sample countries, 2007**

Indicator	Brazil	Chile	Mauritius	South Africa
GDP per capita, PPP (current international dollars)	9,570	13,886	11,278	9,736
Population, total (millions)	191.6	16.6	1.3	47.6
Population age 65 and above (percent of total)	6.4	8.5	6.8	4.5
Total fertility rate (births per woman)	2.3	2.0	2.0	2.7
Life expectancy at birth (years)	72.1	78.3	73.2	50.7
Life expectancy at birth, female (years)	75.8	81.4	76.6	52.5
Life expectancy at birth, male (years)	68.5	75.4	69.9	49.0

SOURCE: World Bank 2008a.

NOTE: PPP, purchasing power parity. Fertility rate and life expectancy data are for 2006.

their fiscal impacts, and unintended consequences for labor markets. A general design framework is proposed to address these issues over the medium term.

Overview of Pension Systems in the Sample Countries

This section reviews the main design features of the social pension systems in Brazil, Chile, Mauritius, and South Africa, as well as key indicators of performance in terms of coverage and costs. For each of the countries we also identify some of the main achievements of the social pension systems to date and the challenges going forward.

BRAZIL

Bismarckian social insurance covering pensions, health care, and social assistance is part of the broad concept of social security established under the Brazilian Federal Constitution of 1989. Private sector workers are covered under the General Social Security Scheme (Regime Geral de Previdência Social, RGPS), a public contributory scheme compulsory for all formal sector employees not covered by their own pension programs. The latest available figures show that 64 percent of employed workers have social protection. There is, however, considerable variation among the five major geographic regions because of profound socioeconomic inequalities (Ansiliero and Paiva 2008). A significant divide exists between the participation of men and women, and of whites and blacks, in the formal employment sector and as contributors to the social security program. Public servants and military personnel have their own social security scheme (the Regime Próprio de Previdência Social, RPPS), but recent reforms have reduced the differences between these schemes and the RGPS.

Beginning in the 1980s, pressures for reform increased, thanks in large part to the political activism of the elderly themselves. Reforms instituted in 1991 established qualifying conditions for men and women in rural areas, reduced the minimum age for the award of retirement benefits to 60 (men) or 55 (women), and established a uniform minimum welfare benefit for all insured persons. (Rural workers had previously received old-age pensions at levels of up to 50 percent of the minimum wage, and spouses and children had received survivor pensions limited to 30 percent of the benefit paid or payable to the deceased.) Whereas before 1991 only heads of household were entitled to a pension, the reforms extended entitlement to all qualifying workers, thus expanding coverage to female rural workers who were not heads of household. Entitlement to old-age, disability, and survivor pensions was broadened to workers in subsistence activities in agriculture, fishing, and mining and to those in informal employment. Women engaging in unpaid family work and independent (mostly self-employed) workers were encouraged to participate. These nontraditional contributors to the RGPS are known as special insured persons (SIPs).[4]

At the same time, the government introduced the noncontributory continuous welfare benefit pension (*benefício de prestação continuada,* BPC) for persons not covered by a compulsory contributory scheme. Beneficiaries receive a uniform welfare benefit set at the level of the minimum wage. An estimated 5.3 million people are served by this scheme (Barrientos 2005). A key aspect of the program is that access to pension entitlements does not require earnings tests or inactivity tests. Delgado and Cardoso (2000) found high levels of satisfaction with the quality of service of public agencies and with the promptness of payment.

The sources of financing for noncontributory benefits include transfers from the social insurance programs (which in turn collect contributions from employers and employees in formal employment) and revenues from excise duties and taxes on large firms. For the rural pension program, a tax is also levied on sales of agricultural produce, although the revenues from this tax cover only one-tenth of benefits, and most funding still comes from the urban social insurance scheme and government revenues (Schwarzer and Delgado 2002).Table 6.2 shows the coverage of the employed population in Brazil in 2006.[5] Of the country's 52 million workers, 64 percent were covered by social protection and 36 percent were not. Nearly 10 percent of those covered were special insured persons under the RGPS. Only 1.6 percent of the employed population is receiving benefits from the noncontributory social pension scheme, but this figure considerably understates the importance of the scheme for the elderly population.

Brazil's programs have been very successful in expanding coverage and reducing poverty among the elderly. (For a review see Robalino et al., forthcoming, ch. 4.) At the same time, there are concerns about the financial sustainability of the programs and about potential distortions in labor markets. Expenditures in the social insurance system (excluding health) amounted to 7.6 percent of gross domestic product (GDP) in 2007; of those expenditures, 8 percent is related to the noncontributory programs. Thus, the tax burden of the system is not negligible. The financing is partly based on dedicated value added or sales taxes, but payroll taxes and social security contributions remain important. The average employer pays 30 percent of the payroll to the social security system to finance pensions, insurance against work accidents, and individual unemployment savings accounts (see World Bank 2008c), and the average worker

TABLE 6.2 **Social protection of the employed population age 16–59, Brazil, 2006**

Category	Number of workers	Percent
1. RGPS contributors	36,931,870	45.6
2. RPPS contributors	5,637,203	7.0
Military	271,169	0.3
Public servants	5,366,034	6.6
3. Special insured persons (RGPS)[a]	8,049,773	9.9
4. Noncontributors	30,319,474	37.5
Total, rows 1, 2, 3, and 4	80,938,320	100.0
5. Noncontributing beneficiaries[b]	1,285,007	1.6
Workers covered by social protection (rows 1, 2, 3, and 5)	51,903,853	64.1
Workers without social protection (row 4 – row 5)	29,034,467	35.9
With incomes of less than minimum wage	13,277,493	16.4
With incomes equal to or greater than minimum wage	15,429,425	19.1
With unknown incomes	327,549	0.4

SOURCE: Ansiliero and Paiva 2008.

NOTE: RGPS, General Social Security Scheme (Regime Geral de Previdência Social); RPPS, Civil Servants' System (Regime Próprio de Previdência Social). Data do not take income criteria into account.

a. Inhabitants of rural areas working in agriculture in the following categories: unregistered, self-employed, producing for own consumption, building for own use, and unremunerated.

b. Employed workers (excluding special insured persons) who, although not contributing, receive a welfare benefit.

contributes around 8 percent. In addition, employers pay value added taxes and sales taxes (0.65 percent of gross revenues in the services sector and 1.65 percent of value added in industry) to finance unemployment benefits (World Bank 2008c). Recent studies suggest that without higher contributions, the pension system is not sustainable (see World Bank 2007). Yet, given the current tax wedge (above 30 percent), further increases could aggravate labor market distortions.

There are also concerns about the incentive effects of the programs. The fact that the minimum pension is equal to the minimum wage is obviously not a good incentive for work. Incentives issues are discussed in more detail in chapter 10 in this volume, but overall, there is good evidence showing that the rural pension has reduced labor supply at the ages close to retirement and that the current structure of the minimum pension guarantee in the contributory system is likely to reduce contribution densities, defined as the number of months in which an individual has made social security contributions as a proportion of months of membership in the system.

CHILE

Chile's 1981 pension reforms have been extensively discussed in the social security literature and have had considerable influence in policy debates (Mesa-Lago 2008). The reforms resulted in a switch from a public pay-as-you-go defined benefit system to a mandatory defined contribution system in which individual accounts are managed by competing private sector firms. Once hailed as a model for social security reformers everywhere, after nearly three decades of experience with the pension system the Chilean reform is now being reassessed as to the extent to which it has achieved its objectives, particularly with respect to coverage and adequacy.

In 2003 the ratio of contributors to the pension system to the economically active population was 59 percent, a decline from 62 percent in 1990. Similar declines have been observed for the ratio of contributors to wage earners (Rofman and Lucchetti 2006). The ratio of pension beneficiaries to the population age 65 and over declined from 73 percent in 1990 to 63 percent in 2003. The decrease was particularly sharp among women, from 67 to 56 percent. At present, about 40 percent of employed persons do not contribute to the fully funded defined contribution pension scheme. Current capital market volatility has reinforced the need to reexamine the program.[6]

The basic tenet of Chile's system is that each worker is responsible for financing his own pension. Nevertheless, the state has long provided some assistance for those unable to fund their retirement. Before the recent reforms (discussed below), this was achieved through two mechanisms:

- The *pensión asistencial (PASIS)*—a publicly funded means-tested social assistance pension provided to the poorest aged, irrespective of their contribution history. The government limits the number of PASIS pensions granted in order to control expenditures, and so there is always a waiting list for them.

- The *minimum pension guarantee (MPG)*—a benefit provided to all individuals who have contributed to the system for at least 20 years (specifically, who have made at least 240 monthly contributions) but have not accumulated enough to qualify for a minimum pension. The guarantee applies only when a member does not have an accumulation sufficient to enable him or her to draw a prespecified minimum benefit. Then, the state simply tops up the members' account by the required amount. The minimum pension is set at approximately three-fourths of Chile's minimum wage or one-fourth of the average wage. At present, it is about US$180 per month.

There are other, covert, guarantees provided by the state. If a pension management company (*administradoras de fondo de pensiones,* AFP) goes bankrupt, the pension funds belonging to the members do not suffer; instead the worker simply transfers them to another AFP. In case of the bankruptcy of an insurance company, the state guarantees 100 percent of the minimum pension plus 75 percent of the difference between the amount the pensioner was receiving and the minimum pension, with a ceiling of US$45 per month.

The pension system in Chile has seen a number of changes since its inception, with the aim of improving coverage, adequacy, and equity (Asher and Vasudevan 2008; Mesa-Lago 2008; Rofman, Fajnzylber, and Herrera 2008; Valdes-Prieto 2008). In March 2006 newly elected President Michelle Bachelet set up a presidential advisory council on pension reform under the chairmanship of Inter-American Development Bank economist Mario Marcel to evaluate the existing pension system. In March 2008 a new Pension Act was passed.

The new pension system is based on the three-tier structure, modified to suit changing needs:

- *Pillar 0.* A government-financed social safety net, the System of Solidarity Pensions (SPS)
- *Pillar 2.* The mandatory contributory second pillar, the basic design of which remains unchanged although its scope will be widened to cover currently excluded workers (Asher and Vasudevan 2008)
- *Pillar 3.* Additional voluntary savings (*ahorro previsional voluntario,* APV).

The most important reform proposed by the committee is a measure to make the APV more inclusive. Currently only those independent workers who are affiliated with an AFP are permitted to contribute to an APV, but this restriction is to be removed to allow access for all independent workers.

The new System of Solidarity Pensions will replace the existing PASIS scheme and the minimum pension guarantee provided by the government. The aim of creating this pillar is to provide universal pension coverage to all Chileans and to minimize old-age poverty by assisting those with lower capacity to contribute toward their pensions. The SPS also offers a more integrated structure between contributory and noncontributory benefits and is expected to reduce incentives for informal sector work (see Valdés-Prieto 2008).

The SPS will benefit men and women age 65 years and older who belong to the poorest 60 percent of the population. To be eligible for SPS benefits, the applicant, in addition, should have lived for 20 years in Chile, including the 5 years preceding the application. The main benefits under the SPS include the universal basic pension (PBU) and the solidarity contributory pension (APS). Beginning July 1, 2008, all persons who did not contribute to the system and have no other source of pension will receive a minimum solidarity pension if eligible for the SPS. Such persons will receive a basic pension amounting to 60,000 Chilean

TABLE 6.3 **Transition to the System of Solidarity Pensions, Chile, 2008–2012**

Year	Universal basic pension (PBU)		Maximum pension with solidarity contribution (PMAS)	
	Chilean pesos	U.S. dollars	Chilean pesos	U.S. dollars
2008	60,000	111	60,000	111
2009	75,000	139	75,000	139
2010	75,000	139	100,000	185
2011	75,000	139	150,000	278
2012	75,000	139	200,000	371

SOURCE: Asher and Vasudevan (2008), table 23, p. 89 (based on Chile, "Reforma Previsional: Protección para la vejez en el nuevo milenio," December 2006).

NOTE: Data are as of July 1 in each year. Exchange rate: 540 Chilean pesos = 1 U.S. dollar.

pesos (Ch$), or US$111 per month; this will increase to Ch$75,000 (US$139) by 2009.

Persons who have some contributory pension and are eligible under the SPS will receive a top-up that will decline as the member's own pension increases and will finally cease when the self-financed contributory pension reaches the maximum pension with solidarity contribution (PMAS). The PMAS will be set at Ch$60,000 (US$111) per month in 2008 and will rise to Ch$200,000 (US$371) per month by 2012. PMAS values during the five-year transition period are shown in table 6.3. The rate of withdrawal of the top-up is designed in such a way that the total pension always increases in response to higher contributory effort. (See chapter 10 in this volume for a discussion of gradual withdrawal or claw-back rates.)

The groups that will benefit most from this reform include workers with low contribution densities; workers with volatile income, such as seasonal and independent workers; persons who have devoted an important part of their active lives to unremunerated work at home; less-educated workers; and old people with very low pensions.

According to projections by the advisory council, when the system starts operating in 2008, about 40 percent of the population over age 65 will receive a basic solidarity pension. This represents an increase of 100,000 people over the current number of beneficiaries of PASIS assistance pensions. By the fifth year of operation, it is expected that 60 percent of the poorest in Chile, or over 1 million persons, will benefit from the scheme.

In addition to expanding coverage, the scheme has the advantage that, by creating a link between the smallest marginal contribution and additional pension received, it maintains the incentive to make regular contributions. The solidarity pension is integrated smoothly into the contributory scheme. Thus, if workers contribute regularly to their individual pension accounts, the contributory pillar ensures that they will receive a worthwhile pension. If for some reason they do not contribute at all, or do so infrequently, they are supported by the solidarity pillar, which not only guarantees a basic pension but also ensures higher pensions based on their contributions. Among the disadvantages is cost; in comparison with other countries that provide social pensions, Chile's cost incurred is relatively high, at 5 percent of GDP.

MAURITIUS

The National Pensions Scheme in Mauritius, governed by the National Pensions Act of 1976, includes both contributory and noncontributory elements. Whereas the noncontributory benefits are entirely financed by the government and are payable to every citizen, with some residency conditions, the contributory benefits are payable only to (or on behalf of) those who have contributed to the National Pensions Fund (NPF). The contributory pensions include old-age, disability, and widow and orphan pensions, in addition to industrial injury allowances. The contributory retirement pension begins at age 60 and provides a pension equivalent to one-third of average earnings, after 40 years of contributions, to employees contributing at a standard rate of 9 percent. A pension of one-half of earnings is paid to those contributing at the higher rate of 13.5 percent of basic income, subject to a ceiling.

All basic benefits are noncontributory and are paid on a universal basis. The noncontributory benefits include the basic retirement pension (BRP), the basic widow's pension (BWP), the basic invalid's pension (BIP), the basic orphan's pension and guardian's allowance (BOP), and the child allowance. Other noncontributory social benefits are provided through schemes such as Social Aid (an income-tested scheme), Food Aid, and Unemployment Hardship Relief (UHR).

Mauritius's provision of a pension to the whole population places it among a small group of African nations that includes Botswana, Lesotho, and Namibia. The country introduced its noncontributory pension system in 1950. Pensions were originally paid on a means-tested basis but were made universal in 1958. The introduction of a compulsory contributory scheme for workers in the private sector, operational since July 1978, endeavors to ensure that the elderly receive enough to live comfortably.

The basic retirement pension (BRP) or social pension—the main noncontributory scheme—is payable to persons over age 60.[7] As of July 1, 2008, the BRP was 2,802 Mauritian rupees (MUR) per month for persons between ages 60 and 89; MUR 8,335 for those between ages 90 and 99; and MUR 9,461 for those 100 and older. The pension thus increases with age and is paid until the person dies, placing longevity risk on the shoulders of the government. The graduated system of pensions has a number of advantages. It recognizes that the very aged likely will have outlived their savings, as well as their potential caregivers, and will be incapable of earning income. The BRP for severely handicapped persons is MUR 1,766 per month, which comes on top of the standard amounts. As a proportion of per capita GDP, these pensions range from about 18 percent for the smallest, most common pension to 92 percent for that of a person age 100 or older. Under the existing system it is also customary to pay all pensioners a 13th-month bonus at the end of each year.

The basic pension is neither income nor retirement tested. It is taxable as ordinary income. Although the income tax rate is nearly flat, most pensioners above age 90 pay some income tax, even if they have no other income, unless they have deductions for dependents or other allowable expenses. Social pension expenditure, totaling US$161 million, is financed through tax revenue.

As in Brazil, the program in Mauritius has been successful in expanding coverage and preventing poverty. There is concern, however, about its sustainability. According to the Ministry of Finance, in 2005/06 government expenditure on social security and welfare amounted to MUR 11.4 billion, equivalent to 23.3 percent of total government expenditure and 5.8 percent of GDP (Mauritius 2007). The amount distributed under the BRP was MUR 4.1 billion, or 36.0 percent of total expenditure on social security and welfare. The corresponding proportions were 6.0 percent for the basic widow's pension, 8.7 percent for the basic invalid's pension, and 3.1 percent for the social assistance scheme. The share of contributory pensions in total expenditure was 4.8 percent. The official projections are that the number of beneficiaries of the BRP will increase by about 80 percent, from 126,000 (nearly 10 percent of the total population) in June 2006 to 228,000 by 2021. Under this scenario, the costs of the BRP will increase by about 75 percent, from MUR 4.1 billion in 2005/6 to MUR 7.3 billion in 2020/21. In addition, 71,000 people (5.5 percent of the total population) received other types of social pensions and child allowances in 2005/6. Social pension coverage is therefore quite high, and the challenge for Mauritius will be to maintain it.

SOUTH AFRICA

For a long time, South Africa's pension policy was supply driven and served political ends. Today it is demand driven, with the aim of meeting the welfare objectives of reducing poverty and promoting equality.

South Africa was the first country in Africa to institute a state pension. In 1922 it introduced a universal pension of US$59 for whites age 65 and US$34 for "coloreds." In 1937 the age of pension eligibility for women, white and colored, was reduced to 60 years; the current eligibility age is 60 for women and 65 for men. In 1944 pensions were extended to all citizens, but black South Africans received a lower pension than whites and colored. There were also differentials based on residence; for example, black South Africans in urban areas received higher pensions than those in rural areas.

With the end of apartheid in 1994, pensions were equalized for all citizens meeting the age test. Pension payments are subject to means testing, which excludes most of the white population and about 20 percent of the black population. In early 2008 the amount of the old-age pension (OAP) was 870 rand (R) a month for a single pensioner; married couples received double that amount. There is a provision for a grant-in-aid allowance (R 180 per month) for those receiving the OAP who require the full-time attendance of another person because of a mental or physical condition. The OAP is noncontributory, with the government bearing the total cost. Family allowances cover low-income persons who have children younger than age 18. The total cost of this program is also borne by the government.

Studies of South Africa's experience with social pensions almost uniformly show a significant reduction in poverty rates for the elderly. Barrientos (2003) estimates that among sampled households in South Africa, the poverty headcount would be 1.9 percentage points higher without social pensions. The reduction is attributed to high coverage and large benefits relative to incomes, particularly for the black population (Palacios and Sluchynsky 2006). In 2007, 2.2 million beneficiaries received social pensions, and 33,000 benefited from the grant-in-aid program (Patel and Triegaardt 2008). There is also evidence that social pensions and other noncontributory income support programs have had a positive effect on access by women (Patel and Triegaardt 2008).

For the time being, the rate of graduation of the elderly to a pension in South Africa is slower than the rate of increase of South Africa's elderly population, and so the system is still fiscally manageable. There is, however, concern as to whether the country will be able to sustain such ambitious social pensions and related programs in the medium term because of fiscal affordability and limited institutional capacities. Another concern is corruption, which, even with improved oversight, is estimated to account for 15 percent of all claims.

The success of the social pension has not stopped South African policy makers from seeking to strengthen other components of the pension system. On February 23, 2007, the minister of finance released the report *Social Security and Pension Reform: A Second Discussion* (South Africa, Ministry of Finance, 2007). The new system is likely to contain four broad elements:

- Noncontributory social assistance to deal with poverty
- A contributory social insurance component to partially cover retirement, as well as unemployment, disability, and injury
- Mandatory retirement savings, designed to provide a higher replacement rate and increase national savings
- A voluntary savings and insurance arrangement.

For very low income earners, the introduction of a wage subsidy will seek to offset the mandatory contribution.

Policy Questions

The examples given here show that social pensions are a feasible approach for providing income in old age, given the still limited coverage of contributory systems. Middle-income countries, however, are in a delicate position. Although they cannot afford the sort of comprehensive pension systems that high-income countries have instituted (and are in many cases trying to rein in), they must meet their citizens' legitimate and growing expectations regarding leisure, well-being, and income security in old age. At the same time, populations are aging and this will likely increase the cost of the programs. Fiscal sustainability would involve a combination of tighter eligibility conditions and lower benefits—options that are not politically popular and that could reduce the impact of the programs on poverty.

Middle-income countries will thus need to address three issues: how to better target social pensions to reduce fiscal costs; how to better integrate social pensions with other social assistance programs; and how to better integrate social pensions with contributory programs in order to improve incentives to contribute and save and thus reduce the long-term costs of the programs.

On the first issue, means-tested social pensions can induce important savings and improve the antipoverty aspect of the programs. It has been argued that means testing can be administratively costly, that there are errors of exclusion, and that testing can carry a threat of stigma, leading to low take-up. HelpAge International (HAI 2008) summarizes international experience suggesting that means-tested social benefits have failed to reach the poorest elderly in countries as diverse as India and Chile. Willmore (2007) argues that if means testing is necessary to control the fiscal impact of a universal pension, it would be best to do it ex post through the tax system, not ex ante. Not all countries, however, have an efficiently functioning tax system. Still, the discussions in chapter 12 and 14 of this volume suggest that efficient means testing could be feasible through proxy means tests. These programs have been very successful in the implementation of conditional cash transfers and could also be applied to social pensions.

Related to this is the issue of whether social pensions should be maintained as separate programs or merged with overall social assistance. There is considerable evidence indicating that when the elderly are direct beneficiaries of an age-based benefit, their status within the household is significantly enhanced (Schwartz 2003). In an aging society, and one experiencing rapid social change, this is not an insignificant advantage. At the same time, chapter 12 shows that allocating resources to social pensions diverts resources from other antipoverty programs. Many of the elderly are poor, but there are also many poor who are not elderly, and many elderly who are not poor. Better-integrated programs could be more effective in reducing overall poverty, and they would involve lower administrative costs.

Finally, there are issues related to the integration of contributory and noncontributory systems to improve incentives and reduce costs. For universal programs, incentive effects in the labor market are likely to be less important as long as the transfers are not too high and eligibility conditions are not too lax. Indeed, eligibility applies regardless of whether individuals have access to contributory pensions. Still, universal programs can be costly, and thus it is important that the contributory part of the pension system be self-sustainable and nonredistributive (see Robalino et al., forthcoming).

Incentive effects become an issue when noncontributory programs target certain groups (e.g., informal sector workers or uncovered agricultural workers) or sharply reduce transfers as a function of earnings (including contributory pensions). The first is the case of Brazil and the second the case in Chile, before the reform. The result can be weak incentives for low-income individuals to enroll and contribute. One solution is to delink access to the noncontributory programs from employment status and to base eligibility solely on income. The other is to reduce the transfer only gradually as a function of earnings—that is, to have a low marginal tax on the transfer. The new reform in Chile is implementing both types of policy. In addition, countries can consider providing ex ante transfers to motivate enrollment and savings in the contributory system, thus reducing the long-term costs of social pensions. This novel approach is discussed in detail in chapter 13.

Conclusions

To put the matter in a nutshell, policy analysis regarding social pensions in any country should revolve around three issues: the impact on poverty, the impact on incentives, and the fiscal impact. The four case studies examined in this chapter suggest that social pensions have the potential to substantially improve the coverage of social security systems, given political commitment and reasonably effective delivery mechanisms. In general, there is also evidence that the programs have contributed to reducing old-age poverty.

It is important to acknowledge, however, that there are economic and fiscal costs. Although in South Africa there is no evidence of adverse effects on labor supply, these have been a source of concern in prereform Chile and in Brazil (see chapter 10 in this volume). The resources allocated to social pensions will need to increase as a result of aging, and this can compromise fiscal sustainability and the efficiency of public spending. Middle-income countries thus face the challenge of rethinking the design of current noncontributory systems to improve equity and incentives and reduce fiscal costs. Chile is already providing some guidance concerning how these adjustments could take place.

Much more country-specific research is necessary for better understanding of the economic and social impacts of the various designs and implementation strategies for social pensions. The political-economy aspects also require further investigation. The current global economic crisis underscores the need for a multitier system in general, and for noncontributory social pensions and related programs in particular. Simultaneous reforms designed to sustain high growth, improve fiscal health, and promote more effective delivery of government services will be needed.

Notes

1. The proportion of the world population age 60 and above is expected to increase from 10.3 percent in 2005 (673 million persons) to 21.8 percent in 2050 (2,006 million). Global life expectancy at birth is expected to increase from 67.2 years in 2005–10 to 75.4 years in 2045–50 (United Nations 2006).

2. The ongoing global financial turmoil is an emphatic reminder of the possibility of market crashes. Global stock market capitalization fell from close to US$61 trillion in December 2007 to about US$43 trillion in September 2008, a drop of 29.7 percent (http://www.world-exchanges .org/WFE/home.asp?menu=395&nav=ie). Markets have declined further since September 2008, and so the erosion of market capitalization is likely to be even larger. This has adverse impacts on the replacement rate that may be obtained from the contributory schemes, whose assets are invested in the capital markets.

3. The World Bank classification of economies according to 2007 gross national income (GNI) per capita, using the World Bank Atlas method, is as follows: low income, US$935 or less; lower middle income, US$936–US$3,705; upper middle income, US$3,706–US$11,455; and high income, US$11,456 or more (World Bank 2008b).

4. In rural areas, in practice, there are no restrictions on vesting periods, and men and women become eligible for the minimum benefit (equal to the minimum wage) on reaching the eligibility age.

5. Coverage may be measured in different ways (Rofman and Lucchetti 2006). For active workers, coverage may be measured as the ratio of contributors to the economically active population, or as the ratio of contributors to employed workers, or as the ratio of contributors to wage earners. Because social pensions are provided to the aged, the ratio of pension recipients to individuals over age 65 (or age 60), disaggregated by those receiving social pensions and those receiving other types of pension, is an appropriate indicator. In many lower-middle-income countries the ratio of aged individuals residing in households containing pension recipients to individuals over age 65 (or age 60) could provide a better social measure of old-age income security.

6. Between September 2007 and September 2008 Chile's stock market capitalization declined by 21 percent; see World Federation of Exchanges, http://www.world-exchanges.org/WFE/ home.asp?menu=395&nav=ie.

7. The retirement age is being raised to 65 years over a period of 10 years, starting in August 2008.

References

Ansiliero, G., and L. H. Paiva. 2008. "The Recent Evolution of Social Security Coverage in Brazil." *International Social Security Review* 61 (3): 1–28.

Asher, M. G., and D. Vasudevan. 2008. "Lessons for Asian Countries from Pension Reforms in Chile." Discussion Paper 381, Institute of Economic Research, Hitotsubashi University, Tokyo.

Barrientos, Armando. 2003. "Non-Contributory Pensions and Poverty Prevention? A Comparative Study of Brazil and South Africa." Report to the U.K. Department for International Development (DFID), Institute for Development Policy and Management (IDPM), University of Manchester, Manchester, U.K., and HelpAge International, London. www.helpage.org/Resources/Researchreports/main_content/1118335208-0-1/NCPEnglish.pdf.

————. 2005. "Non-Contributory Pensions and Poverty Reduction in Brazil and South Africa." Institute for Development Policy and Management (IDPM), University of Manchester, Manchester, U.K.

Delgado, Guilherme, and José Celso Cardoso, Jr. 2000. "Principais resultados da pesquisa domiciliar sobre previdência rural na Região Sul do Brasil: Projeto avaliação da socioeconômica da previdência rural." Texto para discussão 734. Instituto de Pesquisa Econômica Aplicada (IPEA), Rio de Janeiro.

HAI (HelpAge International). 2008. "Tackling Poverty in Old Age: A Universal Pension for Sri Lanka." HAI, London.

Holzmann, Robert, and Richard Hinz. 2005. *Old Age Income Support in the 21st Century: An International Perspective on Pension Systems and Reform.* Washington, DC: World Bank.

Mauritius, Ministry of Finance. 2007. *Digest of Social Security Statistics 2006.* Port Louis: Central Statistics Office.

Mesa-Lago, Carmelo. 2008. *Reassembling Social Security: A Survey of Pensions and Health Care Reforms in Latin America.* New York: Oxford University Press.

Palacios, Robert J., and Oleksiy Sluchynsky. 2006. "Social Pensions Part I: Their Role in the Overall Pension System." Social Protection Discussion Paper 0601, World Bank, Washington, DC.

Patel, L., and J. Triegaardt. 2008. "South Africa: Social Security, Poverty Alleviation, and Development." In *Social Security, the Economy and Development,* ed., J. Midgley and K. L. Tang, 85–109. New York: Palgrave Macmillan.

Robalino David, Gudivada Venkateswara Rao, and Oleksiy Sluchynsky. 2007. "Preventing Poverty among the Elderly in MENA Countries: Role and Optimal Design of Old-Age Subsidies." Human Development Department, Middle East and North Africa Region, World Bank, Washington, DC.

Robalino, David, Andrew Mason, Helena Ribe, and Ian Walker. Forthcoming. *The Future of Social Protection in Latin America: Adapting Programs to Labor Markets and Rethinking Redistribution.* Washington, DC: World Bank.

Rofman, Rafael, and Leonardo Lucchetti. 2006. "Pension Systems in Latin America: Concepts and Measurements of Coverage." Social Protection Discussion Paper 0616, World Bank, Washington, DC.

Rofman, Rafael, Eduardo Fajnzylber, and German Herrera. 2008. "Reforming the Pension Reforms: The Recent Initiatives and Actions on Pensions in Argentina and Chile." Social Protection Discussion Paper 0831, Pension Reform Primer Series, World Bank, Washington, DC.

Schwartz, Anita M. 2003. "Old Age Security and Social Pensions." Social Protection Department, World Bank, Washington, DC. http://info.worldbank.org/etools/docs/library/78330/3rd%20Workshop/Srmafrica/paristwo/pdf/readings/oldage.pdf.

Schwarzer, Helmut, and Guilherme Delgado. 2002. "The Spread of Benefits: Alleviating Poverty in Brazil." *id21 Insights 42* (June). Institute of Development Studies, University of Sussex, Brighton, U.K. http://www.id21.org/insights/insights42/insights-iss42-art08.html.

South Africa, Ministry of Finance. 2007. *Social Security and Pension Reform: A Second Discussion.* Pretoria: Ministry of Finance.

United Nations. 2006. *World Population Prospects: The 2005 Revision.* Population Division, Department of Economic and Social Affairs, United Nations Secretariat, New York. http://esa.un.org/unpp.

Valdés-Prieto, Salvador. 2008. "A Theory of Contribution Density and Implications for Pension Design." Social Protection Discussion Paper 0828, Pension Reform Primer Series, World Bank, Washington, DC.

Willmore, Larry. 2007. "Universal Pensions for Developing Countries." *World Development* 35 (1): 24–51.

World Bank. 2007. "Federative Republic of Brazil: Towards a Sustainable and Fair Pension System." Human Development Sector Management Unit, Latin America and the Caribbean Region, World Bank, Washington, DC.

———. 2008a, "World Development Indicators, WDI Online." World Bank, Washington, DC. http://web.worldbank.org/; accessed April 13, 2008.

———. 2008b. *World Development Report 2008: Agriculture for Development.* Washington, DC: World Bank.

———. 2008c. "Federative Republic of Brazil: Social Insurance and Labor Supply. Assessing Incentives and Redistribution." Draft Technical Report, Human Development Sector Management Unit, Latin America and the Caribbean Region, World Bank, Washington, DC.

CHAPTER 7

Social Pensions in High-Income Countries

Mark Pearson and Edward Whitehouse

Retirement income provision in high-income countries is both diverse and complex. In low- and middle-income countries, social pensions are entirely separate from earnings-related plans; retirees receive benefits either from the social pension or from the earnings-related scheme. In high-income countries, most people who receive a social pension also receive at least some benefit from the earnings-related scheme, and as a result, there are significant and complex overlaps and interactions between social and earnings-related pensions. This chapter examines the performance of social pensions across 30 high-income countries and looks at the effects of recent reforms on these schemes. It finds that in around half of the 30 countries that are members of the Organisation for Economic Co-operation and Development (OECD), minimum support amounts to 25–35 percent of average earnings but that a substantial number of countries have higher or lower retirement income floors. Recent reforms have increased the role of social pensions in one-third of the countries, weakened them in another third, and left them unchanged in the rest. Even in the last group, cuts in earnings-related benefits imply a greater role for social pensions in the future.

This chapter looks at social pensions in the 30 member countries of the Organisation for Economic Co-operation and Development (OECD). Most of these countries fall into the high-income category. The following section presents background information on demographics and pension coverage in this group. We introduce a typology of social pensions and discuss how these perform across countries, as measured by benefit levels, coverage, and interactions with other components of the retirement package. The effects of recent reforms on social pensions are also examined.

Demographics and Coverage in High-Income Countries

Table 7.1 presents basic data for the 30 member countries of the OECD. As is well known, developed countries currently have an older population structure than prevails in the rest of the world. In half of the countries listed, more than 15 percent of the total population is over age 65. The OECD countries with the oldest populations are Germany, Italy, and Japan.

People in high-income countries have relatively high life expectancies. For example, with few exceptions, newborn girls in those countries can expect to live into their 80s.

The views expressed in this paper are those of the authors alone and do not necessarily reflect views or opinions of the OECD or its Member countries. The authors would like to thank Andrew Reilly for his help in preparing this paper.

TABLE 7.1 **Key indicators, OECD countries, various years**

Country	Population (millions)	Proportion of the population over age 65	Life expectancy at birth, male	Life expectancy at birth, female	GDP per capita (local currency)	Coverage of mandatory pension system (percent of population age 15–64)	Coverage of mandatory pension system (percent of labor force)
Australia	20.6	12.7	77	83	50,407	69.6	92.6
Austria	8.3	16.7	76	82	31,139	68.7	96.4
Belgium	10.5	17.6	76	82	30,017	61.6	94.2
Canada	32.6	13.1	77	83	44,333	71.4	90.5
Czech Republic	10.2	14.2	73	79	315,244	61.5	86.3
Denmark	5.4	15	75	80	302,179	75.0	94.6
Finland	5.3	15.9	75	82	31,718	67.2	88.7
France	61.4	16.6	77	84	29,207	61.4	89.9
Germany	82.4	18.8	76	81	28,192.	65.5	88.2
Greece	11.1	18.2	77	81	19,193	58.5	85.3
Hungary	10.1	15.2	69	77	2,358,974	52.0	86.0
Iceland	0.3	11.8	78	82	3,751,624	79.8	88.7
Ireland	4.2	10.9	76	81	41,253	64.0	88.1
Italy	58.4	20	77	83	25,248	58.4	92.4
Japan	127.8	19.7	78	85	3,983,134	75.0	95.3
Korea, Rep. of	48.3	9.4			17,555,401	54.7	78.0
Luxembourg	0.5	13.8	75	81	73,672	95.5	100.0
Mexico	104.9	5.3	73	78	87,246	22.7	34.5
Netherlands	16.3	14.1	76	81	32,688	70.4	90.3
New Zealand	4.1	12.3	77	81	39,472		
Norway	4.7	15	78	82	461,623	75.8	90.8
Poland	38.1	12.9	70	79	27,741	54.5	84.9
Portugal	10.6	17.1	74	81	14,657	71.9	91.4
Slovak Republic	5.4	11.8	70	78	303,507	55.3	78.5
Spain	44.1	16.5	77	84	22,260	63.2	91.0
Sweden	9.1	17.2	78	83	319,309	72.4	91.0
Switzerland	7.5	16	79	84	64,962	79.1	100.0
Turkey	73.0	5.4	69	71	7,897	24.3	45.0
United Kingdom	60.6	16	76	81	21,488	71.4	92.7
United States	299.4	12.3	75	80	43,864	72.5	92.5

SOURCE: OECD data; World Bank pensions database.

NOTE: Data shown is from the following years: life expectancy, 2004; proportion of population over 65, 2005; population and GDP per capita, 2006.

GDP, gross domestic product; OECD, Organisation for Economic Co-operation and Development.

Average life expectancy at birth is 75 for boys and 81 for girls. This gap between the life expectancy of men and women has persisted. Although it has narrowed in some countries, in others, especially in Central and Eastern Europe, it has grown. Life expectancy continues to increase rapidly, although the improvements in mortality are now tending to happen at older ages than in the past.

Generally, over 90 percent of the labor force in developed countries contributes to the compulsory pension scheme—a much higher proportion than in most low- and

middle-income countries. As a result of comparatively high rates of formal sector employment, over 70 percent of the working-age population is covered. Even this figure can
understate the degree of coverage because most OECD countries have extensive systems
of credits for people outside the labor force. This means that the unemployed, working-
age students, and people caring for children or older family members may be covered even
when they do not contribute.

With such broad coverage by formal pension systems, informality in the labor market is not as great a problem as in less developed countries. Nevertheless, there are still
many people who do not have full contribution records, for one reason or another, and
who therefore in retirement do not receive the "target" or "typical" replacement income
for the particular country. Systems in developed countries therefore usually have some
kind of floor for old-age income, and this is equivalent in function to social pensions as
understood in the rest of the world.

Social Pensions

Figure 7.1 presents a widely used taxonomy of pension systems. The classification separates
mandatory and voluntary provision of retirement income provision. All voluntary schemes—
meaning those that are not legally mandated—are placed in the third tier of this taxonomy.

The great bulk of retirement income support in most countries is provided through
the second tier of pension systems. This tier comprises mandatory programs, linked to the
resources of individuals either through earnings-related schemes or individual accounts.
These second-tier schemes can be managed in either the public or the private sector.

FIGURE 7.1 **Taxonomy of pension systems**

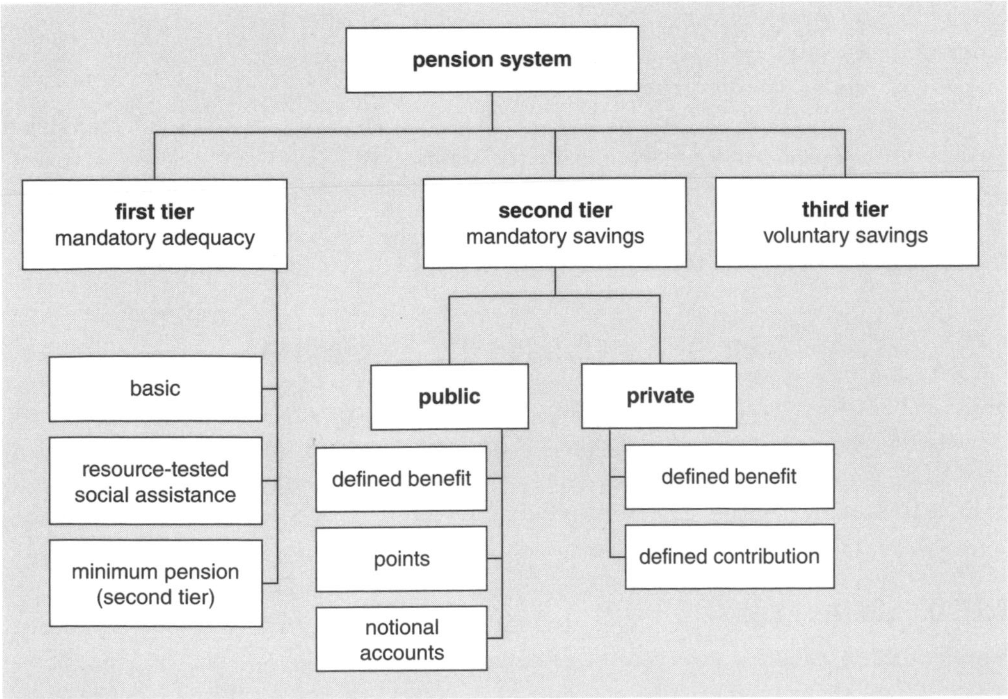

SOURCE: Authors' elaboration; OECD, 2004, 2005, 2007.

It is the first tier of this taxonomy that is of most interest in this study. First-tier programs are designed to address concerns about adequacy of incomes in retirement. They provide the floor below which pension incomes generally will not fall.

There are three main types of first-tier pensions:

- *Basic pensions.* A basic pension, in its purest form, is often called a "demogrant." It is paid at a single rate, regardless of the recipients' other sources of income. Countries with basic pensions usually have provisions, such as residency or contribution tests, that, for example, prevent new immigrants from benefiting in full.

- *Resource-tested programs.* Resource-tested payments for old-age may be separate programs for older people or may be part of a general social assistance scheme for people of all ages. The entitlement depends on income from other sources. Often, it also takes into account the value of assets held.

- *Minimum pensions.* Minimum pensions are similar to resource-tested pensions in that they are targeted at those with the lowest retirement incomes. The important difference is that only one source of income—income from the pension scheme—is taken into account when calculating entitlement to the minimum pension. People who have a very low entitlement to pensions may qualify for the minimum pension payment even if they have high income from other sources.

We call all these first-tier programs "social pensions" in what follows. There are a number of qualifications and clarifications that need to be taken into account when considering this framework.

First, minimum pensions and some basic schemes require contributions to have been paid for a specific number of years. Are such programs really "social" pensions? An important reason for thinking that they are is that most developed countries give credit toward these benefits for periods people spend out of the labor force—because of unemployment, disability, or the need to care for children or elderly relatives—thus helping ensure a minimum level of retirement income.

Second, most OECD countries have social assistance systems. In some countries this is the social pension as analyzed here. In many, social assistance is effectively a second safety net, providing a floor for retirement incomes below the minimum in the pension system. Often, only a handful of people receive social assistance in old age. Social assistance is included in the following analysis only when it plays a prominent role in provision of retirement income.

Social Pensions in OECD Countries

Table 7.2 shows types of social pension in various countries. Around half of the countries listed have only one kind of program. Germany and the United States, for example, have only a resource-tested scheme; Japan, the Netherlands, and New Zealand rely on basic pensions; and Finland and Sweden have only minimum pensions. In most countries, however, we find two of the three types, and the United Kingdom uses all three.

SIZE OF SOCIAL PENSIONS

The existence of multiple social pension programs, often interacting and overlapping in complex ways, means that it does not make sense to analyze the different schemes independently.

Figure 7.2 gives the value of the overall social pension level. The calculations are carried out for people who have been covered by the formal pension system throughout their working lives, either by their own contributions or through credits for unemployment, childcare, and so on.

Social pensions are worth, on average across the OECD countries, 29 percent of national average earnings. About 18 countries are bunched around this average, with social pensions worth about 25 to 35 percent of average earnings. There are, however, quite a few outliers. The basic pension in Japan will be worth just 16 percent of average earnings when adjustments linked to the financial sustainability of the pension system are fully in place. The national pension in Finland and social assistance in Germany are also worth less than 20 percent of average earnings. The largest social pensions are the basic scheme in New Zealand and the minimum pension in Portugal, both of which are worth 40 percent or more of average earnings.

Although a social pension of 25 to 35 percent of average earnings is the norm in OECD countries, there are considerable differences in some cases in the level of the retirement income safety net.

TABLE 7.2 **Social pensions in OECD countries, by type**

Country	Resource tested	Basic	Minimum
Australia	X		
Austria	X		
Belgium	X		X
Canada	X	X	
Czech Republic		X	X
Denmark	X	X	
Finland			X
France	X		X
Germany	X		
Greece	X		X
Hungary			X
Iceland	X	X	
Ireland	X	X	
Italy	X		
Japan		X	
Korea, Rep. of		X	
Luxembourg		X	X
Mexico		X	X
Netherlands		X	
New Zealand		X	
Norway		X	X
Poland			X
Portugal	X		X
Slovak Republic			X
Spain	X		X
Sweden			X
Switzerland	X		X
Turkey	X		X
United Kingdom	X	X	X
United States	X		

SOURCE: OECD 2007.

NOTE: OECD, Organisation for Economic Co-operation and Development.

EFFECT OF RECENT REFORMS ON SOCIAL PENSIONS

Around half of the OECD countries have carried out major pension reforms in the past 15 years (see OECD 2007, pt. II.1). Table 7.3 summarizes the effect of these changes on the role of social pensions. On the left-hand side are listed six reforms that strengthened social pensions. In France, the Republic of Korea, Mexico, and Sweden new social pension programs were introduced, either in addition to or as substitutes for existing provisions.

FIGURE 7.2 **Value of social pensions as share of average earnings, 2007**

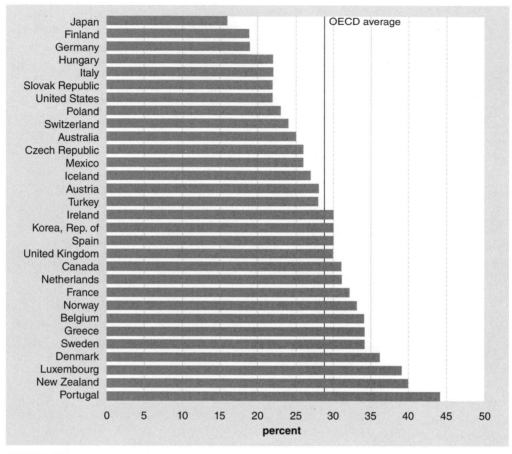

SOURCE: OECD 2007.

NOTE: Calculation based on long-term parameters and rules legislated by 2004.

OECD, Organisation for Economic Co-operation and Development.

On the right-hand side of the table are four countries that abolished their minimum pensions as part of reforms to link pensions more closely to earnings during the working life. Finland, by shifting from a basic to a minimum pension, is also moving toward a smaller role for social pensions in the future.

In the middle of the table are countries whose reforms did not directly affect social pensions because they were focused on cuts in second-tier, earnings-related schemes or on increases in pension eligibility age. These reforms, however, will indirectly affect social pensions in some cases. Lower second-tier benefits will mean that in the future more workers with relatively low earnings will be eligible for social pensions during retirement.

Figure 7.3 explores the effect of pension reforms on the future value of pension entitlements for workers entering the labor market in 2004. It compares the situation of a person who spent a full career under the reformed pension system with the benefits that would have been received had the system not been changed. The results shown are net replacement rates, that is, the value of the pension in retirement (after taxes) compared with the level of earnings when working (after taxes and contributions). Rates are

TABLE 7.3 **Effect of recent pension reforms on social pensions, selected countries**

Stronger social pensions	No direct effect	Weaker social pensions
France New higher minimum income	*Austria* Cuts in earnings-related pension	*Finland* Move from mixed basic/pension-tested benefit to pure pension-tested benefit
Ireland Basic pension increased relative to earnings	*Germany* Cuts in earnings-related pension	*Hungary* Minimum pension abolished
Korea, Rep. of New universal basic pension	*Japan* Cuts in basic and earnings-related pension	*Italy* Minimum pension abolished
Mexico New minimum pension	*New Zealand* Pension age increased	*Poland* Minimum pension abolished
Sweden Basic pension replaced with pension-tested benefit at much higher level	*Portugal* Cuts in earnings-related pension	*Slovak Republic* Minimum pension abolished
United Kingdom Higher minimum income; new minimum credit in earnings-related scheme		

SOURCE: OECD 2007.

presented for low earners—those earning 50 percent of the economywide average each year of their working lives—and for average earners.

The countries are divided into three groups according to the effect of their reforms on the retirement income of workers at different earnings levels. In the top panels are countries that protected low earners from the impact of the reforms. In France and Sweden, for example, the benefits for average earners will be about 20 percent lower as a result of the reforms, while those of low earners hardly change. In Mexico and Portugal the reductions in benefits for average earners are around 50 and 40 percent, respectively, but the reduction for low earners is only about half that. In the United Kingdom recent reforms left the pensions of average earners unchanged but increased the benefits for low earners by nearly 25 percent. Thus, all these reforms increased the targeting of the pension system on people who had low incomes when working.

The bottom panel shows countries with reforms that worked in the opposite way. In Poland benefits for average earners will scarcely change as a result of the reform, but for low earners they will fall by more than 20 percent. Average earners are expected to lose about 5 percent of benefits in the Slovak Republic, in contrast to 13 percent for low earners. These countries explicitly wanted to strengthen the link between pensions in retirement and earnings while working, in the belief that this was fairer than a redistributive system and that it would reduce distortions in the labor market.

SOCIAL PENSIONS IN THE RETIREMENT INCOME PACKAGE

The taxonomy illustrated in figure 7.1 divides retirement income provision into tiers. The most relevant division is that between first-tier schemes, which we call social pensions for short, and second-tier schemes, in which retirement incomes depend on earnings while working. Figure 7.4 shows how retirement income packages (from mandatory schemes) derive

FIGURE 7.3 **Impact of pension reforms on net replacement rates (NRRs), by earnings level, selected countries**

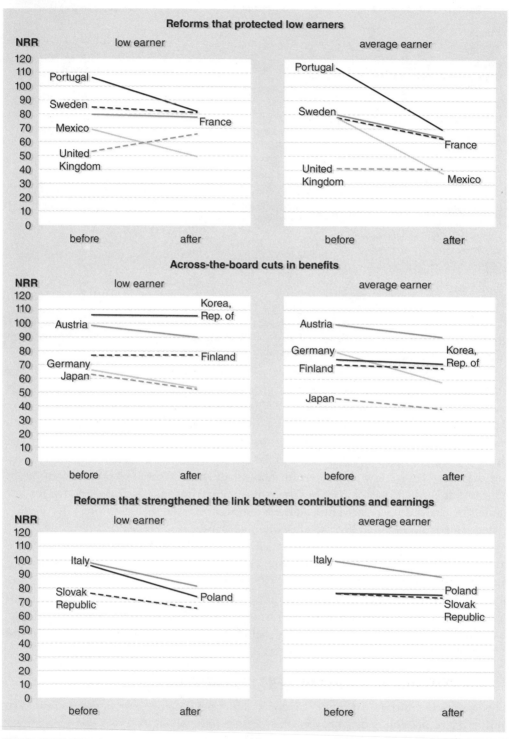

SOURCE: OECD 2007.

FIGURE 7.4 **Pension wealth from first- and second-tier retirement income programs as share of total, OECD countries, 2007**

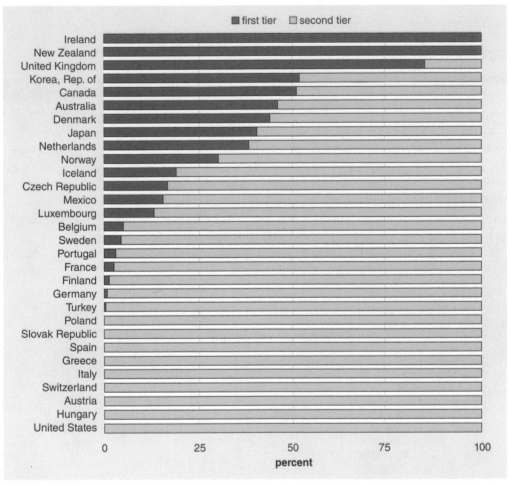

SOURCE: OECD 2007.

NOTE: Calculations based on long-term parameters and rules legislated by 2004.

OECD, Organisation for Economic Co-operation and Development.

from these different programs. The calculations include individuals across the earnings range, from 30 to 300 percent of average (mean) earnings in each country. Data on the distribution of earnings are used to weight the calculated pension entitlements for workers at various earnings levels. The results are only for full-career workers because we do not know the exact career paths of workers at different earnings levels. The outcomes therefore understate the role of first-tier schemes, which are most important for people with less than full careers.

Despite the uncertainties regarding career paths, the chart is a useful description of retirement income systems across countries. Ireland and New Zealand have only basic schemes. In the United Kingdom there is a public earnings-related scheme, but its role is limited, and the recent reform will mean movement to a pure flat-rate scheme. In Korea the value of the pension is based half on individual earnings and half on average earnings. First-tier schemes are also important in Australia, Canada, Denmark, Japan, the

Netherlands, and Norway. At the other end of the scale are countries in which social pensions play an insignificant role in providing old-age incomes for full-career workers. Nevertheless, as the next section shows, social pensions are significant because of their role in covering workers with less than full careers.

COVERAGE OF SOCIAL PENSIONS

The variety of retirement income programs with social pension characteristics among OECD countries and the multiplicity of such programs within countries complicate the presentation of data on coverage of social pensions. The very different paths that OECD countries have followed to guarantee some level of income adequacy in old age reflect divergent public policy decisions about whether it is more effective to rely on resource testing or to provide minimum benefits as an entitlement. The debate as to which approach is the most cost-effective will doubtless continue in the future as OECD countries go on with reforming and readjusting their pension programs. For example, a lively discussion is currently under way in the United States about reintroducing a minimum pension benefit as a way of helping low-income women and minorities in their retirement.

Figure 7.5 presents, for 23 countries, the proportion of people of pension age who are receiving social pension benefits. The figure does not include recipients of basic pensions,

FIGURE 7.5 **Coverage of social pensions as share of population of pension age, selected OECD countries, various years**

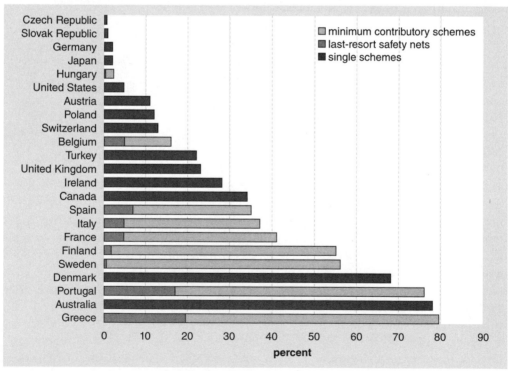

SOURCE: OECD data; European Union (2006); national officials.

Data are most recently available.

OECD, Organisation for Economic Co-operation and Development.

on the grounds that these are by design always nearly universal. In the Netherlands and New Zealand (not shown in the figure), basic pensions are based on adult residency in the country, and so virtually 100 percent of older people receive a benefit. (We return to the issue of basic pensions below.)

Where appropriate, the coverage data are divided between different programs. In Portugal, for example, almost 60 percent of pensioners are on the minimum contributory pension, with an additional 17 percent covered by the noncontributory social pension or the solidarity benefit. Coverage of both minimum contributory benefits and safety net benefits is similarly high in Greece.

In Finland and Sweden more than half of older people receive minimum pensions, but the coverage of the safety net benefit (provided by social assistance) is very narrow in both countries, compared with Greece and Portugal. This probably reflects the history in southern European countries of a large informal sector that must rely on last-resort safety net benefits. The Scandinavian countries have a tiny informal sector and comprehensive protection, through pension credits, for people out of paid work.

In most countries the data in figure 7.5 refer to a single retirement income program. The range of coverage of these programs is huge. For example, whereas in Australia more than 75 percent of older people are eligible for the benefit, in Germany just 2 percent of older people receive social assistance. Both programs are resource tested, but the way they work in practice is fundamentally different. A program such as Australia's has been described as "affluence tested" because the benefit is paid to most older people and is denied only to the richest pensioners (Piggott and Whitehouse 2001). The German program is best characterized as "poverty tested" because benefits under the social assistance program are paid only to the very poorest older people.

Some of the countries shown also have basic pensions. In the United Kingdom, for example, although not quite 25 percent of older people are recipients under the resource-tested programs— the pension credit and the savings credit—about 98 percent receive at least some payment from the basic pension. The situation is similar in Canada, the Czech Republic, Denmark, Ireland, and Japan, where basic pensions have nearly universal coverage. These basic pension schemes are not included in the country models presented in figure 7.5.

Allowing for the role of basic pensions, figure 7.5 shows a huge difference in the coverage of social pensions. Fewer than 5 percent of older people receive social pensions in Germany, the Slovak Republic, and the United States. In the three Scandinavian countries shown, by contrast, more than half of older people get a social pension. In France, Italy, and Spain coverage of social pensions is 35 to 40 percent.

Conclusions

High-income countries have adopted many different means of keeping retirement incomes above a minimum level, and it is therefore important to avoid restricting the analysis of social pensions to last-resort programs. This chapter has accordingly chosen a broad definition of social pensions that includes any program which provides retirement income unrelated to individual contributions or to earnings.

Social pensions are the dominant part of retirement income systems in many high-income countries, including Australia, Canada, the Czech Republic, Denmark, and the

United Kingdom. In addition, Ireland and New Zealand lack mandatory earnings-related pension provision, and so in those countries only basic or resource-tested pensions are mandated. Countries where coverage of social pensions among older people is very broad include Finland, France, Greece, Italy, Portugal, Spain, and Sweden. All together, these countries account for almost half of the OECD membership of 30 countries.

The retirement income floor in half of the OECD countries is set at 25 to 35 percent of average earnings.

A third of OECD countries that have recently reformed their systems have strengthened the role of social pensions, but in another third the importance of social pensions has been weakened. In the remaining third of reforming countries, social pensions were not directly changed, but cuts in earnings-related benefits imply a greater role for social pensions in the future.

References

European Union. 2006. "Minimum Income Provisions for Older People and Their Contribution to Adequacy In Retirement." Special Pensions Study, Social Policy Committee, European Union, Brussels.

OECD (Organisation for Economic Co-operation and Development). 2004. *OECD Classification and Glossary of Private Pensions.* Paris: OECD.

———. 2005. *Pensions at a Glance: Public Policies across OECD Countries.* Paris: OECD.

———. 2007. *Pensions at a Glance: Public Policies across OECD Countries.* Paris: OECD.

Piggott, John, and Edward R. Whitehouse. 2001. "Pensions in Paradise: Modernizing the Mauritian Retirement-Income System." Human Development Department, South Asia Region, World Bank, Washington, DC.

CHAPTER 8

Pension Coverage in Japan

Noriyuki Takayama

Japan has devoted considerable effort to the coverage of all its people through social insurance pension systems. The country has one of the highest coverage rates in the world, with only 1.6 percent of the elderly currently not receiving social security old-age pension benefits. For several reasons, however, the dropout rate from basic protection schemes has recently been increasing. Weak implementation has aggravated the problem. Going forward, improved incentives, compliance, and accountability are needed for maintaining or expanding good coverage. A trustworthy government capable of competent and efficient implementation is also required if coverage is to be broadened.

Japan has mandated social insurance pensions for all residents, with the primary objective of ensuring adequate income in old age. A contribution-based social insurance pension, however, has some disadvantages. Collecting contributions from small companies, atypical employees, and informal sector workers is not easy, since administrative and enforcement costs are relatively high. This may leave low-income workers, in particular, outside the social insurance umbrella. In view of these difficulties, Japan also provides several social pensions to attain higher coverage and minimize the risks of elderly poverty.

This chapter describes Japan's current social insurance pension system, with special emphasis on coverage issues. Extending coverage to the informal sector is still a major challenge, and the introduction of a universal or minimum guaranteed pension has been the subject of heated debate. The Japanese experience furnishes a valuable lesson on what to do and what not to do when extending pension coverage.

Current Provisions of Social Insurance Pensions: A Brief Sketch

Japan already has the oldest population in the world. The proportion of the elderly age 65 and older was more than 25 percent in 2005 (see table 8.1) and will have risen to more than 40 percent by 2050.

Japan has a long history of social insurance pensions, dating back to 1884, when the Kyo-Sai-Nenkin (KSN) was established for civil servants. Basic information on current pension programs—the KSN, the Kokumin Nenkin (KN) for the nonemployed and for full-time housewives, and the Kosei-Nenkin-Hoken (KNH) for private sector employees—is presented in table 8.2. Benefits consist of two tiers. The first-tier flat-rate basic benefit is paid to all participants in the social insurance pension system, and the second-tier earnings-related benefit applies only to employees.[1] The system operates largely as a pay-as-you-go defined benefit program.

The author is very much grateful for the financial support from the academic project on Economic Analysis of Intergenerational Issues, funded by the Grant-in-Aid for Specially Promoted Research from Japan's Ministry of Education (grant number 18002001).

TABLE 8.1 **Japan at a Glance, 2005**

Indicator	Data
Population (millions)	127.8
Population age 65+ (millions)	25.7
As percent of total population	20.1
Total fertility rate (births per woman)	1.26
Gross domestic product (GDP)	
Trillions of yen	504
Trillions of U.S. dollars	4.6
GDP per capita (U.S. dollars)	36,000
Social security pension benefits	
Trillions of yen	46.3
As percent of GDP	9.2
Number of social security pension enrollees (millions)	70.45
As percent of total population	55
Number of social security pension beneficiaries (millions)	32.87
As percent of total population	26
Normal pensionable age	65
Life expectancy at age 65 (additional years)	
Males	18.11
Females	23.16
Labor force participation rate, males (percent)	
Age 60–64	70.3
Age 65+	29.4

SOURCE: Japan, Social Insurance Agency, Annual Reports (In Japanese) and Japan Statistical Association, Statistical Handbook of Japan..

A person is required to contribute for no less than 25 years to receive basic old-age benefits. The full basic old-age pension is payable after 40 years of contributions. The maximum monthly pension of 66,000 yen at 2009 prices (based on the maximum 40 years of contributions) is payable from age 65.[2] The benefit was previously indexed automatically each fiscal year (beginning April 1) to reflect changes in the consumer price index (CPI) since the previous calendar year. Since 2004 this indexation formula has been provisionally suspended, and a new indexation that takes demographic factors into account has been introduced (Takayama 2004, 2006). The pension may be claimed at any age between 60 and 70 years, with an actuarial reduction or increase in benefit.

All employees receive earnings-related benefits. The accrual rate for the earnings-related component of old-age benefits is 0.5481 percent per year. Thus, 40 years of contributions will earn 28.5 percent of career average real monthly earnings.[3]

As a transitional measure, the full earnings-related pension is payable to a fully retired employee beginning at age 60. (Normally, it would start at age 65.) An individual who has reached age 60 but has not fully retired can receive a reduced pension. The current replacement rate (including basic benefits) is close to 60 percent for a typical male retiree (with an average salary earned during 40 years of coverage) and his dependent wife.[4] It will decrease to 50 percent by 2023 under a provisional indexation formula.

Equal percentage contributions are required of employees and their employers. The contributions are based on earnings (which include semiannual bonuses). The total percentage in effect beginning in September 2008 is around 15 percent for the principal program for private sector employees (Kosei-Nenkin-Hoken, KNH). Nonemployed persons between the ages of 20 and 60 pay flat-rate individual contributions as category 1 persons under the Kokumin-Nenkin (KN) program. The current rate, since April 2009, is 660 yen per month. For those who cannot afford that, exemptions will be permitted. The flat-rate basic benefit for the period of exemption will be one-half the normal amount in fiscal 2009.

TABLE 8.2 **Basic statistics of social insurance programs in Japan, March 31, 2007**

Indicator	Kokumin Nenkin (KN)	Kosei-Nenkin-Hoken (KNH)	Kyo-Sai-Nenkin (KSN)	Total
Covered groups	Nonemployed persons and full-time housewives	Private sector employees	Civil servants and others	
Year established	1961	1942	1884	
Insured persons (millions)	32.03	33.79	4.60	70.42
Old-age pensioners (millions)	9.03	11.98	2.34	26.19
Ratio of contributors to pensioners	1.74	2.82	1.96	2.05
Amount of contribution	13,860 yen (per month per person)	14.642 percent	14.767 percent	
Current account surplus or deficit (trillions of yen)	−0.55	−5.26	0.91	−4.90
Funded reserves (trillions of yen)	9.15	132.4	50.88	193.16
Ratio of funded reserves to annual benefits	2.0	3.8	10.46	5.7

SOURCE: Japan, Social Insurance Agency, Annual Reports (in Japanese)..

Beginning with fiscal 2009, the government is subsidizing half of the total cost of the flat-rate basic benefit. There is no subsidy for the earnings-related part. The government pays administrative expenses, as well.

Social Pensions

Japan currently has six types of social pensions, which are paid without individual contributions.

1. *Flat-rate basic pension for full-time housewives.* Under the current system, dependent spouses of regular employees—typically, full-time housewives—are automatically entitled to the flat-rate basic benefits, without being required to make any direct individual payments to the social insurance pension system. In 2007 there were about 10.8 million such persons, equivalent to about 15 percent of the total number of insured persons.

This entitlement raises contentious issues. The number of dual-income couples and single women has been steadily increasing, to such a degree that full-time housewives no longer constitute a majority of working-age women. Single women and dual-income couples have often attacked the current provisions geared toward full-time housewives as unfair. The policy bias is clear, but the issue lies in ideologically contested ground. A purely individualist approach would, for example, logically lead to the abolition of survivors' benefits, even though married women earn far less than their husbands. An alternative solution is to assign some share of husbands' earnings to nonworking wives. (The implicit income share of full-time housewives is currently assumed to be 50 percent.) But this, in turn, could act as a disincentive for married women to work.

2. *Basic disability pensions for those qualified as mentally or physically disabled before age 20.* Those who become mentally or physically disabled before age 20 can receive the basic disability pension from age 20, subject to a generous income test. A thorough medical checkup is carried out before the person is qualified for the pension. The budget is fully financed by transfers from general revenue.

3. *Basic old-age pensions for low-income groups.* Those in low-income groups can be exempted from paying a part or all of the KN flat-rate pension contribution. The upper annual income limit for full or partial exemption varies depending on household size. In a single-member household, for example, the 2008 amount for partial exemption is 1.89 million yen or less. In 2007, 5.84 million people were exempted. Once exempted, they are still qualified to receive half of the full basic old-age pension, which is financed by transfers from general revenue.

4. *Two-tier old-age benefits for those on parental leave.* Japanese parents can enjoy a parental leave of one year (for husband and wife combined) each time they have a baby. During parental leave they are exempted from paying KNH pension contributions but still receive credit toward old-age pensions as if they had continued to earn the same salary that they had just before taking leave. In 2007, 111,000 employees were exempted through this scheme. No special funding arrangement has been made, and consequently these persons' old-age pension benefits accrued during parental leave are ultimately shouldered by contributions made by other participants.

5. *Pension entitlements resulting from a contribution gap.* Employers withdraw their employees' pension contributions from monthly salaries. A small number of employers fail to transfer the contributions to the Social Insurance Agency (SIA), the government body that collects contributions, because of financial difficulties or bankruptcy. The recovery rate at the SIA is usually less than 100 percent, and the contribution gap remains. Contributions made by other participants compensate for the gap by enabling the full payment of KNH pension benefits once the withdrawal of contributions is certified. This arrangement generates moral hazard among employers.

6. *Welfare pensions for aged low-income groups at the start of the program.* The flat-rate basic old-age pension is normally payable to those who have contributed for no fewer than 25 years. When the KN first started, however, those who were between the ages of 36 and 49 in 1961 were specially entitled to receive a smaller amount of basic pension with shorter contribution periods, ranging between 10 to 24 years. Those age 50 and over in 1961 were not entitled to receive basic pensions. Instead, "welfare pensions" were provided to them when they reached age 70, with an income test. Welfare pensions have been financed wholly by transfers from general revenue, and the current monthly benefit is around 34,000 Japanese yen. They are a transitory sunset scheme, and the number of recipients is currently very small, around 20,000 persons in March 2007.

Increasing Dropout Rate

The descriptions given above are just half the story. Several coverage, implementation, and social adequacy problems still confront Japan's social insurance pensions.

The first-tier basic benefit is not yet universal. Nearly 100 percent of regular employees are currently covered by the social insurance pension programs, but atypical employees and nonemployees are not necessarily covered, although their enrollment is mandatory.

In March 2007 around 54 percent of category 1 persons under the KN (independent workers, atypical workers, the self-employed, and persons with no occupation) dropped out from the basic level of protection as a result of exemption (5.84 million persons), delinquency in paying contributions (5.19 million persons), or shunning of the program (363,000 persons).[5] The dropout rate had increased from 35 percent in 1992.

Those who have dropped out will receive a smaller pension or none at all in old age, so they are likely to rely on the means-tested public assistance program. The principal idea of a social insurance pension should be income security in old age without the need to depend on means-tested support. A social insurance system that promises old-age security to all members of the community has its own drawbacks. The current legislation mandating a basic pension is becoming virtually hollow for atypical employees and the nonemployed.

Growing Numbers of Atypical Employees

In 2007 there were 32 million male and 23 million female employees in Japan, and the proportions of regular employees were 82 percent for males and 47 percent for females. These proportions have been gradually declining. Outsourcing, replacement of workers by contracts with outside staffing agencies, and increasing dependence on part-time, temporary, and seasonal workers have all become common. Table 8.3 shows that in 2007 about one-third of workers were not regular employees. A majority of female employees are now nonregular, with most of them engaging in part-time jobs.

The current KNH system does not directly apply to employees who work fewer than 30 hours per week (three-fourths of the normal work week.) These part-time employees are obliged to participate in the KN instead. If they are the spouses of regular employees and their annual pay is less than 1.3 million Japanese yen (US$12,000), they are treated like full-time homemakers, but if their annual pay exceeds 1.3 million yen, they lose the right to be treated as dependent spouses. They are then forced to pay flat-rate pension contributions as category 1 persons.

This arrangement tends to encourage part-time jobs that pay less than 1.3 million yen per year. Critics say that this is the main reason why part-timers remain low-income earners. One solution would be to reduce the upper earnings limit of 1.3 million yen to a negligible level, as in the United States and Germany. Employers in Japan, however, are strongly against this kind of program change because they would rather continue to avoid the higher compliance costs associated with social security. If this solution were implemented, employers might begin to lower part-time workers' wages, since

TABLE 8.3 **Distribution of employees, by type, 2007** (percent)

Type	Males	Females	All employees
Regular	81.7	46.5	66.5
Nonregular	18.3	53.5	33.5
Types of employee as share of nonregular employees			
Part-time	47.4	76.1	67.2
Temporary	9.9	6.7	7.7
Contract	29.9	11.5	17.2
Others	12.8	5.7	7.9

SOURCE: Japan, *2007 Labor Force Survey.*

nonwage costs, including the employers' share of social insurance contributions, would be increased.

The social insurance coverage of earnings-related pension benefits has been on the decline. The reason is that the existing KNH system only covers regular employees and does not apply to such workers as temporary staff members under labor contracts of not more than two months, seasonal employees working not more than four continuous months, or those engaged on contract work for no more than six months—in addition to part-timers, as noted above. Such labor contracts are often made fictitiously to evade paying social insurance contributions, in collusion with employees who want to have higher take-home pay on the spot.

In addition, employers of small business establishments are often reluctant to participate in the compulsory KNH. Typical examples are those who work in the restaurant, lodging, cleaning, barber, beauty salon, amusement, and construction businesses. KNH coverage in these industries is currently around 50 percent, and the remaining employees, including regular ones, are obliged to participate only in the KN.[6]

At first, the KN was supposed to apply mainly to self-employed and nonemployed people, but today it also covers around 9 million atypical employees. Their share in the KN was 37 percent in 2005, making that the highest of all categories. (The shares of nonemployed and self-employed persons were 31 and 18 percent, respectively). Critics say that the KNH for employees is beginning to decline to a mere form.

Distrust of government pension commitments increased in 2007, mainly because of the unexpected announcement of 50 million "floating" pension records. These pensions had not been integrated into the unified personal pension numbers, which were introduced in 1997. Social insurance pension implementation proved to be still quite weak in Japan, inducing a higher dropout rate in the future (see Takayama, forthcoming).

Nonbeneficiaries of Social Security Pensions

In April 2007 around 420,000 people age 65 and over (1.6 percent of those in the 65+ age group) received no social security old-age pension benefits, and it is estimated that 1.18 million persons, including those now under age 65, will be nonbeneficiaries in the near future. The main reasons for noncoverage are failure to file applications and insufficient years of contributions.

In 2005, 556,000 persons among the elderly age 65 and over (2.2 percent of the age group) received means-tested public assistance. Around 65 percent of the elderly with no social insurance pension benefits were forced to receive public assistance. Others among the elderly drew both social insurance pension benefits and public assistance, mainly because of their lower benefit level.

Introducing a Universal or Minimum Guaranteed Pension

Many in Japan have proposed a shift from the current contribution-based basic benefit to a tax-based universal one, with a view toward achieving the long-cherished aim of old-age income security for all residents.[7] The most politically feasible funding source for this move is an earmarked consumption-based tax, replacing the current flat-rate contributions and (part of the) wage-proportional pension contributions.[8] If this change takes place in 2009, an additional increase in the consumption tax rate of 3.5 percent will be required, and the KNH contribution rate can be reduced by 4 percent (see NCSS 2008).

Overall, this can almost be seen as a zero-sum change in funding sources. Current pensioners will be forced to bear additional pension burdens, while employers stand to gain if their portion of KNH contributions is decreased. If, however, the cut in KNH contributions is to be wholly on the employees' portion, the employers' portion will remain unchanged. In this case, the current actively working generations stand to benefit (see Takayama and Miyake 2008).[9]

To mitigate the controversial issues of intergenerational loss and gain, other experts are now recommending, as an alternative, the introduction of a minimum guaranteed pension. The required additional financing sources are estimated to equal around 1.0 trillion Japanese yen in 2009, equivalent to a mere 0.4 percent increase in the consumption tax rate. Still to be determined is whether means-tested, income-tested, pension-tested, claw-back, or tax credit schemes are preferable.

Conclusion

Japan has devoted considerable effort to achieving the coverage of all residents by social insurance pension systems. Coverage, overall, is among the highest in the world, with only 1.6 percent of the elderly currently not receiving social security old-age pension benefits.

Because of its rapidly aging population, Japan has been raising contributions to finance social insurance pensions, and this has induced an increased dropout rate from the basic protection scheme. Weak implementation has aggravated lower coverage. Growing numbers of atypical and irregular employees are losing their entitlement to an earnings-related pension through social insurance programs.

Incentives, compliance, and accountability are basic prerequisites for maintaining or expanding good coverage. A trustworthy government capable of competent and efficient implementation is required for broader coverage, as well. Heavy work still lies ahead.

Notes

1. For a detailed explanation of the Japanese public pension system, see Takayama (1998, 2003).

2. 1,000 yen = US$ 10.18 = UK £ 6.69 = 7.45 euros (as of August 1, 2008).

3. A semiannual bonus equivalent to 3.6 months' salary is typically assumed.

4. The couple's monthly amount of old-age benefits would be 233,000 yen in 2008.

5. This figure of 54 percent for all dropouts is equivalent to around 19 percent of all mandatory contributors. The administrative cost of the KN was about 7.7 percent of the aggregate amount of contributions in 2006, mainly because of the high dropout rate.

6. The enforcement abilities of the Social Insurance Agency remain relatively poor compared with those of tax authorities.

7. Among the proponents of a move to a universal pension are the Democratic Party, the Management Federation, a trade union (Rengo), and the Nikkei Newspaper Group.

8. The rate of the Japanese consumption-based tax was 5.0 percent in 2008. There may be considerable scope for an increase in the consumption tax rate to the minimum 15 percent, which is the norm in European Union countries.

9. There are other problems. One is how to carry out the necessary transitions. Some experts foresee a 40-year transition period, while others propose a 20-year period, as all Japanese have been paying consumption-based taxes for nearly 20 years, since 1989. Another problem is the trade-off between reduction of labor distortions and the integrity of the budget. Moving to consumption taxes will increase the capital-labor ratio, but few empirical studies on this issue have been conducted in Japan.

References

NCSS (National Council on Social Security). 2008. *The Interim Report* [in Japanese]. Tokyo: NCSS.

Takayama, Noriyuki.1998. *The Morning After in Japan: Its Declining Population, Too Generous Pensions and a Weakened Economy.* Tokyo: Maruzen.

———, ed. 2003. *Taste of Pie: Searching for Better Pension Provisions in Developed Countries.* Tokyo: Maruzen.

———. 2004. "Changes in the Pension System." *Japan Echo* 31 (5, October), pp. 9–12.

———. 2006. "Reforming Social Security in Japan: Is NDC the Answer?" In *Pension Reform: Issues and Prospects for Non-Financial Defined Contribution (NDC) Schemes*, ed. Robert Holzmann and Edward Palmer. Washington, DC: World Bank.

———. Forthcoming. "How to Make Public Pensions Reliable and Workable?" *Asian Economic Policy Review.*

Takayama, Noriyuki, and H. Miyake. 2008. "Shifting the Basic Pension to a Tax-Financed Pension in Japan: A Rough Estimate. July 2008 Version [in Japanese]." PIE/CIS Discussion Paper 386, Project on Intergenerational Equity (PIE)/Center for Intergenerational Studies (CIE), Institute of Economic Research, Hitotsubashi University, Tokyo.

CHAPTER 9

The Role of Social Pensions in the Republic of Korea

Hyungpyo Moon

Currently, the Republic of Korea has the highest elderly poverty rate among member countries of the Organisation for Economic Co-operation and Development (OECD), mainly because of the limited role of public pensions and the immaturity of the system. In 2007 the Korean government expanded pension coverage by introducing a new social benefit, in the form of a noncontributory basic old-age pension. This chapter examines the issues and limitations attending the recent pension reform in Korea.

Until 2007, the principal old-age income security system for the general public in the Republic of Korea largely consisted of the National Pension Scheme (NPS), a contributory social insurance system, and the National Basic Livelihood Security (NBLS), a public assistance program. The NPS, first introduced in 1988, is a partially funded defined benefit plan that provides a survivors' pension and disability pension, as well as a relatively generous old-age pension with a 60 percent average replacement rate (assuming 40 years of participation). The scheme, however, is still in its infancy and has yet to come to fruition. Currently, only about 20 percent of senior citizens age 65 and above receive pension benefits. Benefits are rather low because of the short participation period of current beneficiaries.

The National Basic Livelihood Security program, introduced in 2000, is a means-tested public assistance program targeted at poor households. Since more than one-fourth of its recipients are senior households, it actually functions as a zero-pillar old-age income security mechanism.[1] The NBLS's objective is to guarantee basic income by compensating for the gap between actual household income and the poverty threshold officially announced each year. The minimum livelihood costs are set at about 40 percent of average household income. A recipient has to meet criteria based on his or her income and assets, as well as a set of strict rules regarding family support. When the income of a child's household exceeds 120 percent of the combined minimum living costs of both the child's and the parents' households, the right of the elderly household to receive NBLS support is restricted. The actual number of recipients is therefore less than 10 percent of senior households age 65 and older. Thus, only about 30 percent of those age 65 and over are drawing benefits from Korea's public old-age income security system.

Most of the low-income elderly receive no public support, leading to widespread old-age poverty. In addition, many low-income participants, such as informal sector workers, self-employed persons, and small business owners, evade mandatory NPS contributions.

The Korean government reformed the NPS in 2007, reducing overgenerous pension benefits and adding the basic old-age pension scheme, a new noncontributory social pension. This chapter examines the limitations and issues attending the coverage of Korea's old-age income security system and discusses future policy directions for the system on the basis of an assessment of the recent pension reform.

Problems with the Coverage of the Korean National Pension

Among the shortcomings of Korea's pension system are low coverage of the elderly population and a low share of active workers paying contributions. The latter is explained, in part, by the large number of exempt categories, evasion, and administrative shortcomings.

LOW COVERAGE OF THE ELDERLY POPULATION

Despite continuous economic growth, poverty among the elderly remains a critical problem. As illustrated in figure 9.1, poverty can be expected to afflict about one-fourth of all households with a head of household older than age 60 and around half of those where the head of household is over age 70. These figures are, respectively, two and four times higher than the overall poverty rate. Of the member countries of the Organisation of Economic Co-operation and Development (OECD), Korea has both the highest elderly household poverty rate and the widest relative income gap between working families and elderly households (Whitehouse 2008).

One reason for the elevated elderly poverty rate can be easily understood by looking at the sources of income for elderly households—those in which the head of household is age 65 or older. As table 9.1 shows, private transfers, which account for 25.8 percent of total income for elderly Korean households, are the largest income source. Public pensions amount to a mere 12.8 percent, an outcome that stands in stark contrast to the role of public pensions as the most important income source for the elderly in other developed countries. Thus, a majority of elderly Korean households is financially dependent on offspring, continuing a tradition of informal safety nets. Given the limited role of public pensions, elderly households without savings or offspring run a high risk of poverty.

The NPS's narrow coverage will gradually widen as the scheme matures. The National Pension Service predicts that over 70 percent of the population age 65 or

FIGURE 9.1 **Poverty rates by age of household head, Korea, 2006**

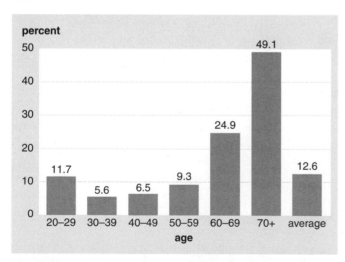

SOURCE: Korea, National Statistical Office, *National Household Survey, 2006.*

NOTE: The poverty line is set at 40 percent of median income, and the number of households is converted by applying an equivalence scale.

TABLE 9.1 **Composition of income, elderly households, Korea, 2006**
(percent)

	Payroll income	Business income	Asset income	Private transfers	Public transfers			Total
					Public pension	Other	Nonordinary income	
Share	22.8	9.7	10.9	25.8	12.8	7.8	10.1	100.0

SOURCE: Korea, National Statistical Office, *National Household Survey*, 2006.

NOTE: Based on households with household head age 65 or older.

over will receive an old-age pension by 2070 and that 90 percent of the elderly will be NPS beneficiaries, when survivors' and disability pensions are included (Korea, CNPFE, 2008). Since more than half of the elderly population is not expected to enjoy pension benefits until 2030, however, the narrow NPS coverage will remain a social issue for the next 20 to 30 years. This implies that measures need to be taken to fill the gap between the NPS and the NBLS—the last-resort social safety net that supports only 8.4 percent of the elderly population.

LOW CONTRIBUTION PAYMENT RATE

Many working-age members of the NPS do not actually pay contributions. Table 9.2 shows that in 2007, 5.1 million participants, or 28 percent of the total, were classified as exempt payers, meaning that they were given a grace period for the time being because they could not afford to contribute. Even more grave is the recent rise in the number of such participants. Since many of them are classified as poor or nearly so, a substantial number will continue to have difficulty accumulating a contribution history sufficient to draw benefits in the future.[2] Exempt payers are subject to a high risk of eventual elderly poverty.

As is highlighted in table 9.3, 90 percent of exempt participants have difficulty keeping their livelihoods; almost 75 percent are unemployed. What is most noteworthy is that the number of exempt payers who are unemployed is far higher than the figure publicly

TABLE 9.2 **Numbers and shares of participants in national pension scheme, Korea, 2005, 2006, and 2007**
(thousands; numbers in parentheses are percent)

Year	Total participants	Workplace participants	Regional participants	Exempt payers
2005	17,074 (100.0)	7,951 (46.6)	4,489 (26.3)	4,634 (27.1)
2006	17,691 (100.0)	8,605 (48.6)	4,150 (23.5)	4,936 (27.9)
2007	18,212 (100.0)	9,149 (50.2)	3,956 (21.7)	5,107 (28.0)

SOURCE: National Pension Service data.

TABLE 9.3 **Numbers and status of exempt payers, by reason for exemption, Korea, 2007**
(thousands; numbers in parentheses are percent)

	Unemployed	On leave	Business closed	Hardship in livelihood	In school or military service	Unknown address	Other	Total
Headcount	3,799 (74.4)	137 (2.7)	428 (8.4)	218 (4.3)	120 (2.3)	396 (7.8)	9 (0.2)	5,107 (100.0)

SOURCE: National Pension Service data.

announced by the government. (According to the National Statistical Office, the number of unemployed at the end of 2007 was 736,000, and the unemployment rate was 3.1 percent.) Because exempt payers include not only the currently unemployed but also a certain portion of the economically inactive who previously contributed, it is difficult to draw a comparison. Many exempt participants may be temporary or daily workers, self-employed persons, or small business owners who underreport income and are not discovered by the National Pension Service.

Delinquency on the part of those who actually do report income is another problem. As of January 2008, about 2.7 million participants were behind in their payments, and half of them were long-term delinquents who had failed to pay for more than two years (National Pension Service data). Many of these long-term delinquents have reasons for their inability to pay, such as insufficient income. (Among the delinquents, only 587,000, or 21.8 percent, have taxable income, according to the National Pension Service.) But administrative deficiencies in the National Pension Scheme bear a portion of the blame.

Evaluation of the 2007 Korean National Pension Reform

The government has identified as priority issues the narrow coverage of the NPS, its low participation rate, and its fragile long-run financial security. Having recognized the problem, the government in 2007 implemented a reform of the NPS that focused on enhancing sustainability and expanding coverage. The reform intended to extend coverage by introducing a noncontributory basic old-age pension. The long-run financial stability of the NPS was addressed by maintaining a 9 percent contribution rate while immediately lowering benefit levels to 50 percent from the current income replacement rate of 60 percent for an average income earner with a 40-year participation history. The benefit reduction is planned to continue at a rate of 0.5 percent per year until the replacement rate reaches 40 percent by 2028. Pension credits for compulsory military service and childbirth pension credits for female participants were introduced, and the elderly were provided with greater incentives to continuing working, in the form of enhanced delayed pensions.

The Basic Old-Age Pension Law, intended to help the low-income elderly, stipulates that an amount equivalent to 5 percent of the average monthly income of NPS participants be paid to those age 65 or over whose income level is lower than a specified threshold. In 2008 the threshold for a single-member household was a monthly income of 400,000 won or less and for a couple, 640,000 won or less. The benefit rate is to be incrementally raised from 5 percent in 2008 to 10 percent in 2028. As of July 2008, 60 percent of the population age 65 and over qualified for the basic pension. The plan was to adjust eligibility so as to reach 70 percent of those age 65 or over by January 2009.

The government believes that the 2007 pension reform will substantially contribute to old age security for all and will increase the long-run financial sustainability of the NPS. In particular, the introduction of the basic old-age pension as a new zero pillar means that the government has officially recognized the coverage gap of the nascent NPS and the issue of elderly poverty. Nonetheless, the recently introduced basic old-age pension scheme raises a number of issues related to its structure and benefit level.

1. It is not clear how the scheme is to be classified. The number of recipients of the basic old-age pension is restricted to 60–70 percent of the population age 65 or over. Thus, it is difficult to characterize the system either as a demogrant-type universal basic pension or as a public assistance pension aimed at poor seniors. In fact, the basic old-age pension is subject to means testing, making it look more like public assistance than like an entitlement. Even so, the 70 percent coverage target seems too high a figure for a policy aimed specifically at the poor elderly. The problem of classification is a by-product of political compromise. When the introduction of the basic old-age pension was first discussed, the government proposed the adoption of a public assistance pension geared toward about 40 percent of the elderly population in poverty, while the opposition party, the Grand National Party, insisted on a demogrant-type universal basic pension. In the course of political deliberations, the coverage of the basic old-age pension was haggled over, and eventually a compromise between the two was reached (Moon 2007)—producing a system that is neither fish nor fowl.

2. The benefit level under the basic old-age pension is too low to relieve poverty among the elderly population. The 2008 benefit level is set at 84,000 won for a single-member household, or 134,000 won for a couple, amounting to 5 percent of NPS participants' average monthly income (1,677,000 won). This is less than one-fifth of the government's official poverty threshold. Even though the pension is to be increased gradually, by 2028 it will account for only 35 percent of minimum livelihood costs. It is doubtful whether, with such a low benefit level, the basic old-age pension can effectively resolve the issue of elderly poverty.

In sum, political considerations have led to wide basic pension coverage, but not broad enough for the scheme to be called universal. Wide coverage has required a very low benefit level in order to make the scheme affordable.

Future Policy Directions

A public old-age income security scheme should, at a minimum, prevent elderly poverty. With this in mind, it is necessary to reevaluate the validity of Korea's recently introduced basic old-age pension system and to examine whether its combination of wide coverage with low benefit levels will be effective in achieving the stated goal. President Lee Myoung-Bak, who was inaugurated in February 2008, stated that he would once again reform the current national pension and the basic old-age pension by reorganizing them into a first-tier noncontributory universal basic pension and a second-tier contributory earnings-related pension. Under his plan, the adjusted benefits of the national pension would be maintained. The basic old-age pension system would be integrated into the NPS and transformed into a tax-financed basic pension that guarantees a minimum income for elderly citizens, and the prefunded national pension would maintain its actuarial balance (Korea, President's Transition Committee, 2008). Although the details, such as the scope of coverage and the level of benefits, are not yet determined, the new administration is clearly making a priority of extending the scope of pension coverage by introducing a universal pension scheme. Yet the fiscal cost needs to be considered. According to one estimate (Moon 2007), if 15 percent of the average income of national pension participants were paid to 80 percent of those age 65 years and over, the total payment would amount to 5.8 percent of GDP in 2050. A level of 20 percent of average income would take up 7.7 percent of GDP. If value added tax revenue were appropriated for these expenses, the tax would have to be raised to 21 percent level in 2050 (25 percent, under the 20 percent average income scenario), from the current level of 10 percent.

In conclusion, coverage in Korea continues to be inadequate, and old-age poverty remains a problem, despite pension reform. The current priority appears to be the extension of coverage, in part through the provision of a universal basic pension. This is laudable, but the fiscal costs can be considerable.

Notes

1. In 2006, 25.8 percent of all recipients in the NBLS program were age 65 or older. This group accounted for 8.1 percent of the total population age 65 and older (Korea, Ministry of Health and Welfare, 2007).

2. According to National Pension Service data, as of December 2007, among the 5,107 exempt payers, 79.9 percent (4,079 persons) had been in that category for one year or more, and 53.2 percent (2,716 persons) had been in exempt status for three or more years.

References

Korea, CNPFE (Committee on the National Pension's Financial Evaluation). 2008. "The 2nd Long-Term Financial Estimates on National Pension, March 2008." CNPFE, Seoul.

Korea, Ministry of Health and Welfare. 2007. *The 2006 Report on the National Basic Livelihood Security Program.* Seoul: Ministry of Health and Welfare.

Korea, National Statistical Office. 2006. *National Household Survey.* Seoul: National Statistical Office.

Korea, President's Transition Committee. 2008. *Transition Committee White Paper.* Seoul: President's Transition Committee.

Moon, Hyungpyo. 2007. "The 2007 National Pension Reform: Evaluation and Future Policy Issues." In *The Comprehensive Study on the Old Age Income Security System in Korea,* ed. Hyungpyo Moon. Seoul: Korean Development Institute.

Whitehouse, Edward. 2008. "Socioeconomic Status of Older People." Presented at the World Bank–Hitotsubashi University–Ministry of Finance workshop, "Closing the Coverage Gap: The Role of Social Pensions," Tokyo, February 20–22.

CHAPTER 10

Incentive Effects of Retirement Income Transfers

John Piggott, David A. Robalino, and Sergi Jimenez-Martin

This chapter explores the incentive effects of retirement income transfers—essentially, noncontributory cash transfers aimed at reducing poverty among the elderly. A literature review reveals how little academic analysis of the impact of these transfers has been carried out. Following the introduction of a taxonomy of retirement income transfers, a simple framework for examining incentive impacts of the transfers is presented. Drawing on theory and the available empirical evidence, the authors derive several policy-relevant findings. First, incentive effects depend on the level of the transfer in relation to average earnings and the degree of integration between the formal and informal sectors in the economy. In general, where transfers are modest, negative impacts on saving and the labor supply will be contained. Second, there is a trade-off between maintaining low effective marginal tax rates (EMTRs), to reduce distortions, and keeping program costs at affordable levels; this trade-off suggests that universal programs are suboptimal. Third, it is important to implement a gradual withdrawal of the benefit—to avoid crowding out contributory pensions among low-income individuals—and to index the eligibility age to life expectancy, to contain costs. Finally, matching contributions can be a promising instrument for promoting saving among individuals with limited saving capacity.

All the countries of the Organisation for Economic Co-operation and Development (OECD), and many other nations around the world, have implemented some form of transfer to guarantee a minimum income during old age. Most of the time, these are transfers that take place after retirement, often called "social pensions." Some countries, however, are starting to explore matching contributions—transfers that are made while individuals are active—to deliver a prefunded social pension. Both types of program can take a range of forms, and they vary in the degree of integration with other policies aimed at providing public support for the retired and elderly. But they have in common provision of cash, usually with some minimum level stipulated, to alleviate poverty among the elderly.

This chapter developed from presentations and discussions at the World Bank–Hitosubashi University–Ministry of Finance conference, "Reducing the Coverage Gap," held in Tokyo in February 2008. We are grateful to the conference organizers, Noriyuki Takayama and Robert Holzmann, for involving us in this project and to conference participants for comments that improved the paper. Lu Bei, Cagri Kumru, and Renuka Sane provided valuable research assistance; Mario di Filippo carried out simulations on fiscal impacts; and Eduardo Zylberstajn worked on the simulations based on the life-cycle model. We appreciate their contributions. Finally, John Piggot and Sergi Jimenez-Martin thank respectively the Australian Research Council and the Spanish Ministry of Education project # ECO2008-06395-C05-01 for financial support.

Social pensions are offered primarily on a noncontributory basis.[1] It is this that makes them central to any effort to reduce the coverage gap in emerging economies, where the informal sector is large and where much of the population lacks access to standard social security. Matching contributions, by contrast, are linked to individual contributions. While also serving the goal of guaranteeing a minimum level of income during old age, matching contributions can provide incentives for long-term saving, particularly for individuals with some but limited saving capacity who operate outside the formal sector (see chapter 13 in this volume).

Academic analysis of social pensions and matching contributions has been sparse. One reason may be lack of data. Another is that the incentives to evaluate these programs are low because these schemes usually involve relatively small outlays, compared with standard social security and in-kind provision programs such as health. If, however, coverage of the financial risks and shortfalls faced by the elderly in emerging economies is to be substantially increased over any short period, it is likely that retirement income transfers will become a more significant international policy paradigm, driven by the global demographic shift currently under way. As is shown in chapter 2 in this volume, formal retirement income schemes are thought to cover fewer than 2 percent of the world's working-age population. Most of those working without coverage live in developing countries (Willmore 2007). It is therefore timely to document what we do know about the impacts of retirement income transfers and to consider what might be the most useful framework for further analysis.

Following the presentation in the next section of a taxonomy of retirement income transfers, we go on to provide a simple framework for thinking about the potential incentive impacts of social pensions. We then briefly survey the economic literature on the incentive impacts of retirement transfers, mostly focusing on social pensions. Although excellent reviews of the literature on social assistance programs exist (for example, Atkinson and Micklewright 1991; Moffitt 1992), they do not cover retirement income programs, so even a brief overview may be of use. Next, we use a stochastic simulation model of the pension system in the Arab Republic of Egypt to illustrate the revenue requirements and the associated fiscal burdens of alternative social pension designs. Finally, we offer some conclusions.

Taxonomy of Retirement Income Transfers

As mentioned above, we distinguish between transfers that take place before and after retirement age—ex ante and ex post transfers, respectively. (For a discussion, see Robalino, Rao, and Sluchynsky 2007.) We later show that the two types of transfer can have different effects on individual behaviors. Therefore, when analyzing how to secure a minimum level of income during old age for different population groups, it is important to take an integrated approach and consider the costs and benefits of both interventions simultaneously.

Ex post transfers are by far the most common. Four types can be readily observed: social assistance, targeted pensions, basic (universal) pensions, and minimum pensions (OECD 2005). Social assistance refers to general programs that also cover older people. Targeted pensions cover specific schemes for older people that are resource tested. Basic schemes are universal, noncontributory, flat-rate programs. Minimum pensions are a specification within a more standard social security scheme; qualified members receive a minimum pension, sometimes conditioned on a certain contribution history.[2] Minimum pensions represent a special case of targeted pensions in which the test is based on the pension income generated by the contributory system (see below).

Ex ante interventions are more recent additions to the policy agenda of governments. They basically involve government matching of the contributions that individuals make to a given pension plan, which can be defined benefit or defined contribution, funded or unfunded. By design these transfers are resource tested.

Among targeted pensions, it is possible to distinguish three types: those that are tested only against pension income; those that employ a broader definition of income for the test; and broader means-tested schemes that take into account, for example, assets.[3] Means testing of the last type is feasible only if the state can measure personal consumption at a modest incremental cost. This requires a bureaucracy capable of observing personal income and holdings of durable consumption goods. Under these conditions, targeting allows both a reduction of fiscal cost and stronger redistribution. These conditions are also considered necessary for the implementation of matching contributions. Although not all emerging economies have this type of institutional capacity (see Valdés-Prieto 2008), important progress has been made in the development of proxy means tests (PMTs). These programs have been applied successfully to the targeting of conditional cash transfers and therefore could form the basis for the development of resource-tested social pensions (see chapter 12 in this volume).

Within the OECD, all countries have at least one of these types of pension in operation (see chapter 7 in this volume). Most offer a targeted pension; the next most common type is the minimum pension. Social assistance and the basic pension are less frequently encountered. Only five countries rely on general social assistance programs as the only noncontributory program for the old. In middle- and low-income countries, minimum pensions in the contributory system are also prevalent (see chapter 1 in this volume). Several countries have, in addition, adopted some form of social pension (see chapters 4 and 5 in this volume). Matching contributions are more recent initiatives (see chapter 13 in this volume), with pilots in the Dominican Republic (law passed), India (program implemented in West Bengal State), Mexico (program implemented), and Vietnam (law under consideration).

Analyzing Incentive Effects: A Conceptual Framework

Like any other tax-financed financial transfer, retirement income transfers affect incentives at two points in economic transactions: when the tax is levied, and when the transfer is received. In contrast to social security plans, where it may be argued that some dimensions of behavioral impact are neutralized through the actuarial link between contribution and benefit, social pensions are by definition redistributive, and the two points of price distortion need to be considered separately.[4]

To capture both points of intervention, it is necessary to adopt an economywide conceptual framework. Indeed, there are complex interactions between the effective marginal tax rates facing those eligible to receive transfers, those not eligible, and those who are being taxed to finance the transfers. The problem is complicated by dynamic intertemporal effects: for example, the prospect of benefiting from a transfer during old age might affect decisions about labor supply and saving during active life. In fact, even if the transfer is not targeted (i.e., if there are no conditionalities of any type) and therefore generates a pure income effect, individuals might have incentives to change labor supply and saving rates over the life cycle.

RETIREMENT INCOME TRANSFERS AND EFFECTIVE MARGINAL TAX RATES

The usual place to start when assessing the incentive effects of retirement income transfers, and social assistance programs in general, is to look at the effective marginal tax rates (EMTRs) facing potential beneficiaries. The thinking is that targeted programs can induce large EMTRs and can reduce incentives to work and save for individuals close to the eligibility line. Because efficiency costs or excess burdens increase disproportionately with increasing EMTRs, their estimation is a natural focus for analysis.[5] There are, however, potentially important trade-offs between the EMTR, the number of people affected by the targeting, and other explicit taxes in the economy. We discuss these issues next.

Assume for the moment that we wish to compare a targeted with a universal social pension. First, whereas a means-tested pension will impose high EMTRs on those at the margin of eligibility, where withdrawal of the pension is operative, many individuals potentially affected by a universal pension will not be affected by a targeted pension. The rate of withdrawal of the means-tested pension, sometimes called the taper rate, or claw-back, will have an effect on the number of people affected by the policy and the EMTR they face. The lower the taper rate, the lower will be the EMTR, but the greater will be the number of people affected.[6] Second, as the taper rate and the associated EMTR are reduced, the overall revenue requirement of the program will increase, requiring higher tax rates to be applied to others in the economy, probably workers. If these persons already pay high taxes, as is the case in developed countries, the argument about disproportionate efficiency costs of high marginal tax rates will apply, offsetting the EMTR reduction among pension recipients. On the other hand, if the economy is less developed, with low tax rates, it is likely that the tax imposition will retard the development of the formal sector or (when programs are financed through payroll taxes, the common approach in the case of minimum pensions), will affect employment levels. Overall, the efficiency impact of the two designs will be a somewhat subtle trade-off between maintaining a low EMTR for potential beneficiaries and keeping the tax burden on the economy at affordable levels.

Figure 10.1 captures these effects graphically. The upper part of the figure maps gross income into net income; M gives the level of minimum income available under the assistance scheme.[7] A 100 percent taper—that is, a dollar-for-dollar withdrawal of the transfer with increments in gross income—is represented by the horizontal line

FIGURE 10.1 **Means-tested transfers and incentive effects**

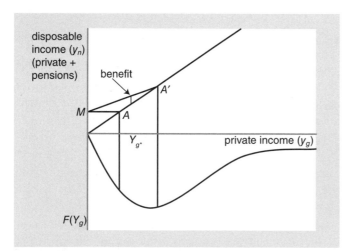

SOURCE: Authors' elaboration.

NOTE: M is the level of minimum income available under the assistance scheme. The line MA represents a 100 percent taper; MA' shows a 50 percent taper. The values Y_g and Y_n represent gross income and net income, respectively. $F(y_g)$ is the function defining the distribution of income.

MA, and a 50 percent taper is shown by *MA'*. The cost of the pension, for an individual at any income level, is given by the vertical distance between the 45 degree line and the relevant disposable income line, *MA* or *MA'*. The fiscal cost of the program depends on the number of recipients, whose frequency is mapped in the lower part of the figure. Although the frequency distribution shown is illustrative, it is consistent with the available evidence. The revenue cost increases dramatically as the taper rate is reduced, necessitating increases in distortionary taxes elsewhere in the economy. Moreover, the income effect generated among those not affected by the claw-back can still change behaviors regarding labor supply, saving, and retirement.

Unfortunately, the net impacts of these distortions on labor supply and saving are difficult to estimate, and, as the next section makes clear, the empirical evidence to date is limited. To provide further insights, we take a partial equilibrium approach, looking in a dynamic setting at the effects of the transfer and related EMRTs on the labor supply of potential beneficiaries. We also use a simple two-period consumption model to look at the plausible impacts on saving. General equilibrium effects resulting from the trade-offs between the level of the EMTR and other explicit taxes are not considered. The subsequent section nevertheless attempts to estimate the magnitude of this trade-off and discusses potential implications.

POTENTIAL INCENTIVE EFFECTS ON LABOR SUPPLY

We are mainly interested in the potential effects of retirement income transfers on densities of contributions to social security (i.e., formal work) and on retirement ages. Accordingly, we use a life-cycle behavioral model, in which individuals are assumed to make decisions about how long and where to work and how much to save, with the objective of maximizing intertemporal utility, which depends on consumption.[8] More precisely, at each time *t*, representative consumers choose their saving rate and decide whether to retire and what level of effort to invest in keeping or finding formal sector jobs.[9] Thus, the model can be used to understand trade-offs between formal and informal sector work. The implicit assumption is that individuals have some degree of mobility between formal and informal sector jobs (and vice versa); the labor market is not fully segmented. Transition probabilities between formal and informal jobs (including self-employment) then have two components: an exogenous component that does not depend on individual decisions, although it can be correlated with individual characteristics (e.g., formal firms that shut down or downsize), and an endogenous component that depends on individual preferences and choices. In this setting, which seems to be an accurate description of the labor market in middle-income countries such as Brazil, Chile, and Mexico (see for instance Bosh and Maloney 2007), the design of the transfer program would affect not only saving rates and retirement ages but also contribution densities in social security. This may have a major impact on development if the informal sector uses less productive technology.[10] The formal-informal split, of course, would be less important or nonexistent in countries where the labor market is segmented and the informal sector takes the form of a warehouse for residual labor.

We simulate the effects of introducing social pensions with three claw-backs (100, 30, and 0 percent) and a matching contribution program designed to cost, in present value, the equivalent of a flat pension equal to 42 percent of average earnings, paid at age 60 after 40 years of contribution.[11] Because choices depend on preferences regarding future and present consumption, attitudes toward risk, and views regarding formal versus informal sector jobs, we consider a large range of possible behavioral responses (i.e., individual preferences).[12]

The main results from the analysis are summarized in figure 10.2. Each panel graphs the change in contribution densities and retirement ages relative to the relevant counterfactual. Each point refers to a given combination of the parameters determining individual preferences. There are three main insights. First, introducing a minimum pension in the form of a top-up (i.e., 100 percent EMTR) can induce important reductions in contribution densities and retirement ages, depending on the level of the transfer in relation to average earnings. For instance, in our simulations a pension equivalent to 42 percent of an individual's earnings (the case of Brazil for the average worker) reduces contribution densities by up to 30 percentage points and the retirement age by up to seven years (panel A, figure 10.2). A more modest minimum pension equivalent to 25 percent of average earnings reduces contribution densities by less than 10 percentage points and retirement ages by less than two years in most cases (panel B, figure 10.2). Retirement

FIGURE 10.2 **Effects of transfers on contribution densities and average retirement age**

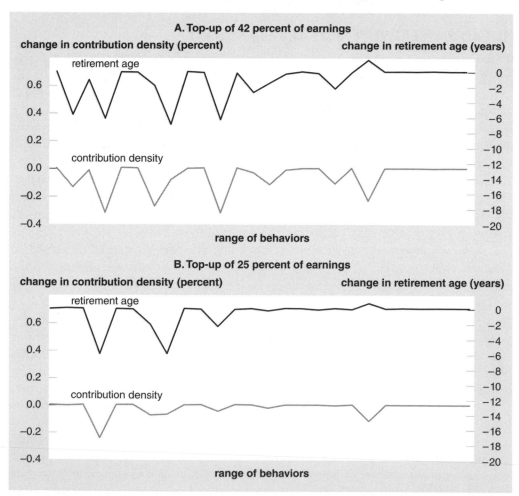

FIGURE 10.2 (continued) **Effects of transfers on contribution densities and average retirement age**

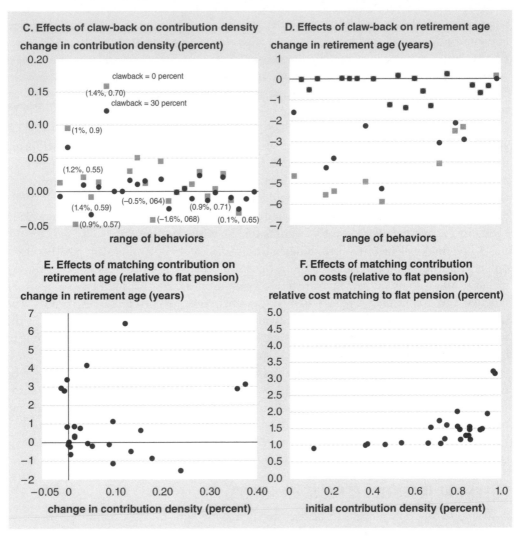

SOURCE: Authors' calculations.

NOTE: In panel C, numbers in parentheses are the elasticity of utility relative to consumption and the rate of time preference.

ages fall as a result of the income effect that makes early retirement more affordable. At the same time, the EMTR that is created by the top-up penalizes formal sector work: the individual can receive higher net earnings and enjoy a higher level of present consumption by working in the formal sector, but this reduces the level of the transfer, and therefore consumption, in the future. The rational response to this intertemporal trade-off is to participate less in social security.

A second insight is that a gradual claw-back of the minimum pension—in essence, a reduction of the EMTR—can increase contribution densities in comparison with a 100 percent EMTR. The exceptions are where individuals have high intertemporal substitution rates and strong preferences concerning leisure (see panel C, figure 10.2). These individuals value future utility less and therefore care less about the level of the future transfer. They also value current consumption less and are willing to accept lower lifetime earnings in exchange for greater flexibility in work arrangements (i.e., by investing less effort in finding and keeping formal sector jobs). In this case, the income effect of a lower EMTR induces decreased participation in social security. For individuals with stronger preferences for consumption over leisure and lower rates of time preference (the more common case), a claw-back of 30 percent increases contribution densities relative to the top-up by 1 to 12 percentage points. At the extreme, a flat transfer (a 0 percent EMTR) can increase contribution densities by 5 to 15 percentage points. Clearly, a lower EMTR also increases the cost of the transfer, in a way that depends on preretirement contribution density. For densities below 40 percent, the increase in costs is less than 6 percent in the case of the flat pension and 3.8 percent for the 30 percent claw-back. For higher contribution densities, the increase in the cost is much higher; for full career workers, low EMTRs can increase the cost of the transfer dramatically, mainly because in the absence of a claw-back most individuals would not be eligible for the minimum pension.

The final insight is that matching contributions can have a significant positive effect on contribution densities (panels E and F, figure 10.2). For most preferences, contribution densities and retirement ages increase. For contribution density, the increase can be in the range of 1 to 30 percentage points, in most cases between 5 and 10 percentage points. The result is not surprising: the more the individual contributes, the higher is the level of the transfer. One would expect, therefore, that higher contribution densities would come at high costs. As with claw-backs, however, high costs are only associated with high pretransfer contribution densities. For contribution densities below 60 percent, which would be the most common case in middle- and low-income countries, the cost of the matching would be similar to that of the flat pension. Adding restrictions such as a maximum cap on transferred capital could bring costs down further, but, of course, this creates a positive EMTR on contributions that would also reduce the contribution density. There lies the trade-off between lower distortions in labor markets and lower fiscal costs.

POTENTIAL INCENTIVE EFFECTS ON SAVING

A simple two-period model can be used to shed some light on the question of incentive effects on saving. Figure 10.3 shows the present value of utility as a function of consumption in period 1, which, given income, determines consumption in period 2. The left-hand panel shows the effects of a social pension equal to 20 percent of average earnings (targeted to individuals with earnings below 30 percent) and combinations of the social pension and various levels of matching in a system based on a 10 percent contribution rate. The social pension creates a "kink" in intertemporal utility that makes it optimal to increase consumption in period 1. Matching contributions, by contrast, move the utility function up.

A first observation is that matching contribution systems would be attractive even when social pensions are available; individuals would have incentives to enroll, since the matching increases intertemporal utility. But the level of the matching is important. If the matching is too low ($M = 1$), individuals will have incentives to enroll in the matching system and yet benefit from the social pension at the end by further reducing saving rates (see chapter 13 in this volume). In the first panel of figure 10.3, it is only when $M = 3$ that individuals can no longer "reach" the social pension (i.e., even with very low saving rates,

FIGURE 10.3 **Matching contributions and social pensions (SPs)**

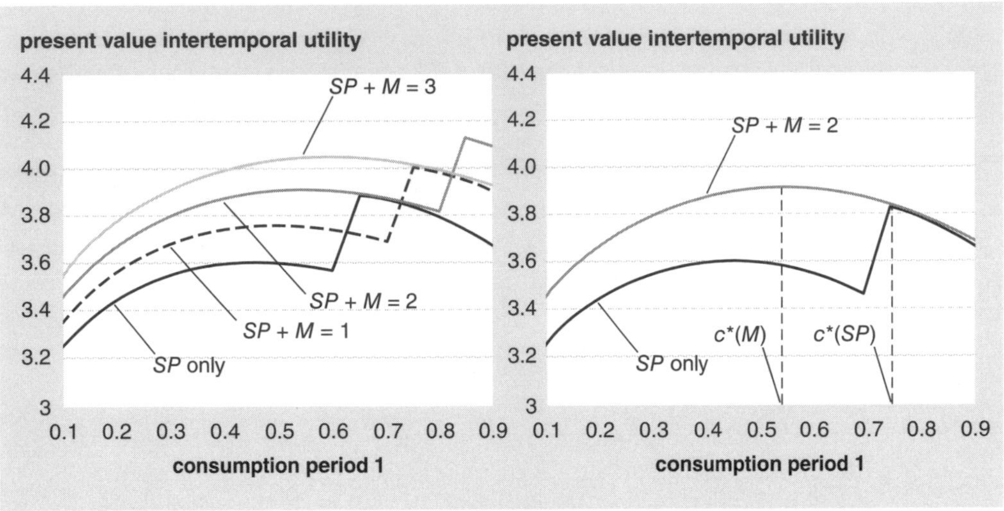

SOURCE: Authors' calculations.

NOTE: M, matching contribution; c^*, optimal consumption.

they would not be eligible). At $M = 3$, however, the matching costs more than the social pension (0.3 of average earnings instead of 0.2). But these costs can be reduced by bringing down the ceiling for eligibility for the social pension. This is done in the right-hand panel of figure 10.3, where the ceiling is set at 20 percent of average earnings. There, a matching of twice the contribution rate (costing the same as the social pension) generates levels of utility higher than or similar to those of the social pension but provides incentives for higher saving while young.

Empirical Evidence of Economic Effects of Social Pensions

The literature on the incentive effects of social pensions is sparse. This is partly because of the limited range of natural experiments that have presented themselves as candidates for empirical analysis. In what follows, we briefly review five studies. The first study centers on the Supplemental Security Income scheme in the United States, a sharply means-tested instrument available to all age groups but importantly used by the poor elderly who are not eligible for social security benefits. Aside from the specific findings on incentive impacts, this work also points up the importance of interactions between programs—an issue that policymakers tend to ignore when designing a new policy instrument or reforming an old one. (See also Robalino et al., forthcoming b, ch. 7, for a discussion of program interactions.) Next, we turn to the Chilean system before the 2008 reform. Chile had a mandatory funded scheme with a minimum pension guarantee that was available after 20 years of contributions and an underlying, but very modest, welfare payment plan. We focus on the potential effects of the system on formal employment. Our third instance is South Africa, where a means-tested pension is available to, and is taken up by, about 80 percent of the elderly, predominantly black. Here, the impact of a pension on other members of a household is examined, with surprising outcomes. The fourth case study is Brazil, which has implemented a targeted social pension for the elderly poor, as well as a universal rural pension; issues related to labor supply are included in the discussion. Finally, we turn to minimum pensions in Europe, focusing especially on Spain, and look at its impact on retirement ages. Our review is not by any means comprehensive, but we hope that it is representative and covers at least some of the important studies.[13]

It is worth emphasizing at the outset that identifying and quantifying the incentive effects of social pension programs is a more than usually challenging exercise, and the results are generally to be treated with caution. The recipients of means-tested benefits are, after all, meant to be different in germane ways from their non-pension-recipient counterparts. In addition, and especially in emerging economies, data reliability may be poor. As Case and Deaton put it:

> Simple correlations and regressions have a tendency to link pension receipt with undesirable outcomes, but these results can reasonably be attributed to the fact that pension recipients are different from others—in particular they are poorer and less well educated—or more subtly, to measurement error in income, so that even conditional on low measured income, the receipt of the pension may indicate low economic status. (Case and Deaton 1998, 1360)

THE U.S. SUPPLEMENTAL SECURITY INCOME PROGRAM: EFFECTS ON SAVING AND LABOR SUPPLY

The U.S. Supplemental Security Income (SSI) Program is a means-tested monthly stipend provided to persons who are aged (legally deemed to be 65 or older), blind, or disabled. It is paid by the federal government, but many states provide supplements to the federal benefit. The program was created by the Nixon administration in 1974 to replace various state-administered programs that served the same purpose.

In 2006 the federal payment stood at US$637 a month for a single person, or US$956 for a couple. The means-test income limits may vary depending on the state the individual lives in, his or her living arrangement, the number of people living in the residence, and the type of income. The resource limit is about $2,000 for a single individual and $3,000 for a married couple, in addition to an owner-occupied residence and a motor vehicle. There were about 7.4 million beneficiaries as of March 2008, costing approximately 0.3 percent of gross domestic product (GDP). The program is administered by the Social Security Administration (SSA). It is largely separate from social security, but eligible persons must apply for social security before qualifying for SSI.[14] In 2007, 11.1 percent of federal SSI payments were received by aged but not disabled individuals, and 8.4 percent of payments went to individuals who were both aged and disabled. According to the SSA's 2008 annual report on the program, most payments were received by disabled individuals under age 65.

In two related studies, Neumark and Powers (1998, 2000) investigate the impact of the SSI on saving and preretirement labor supply, respectively. In the 1998 study they exploit state variations in SSI benefits to estimate the effects of SSI on saving, using data from the SSA's 1984 Survey of Income Program Participation. To derive their main result, they control for possible correlations between disability and income support by dropping individuals with any self-reported work-impairing disability from their sample. By using the restricted sample, they are able to show that a US$100 increase in annual benefits reduces saving by US$281 among likely participants between ages 60 and 64. Their results suggest that a means-tested retirement program can distort the saving decisions of a portion of the population. They caution against applying their findings to social security systems more broadly because the SSI program serves a poor population with relatively low lifetime labor supply, whereas social security, in general, serves a higher-income population with higher lifetime labor supply.

The 2000 study focuses on preretirement labor supply. Using a similar empirical approach, the authors find evidence that generous SSI benefits reduce the preretirement labor supply (and earnings) of men nearing the eligibility age who are likely to participate in SSI after retirement. This is especially true of men who are eligible for early social security benefits that may be used to offset their reduced labor income. The authors' basic results show that a generous SSI supplement reduces the probability of employment between ages 60 and 64 by 10 percent. The findings here are more robust, and secondary evidence suggests a causal relationship between the availability of SSI and labor supply behavior in this group.

The strongest effects are for those age 62–64 who are able to take early social security entitlements. That is, the existence of SSI might encourage participation in another program at an earlier age than would otherwise be the case. This points to a subtle but extremely important feature in social pension design: interactions with other programs may produce incentive effects not envisioned by policy makers concerned with the integrity of the social pension itself.[15]

CHILE'S MINIMUM PENSION GUARANTEE AND ASSISTANCE PENSION: EFFECTS ON INFORMAL SECTOR WORK

The current Chilean pension system can be decomposed into a poverty prevention pillar, a contributory pillar, and a voluntary pillar. Before the 2008 reform, the poverty prevention pillar was based on two components: a means-tested assistance pension (*pensión asistencial*, PASIS), and the minimum pension guarantee (MPG) for individuals who contributed to the individual capitalization scheme for at least 20 years but were not able to finance a minimum amount for their retirement.[16] A recent study argues that the prereform noncontributory system led to reduced contribution densities and provided incentives for informal rather than formal sector work (Valdés-Prieto 2008). First, the PASIS gave low-income workers incentives to contribute only to the point at which the contributory pension exceeded 50 percent of the minimum pension. After that, the PASIS fell to zero—in essence, a very large marginal tax on additional pension income. Similarly, the MPG provided incentives to contribute only to the point of eligibility (20 years). Additional contributions afterward would have not increased the value of the total pension (the contributory pension plus the subsidy) paid by the contributory system. This implies a 100 percent marginal tax on additional pension income, resulting in a strong incentive to take informal sector jobs (despite the potential loss of productivity) in order to save on mandatory contributions to the pension system and avoid paying implicit taxes on pension subsidies. Although to date there are no rigorous impact evaluations of this effect, general statistics suggest that it was important. Thus, the coverage of the PASIS rose from 7.7 to 18.6 percent between 1992 and 2003, a period when the value of the MPG and the PASIS increased considerably in relation to economywide average earnings (see Valdés-Prieto 2008). This suggests that a larger share of workers, including those who had before regarded the transfer as too low, *chose* to maintain low contribution densities. The problem of low contribution densities in Chile, where more than half of workers have contribution densities below 50 percent, is well documented by Berstein, Larrain, and Pino (2006). A similar phenomenon is observed in Argentina and Uruguay (see table 10.1).

The 2008 reform replaces these programs with a unique scheme which guarantees that all individuals in the less affluent 60 percent of the population will have a guaranteed basic pension, regardless of their contribution histories. The new program provides old-age and disability subsidies, financed by general revenues of the state. Individuals with no contributions are entitled to an old-age basic solidarity pension (*pensión básica solidaria*, PBS) once they reach age 65 and fulfill the affluence and residence requirements. Individuals who make contributions can still receive part of the subsidy. Indeed, there is a claw-back based on the value of the contributory pension that will be close to 37 percent in the steady state, as opposed to the current 100 percent (see Valdés-Prieto 2008). The resulting subsidy, the solidarity complement (*aporte previsional solidario*, APS), has the same affluence and residence requirements as the PBS. (See Rofman, Fajnzylber, and Herrera 2008 for a more detailed description of the reformed noncontributory system.)

Given the more gradual withdrawal of the subsidy, the reform is expected to improve incentives to contribute and therefore reduce incentives for informal sector work. Clearly, other things being equal, reducing the claw-back rate also increases the cost of the system, thus requiring higher fiscal revenues and higher explicit taxes (see the discussion in the next section). Some have therefore argued that there is an optimal claw-back rate at which the marginal benefits of improved incentives to contribute equal the marginal costs of higher taxes. In the case of Chile this optimal claw-back would be around 20 percent (Poblete 2005).

Regardless of the claw-back rate, a persistent problem with the reformed system has to do with the level of the PBS, which is expected to reach 82 percent of the median salary by 2009 (Valdés-Prieto 2008). Regardless of the progressive claw-back rate, the high PBS is very likely to reduce incentives for formal sector work.

EFFECTS OF BRAZIL'S RURAL PENSION ON LABOR SUPPLY AND RETIREMENT DECISIONS

The Brazilian national pension system is managed by the National Social Security Institute (INSS) and includes contributory and noncontributory arrangements. The contributory system for private sector workers offers old-age, disability, and survivor pensions under the Regime Geral de Previdencia Social (RGPS). This is a defined benefit plan with pay-as-you-go financing. In addition, Brazil offers a means-tested flat pension for the elderly poor (BPC) and an old-age pension for agricultural workers. The latter offers a pension that can be a function of past earnings or equal to the minimum pension guarantee (*pisso providenciario*), whichever is higher. Most rural workers have short contribution histories and therefore retire with the minimum pension, which today is equal to the minimum wage. (For a recent assessment of redistribution and incentives in the Brazilian system, see World Bank forthcoming.)

A recent study exploited a reform implemented in 1991 to estimate the effect of the rural pension on retirement decisions and labor supply (de Carvalho Filho 2008). The reform in question reduced the minimum eligibility age for old-age benefits for rural workers from 65 to 60 for men and to 55 for women; increased the minimum benefit paid to rural old-age beneficiaries from 50 to 100 percent of the minimum wage; and extended old-age benefits to rural workers who were not heads of households, thus expanding coverage to many married female rural workers. Because the minimum pension is not means tested and there are no conditions regarding contribution histories (no vesting period), this pension generates a pure income effect.

The author uses a triple differences-in-differences approach to determine the effect of the rural pension. The first difference involves a treated group (rural workers) and a control group (urban workers not eligible for the rural pension). The second difference involves affected and unaffected workers within the treated group. (The 55–59 and 65–69 age groups were, if anything, less affected by the reform than the 60–64 age group.) The results show a statistically significant increase of 25.40 percentage points in the benefit take-up rates of rural workers age 60–64. In addition, the proportion of workers age 60–64 who "did not work in the week of reference" increased by 12.56 percentage points more for rural workers than for urban workers of the same age (difference-in-differences), during the period immediately before and after the reform. This difference was not observed among the unaffected groups. Triple-differences estimates show a statistically significant increase of 10.96 and 6.03 percentage points in the proportion of rural workers age 60–64 who "did not work in the week of reference" when the unaffected group consists of males age 55–59 and 65–69, respectively. Furthermore, "total hours of work in all jobs" for rural workers of the "affected age" decreased relative to urban workers by 5.80 hours per week during the period immediately before and after the reform. The triple-differences estimates show a relative reduction of 6.49 and 2.81 hours of work per week for rural workers age 60–64 relative to the 55–59 and 65–69 age groups, respectively. Only the first number is statistically significant.

The author therefore argues that estimates of the poverty reduction effect of old-age benefits in developing countries should take into account the negative labor supply impact of those benefits. Furthermore, the finding of a sizeable pure income effect suggests that means testing is more desirable than otherwise, since an important cost of means testing is its negative labor supply consequences. The paper also showed that more-educated workers are more able to benefit from social programs than less-educated ones, perhaps because they are better able to understand the formal rules of the game or because they are in general better informed.

EFFECTS OF SOUTH AFRICA'S MEANS-TESTED AGE PENSION ON LABOR SUPPLY AND JOB-SEEKING EFFORT

South Africa's social pension has been in existence since 1928, although much analysis focuses on the period after 1993, when the scheme was reformed. The pension is available to women age 60 or older and to men age 65 or older. In practice, the maximum each month (in 2007, 820 rand, or about US$105) is paid to anyone without a private pension (Ardington, Case, and Hosegood 2007). The social pension is about twice median per capita income, or about 20 percent of GDP per capita, and is thus a very important income source for many Africans. Altogether, there were more than 2 million households with pension beneficiaries in 2007. The International Monetary Fund (IMF) estimated South Africa's GDP per capita at US$5,906 (approximately US$492 per month) in 2007. The cost of the pension was estimated at 1.4 percent of GDP in 2006.[17]

The program has received a good deal of academic attention, perhaps because of its importance as a potential model for the developing world. The most recent and most comprehensive study is that of Ardington, Case, and Hosegood (2007), who focus on the implications of pension receipt for the whole household, assuming some form of income sharing. Standard analysis assumes that households pool income, so that labor supplied by prime-age workers is reduced as a result of social pensions. Alternatively, however, as the authors put it:

> If social transfers allow households to overcome credit constraints, enabling house-holds to bankroll potential migrants or potential work seekers who need financial support to look for jobs, then social transfers like the pension may promote employment and help households to break out of poverty traps. (Ardington, Case, and Hosegood 2007, 2)

Early studies suggested that the pension had the expected impact of reducing labor supply (Bertrand, Mullainathan, and Miller 2003). Later research, however, pointed to an interesting interaction between household receipt of an old-age pension and the probability that a younger member of the household will migrate to find work. While the standard result held for workers resident in the household, the ability of households receiving a pension to help their younger members find work elsewhere offset this result (Ardington, Case, and Hosegood 2007). This effect appears to operate both by simply relieving the credit constraint and by freeing older household members from work to care for children, thus giving more productive younger workers an opportunity to seek employment.

This finding expands the range of potential impacts of the social pension in developing countries where coverage rates are low. It suggests that, at least in developing countries, the role of the social pension might be much more varied than economists and policy makers have supposed and that these potential impacts should be assessed when such policies are being considered.

EFFECTS OF SPAIN'S MINIMUM PENSION ON RETIREMENT AND SAVING DECISIONS

Minimum pensions that are part of the national contributory system are quite prevalent in Europe (see chapter 7 in this volume). Recent evaluations have shown that current systems have deficiencies of various kinds when compared with the European minimum pension standard and that the effects are highly uneven across countries (Atkinson et al. 2002). Much attention has been given to the analysis of the effects on retirement decisions through different approaches. Some important areas of research are the study of implicit incentives (Blöndal and Scarpetta 1998; Gruber and Wise 1999); reduced-form models of retirement (Samwick1998); and models of conditional consumer decisions in a given economic environment (Stock and Wise 1990; Rust and Phelan 1997; Boldrin, Jiménez-Martín, and Peracchi 2004).

In the remainder of this section we focus on the minimum pension in Spain analyzed in Jiménez-Martín and Sánchez-Martín (2006). The authors quantitatively assess the impact of the Spanish pension rules, especially the minimum pension scheme, on the retirement and saving patterns of Spanish workers.[18]

The public Spanish pension system (comprising old-age, survivorship, and disability benefits) has two components. The first is a compulsory state pension system, universal and financed by taxes, that guarantees a minimum source of income to all individuals. The second is a defined benefit plan financed by contributions on a pay-as-you-go basis.

The crucial element for redistribution and solidarity is the minimum pension. During the late 1970s and early 1980s, close to 70 percent of Spanish pensioners received a minimum pension. In 2001 this proportion was still a sizeable 32 percent, with about 25 percent of new recipients starting out with a minimum pension. The minimum pension has been growing faster than the minimum wage, and since 2000 it was been higher than the minimum wage. Data on retirement patterns suggest that this minimum pension is far from neutral in a labor supply sense because it increases retirement probabilities for an important fraction of workers, especially low-income workers, who are potentially affected by the minimum pension.

The authors show that the minimum pension increases the opportunity cost of the forgone pension income and utterly eliminates the incentive to work arising from early retirement penalties. These two effects make it optimal for most low-income workers to retire at the earliest possible age (i.e., the early retirement age, ERA). This substitution effect is accompanied by an income effect, as the minimum pension effectively increases individuals' life-cycle wealth. This income effect also weakens the incentive to keep working in preretirement ages. These outcomes are reminiscent of the findings of Neumark and Powers (1998, 2000) on SSI. The net effect is a change in the shape of the retirement distribution in a fundamental way, shifting substantial amounts of probability mass from age 65 and the immediately preceding early retirement ages (61–64) to the ERA, age 60 (figure 10.4). As minimum pensions carry the retirement age of large groups of individuals forward, the distribution changes from a unimodal shape with a single peak at age 65 to a bimodal one with peaks at ages 60 and 65. A remarkable spike emerges at age 60 as the probability of retiring exactly at the early retirement age almost triples, from 6.6 to 18.0 percent. Increases in the incidence of preretirement (retirement before age 60) are mirrored by decreases in retirement after the early retirement age. Early retirement before age 65 is reduced by 15.5 percent, and retirement at the normal retirement age drops by 30 percent. Overall, the introduction of the minimum pension implies a 10 percent increase in early retirement and preretirement. The introduction of minimum pensions, together with the other caps and ceilings, reduces the average retirement age by four months, from age 63.0 to age 62.66. Most changes occur at the low end of the income distribution.

The authors also show that the minimum pension has effects on individual saving behaviors. The wealth effects implied by the guaranteed minimum can be quite substantial, leading to an upward shift in the life-cycle profile of consumption. This, in turn,

FIGURE 10.4 **Simulated aggregate retirement probabilities by age, with and without the minimum pension scheme**

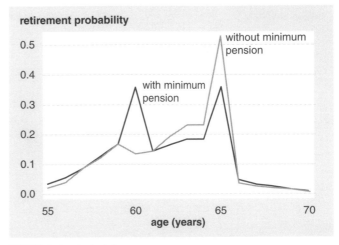

SOURCE: Authors' calculations.

implies lower savings in the first stages of the life cycle and lower accumulated assets (figure 10.5).

But do these behavioral changes have meaningful effects on welfare? To determine whether they do, the welfare loss or gain resulting from the redistributive function of the minimum pension is computed.[19] The minimum pension does benefit low-income workers, but it also imposes higher contribution rates on the overall population. The question then is, how much "extra" life-cycle consumption one would need to give each individual in the sample to make that individual indifferent to the simultaneous elimination of the minimum pension and reduction in the contribution rate.[20] The results show that the welfare impact of the minimum pension is quite modest, amounting to a 0.6 percent increase in the life-cycle consumption of the median worker in the economy. This low figure is, of course, the result of the cancellation of effects of opposite sign for different individuals. The gain for a low-income worker who retires at age 60 is a substantial 3.3 percent

FIGURE 10.5 **Impact of minimum pension regulation on consumption, income, savings, and assets**

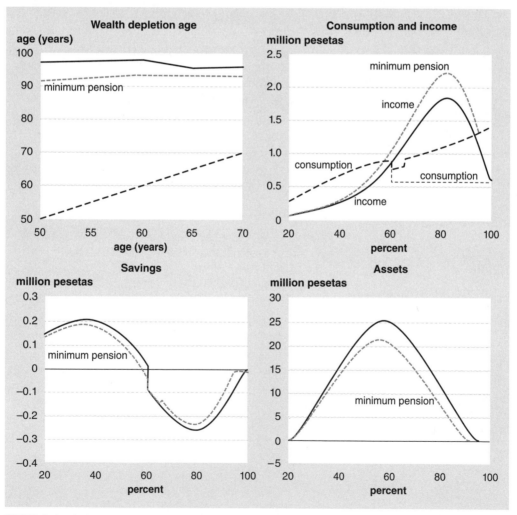

SOURCE: Authors' calculations.

of his or her life-cycle consumption. For a worker of average earnings who stays active until age 65, the losses from higher contributions amount to almost 1 percent of life-cycle consumption. It is important to note, however, that these figures are extremely sensitive to changes in the growth rate of the minimum pension. Furthermore, the economic costs of a reduction in labor supply as a result of early retirement are ignored.

These findings make it clear that minimum pensions should receive more attention in the current debate about the reform of the pension system in Spain (or any country with a similar system). Indeed, it makes little sense to discuss changes aimed at fostering older workers' labor participation while ignoring the strong disincentive effects of minimum pensions.

The Fiscal Cost of Retirement Income Transfers

As discussed above, beyond the potential impacts of retirement income transfers on saving and labor supply, one of the main sources of distortion is the cost of the transfer itself, which has to be financed out of general revenues through some form of tax (see chapter 11 in this volume). In the case of minimum pensions offered within contributory systems, the financing mechanism usually involves payroll taxes and employee contributions that increase the tax wedge and can reduce the level of formal employment. Evidence at the international level, for instance, suggests that a 1 percentage point increase in the tax wedge can be associated with a 0.4 percentage point reduction in the level of employment (see Robalino et al., forthcoming b, ch. 7). In this section we use the case of Egypt to illustrate the trade-off between a lower EMTR (which presumably reduces distortions in labor markets and provides better incentives to contribute) and higher fiscal costs. We also look at the fiscal impact of the eligibility age.

Egypt is an interesting case because the country is in the process of reforming its pension system; a classic defined benefit plan financed on a pay-as-you-go basis that includes a quasi-noncontributory scheme to cover casual workers (World Bank 2006).[21] Under current arrangements, eligible casual workers contribute 1 Egyptian pound per month and receive on retirement a flat pension equal to 80 pounds per month (around US$8). The contributory system also offers to plan members a minimum pension guarantee estimated at around 20 percent of economywide average earnings. Under the reform, these two programs are integrated into a new scheme that is reminiscent of the recent Chilean reform discussed above. In essence, all individuals age 65 or older (the eligibility age is automatically indexed with life expectancy) become eligible for a basic pension, which is set at 15 percent of economywide average earnings. This basic pension, however, is reduced as a function of the contributory pension (the taper rate is 30 percent; that is, for each monetary unit increase in the contributory pension, the transfer is reduced by 0.3 cents), which, in the reformed system, comes from notional and funded individual accounts. (The contribution rates to the notional defined contribution and funded defined contribution portions are 15 and 5 percent, respectively.) Thus, individuals who never contribute to the public pension system receive the basic pension in full. Those who contribute can draw part of the benefit, depending on their contribution density and level of income.

To evaluate the cost of the program under various designs, we use a stochastic simulation model designed for Egypt that takes into account transitions into and out of the social security system.[22] The results show that, as presented in the draft law, the cost of the new system would start at around 0.7 percent of GDP, increase gradually over the next 30

FIGURE 10.6 **Fiscal cost of alternative retirement income transfers, Arab Republic of Egypt**

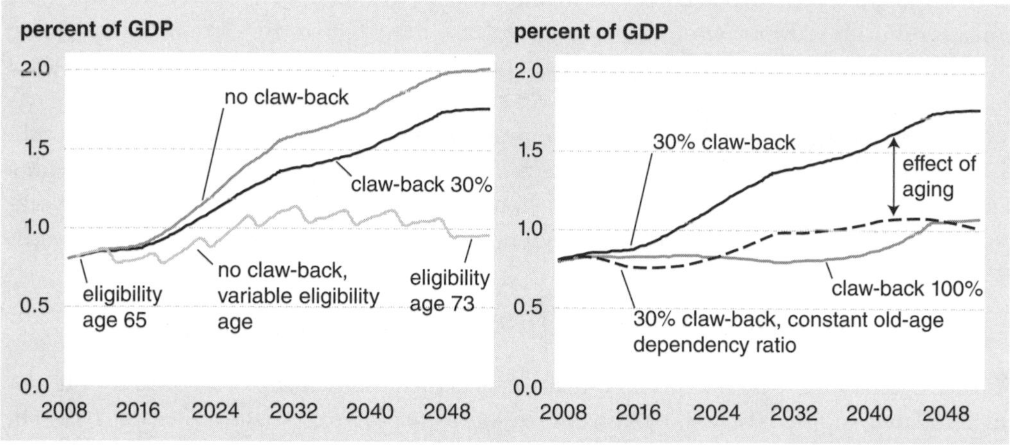

SOURCE: Authors' calculations.

NOTE: GDP, gross domestic product.

years as a result of population aging, and then stabilize below 1 percent of GDP (see dark line in left panel of figure 10.6). The dynamics of these costs, however, are quite sensitive to both the taper rate and the indexation of the eligibility age. Without automatic indexation of the eligibility age, costs would more than double, reaching 1.75 percent of GDP by the end of the simulation period. Indexing the eligibility age thus becomes one of the most important instruments for neutralizing the cost of the program as population ages.

The claw-back rate also has important fiscal implications. With a zero percent claw-back, which is basically the case of a universal pension that would impose the lowest distortion in the labor market, the cost of the program relative to the case with no indexation of the eligibility age could increase by 0.5 percentage point by the end of the simulation period. At the other extreme, imposing a 100 percent claw-back rate would reduce the cost of the program by 1 percentage point over the long term relative to the case with no claw-back (see right panel of figure 10.6). Thus, going from a 100 percent to a 30 percent claw-back rate demands around 0.7 percent of GDP in additional fiscal revenues. As discussed in chapter 11, mobilizing these resources can be an important challenge for many middle- and low-income countries.

This raises the issue of having a broader targeting mechanism, albeit with a gradual taper rate. The cost and benefits of targeting systems are discussed in chapter 12. As a preamble, however, it is worth emphasizing that the savings from a good targeting system can be considerable. A recent study in countries in the Middle East and North Africa Region, for instance, shows that perfect targeting (meaning that only the elderly poor are eligible) can cost between 2.3 and 24 times less than a universal pension (see Robalino, Rao, and Sluchynsky 2007).

Conclusions

This chapter has discussed the potential distortions of retirement income transfers, focusing on labor market effects, saving decisions, and the fiscal costs of the programs. The analysis was constrained by the small number of rigorous impact evaluations of the various programs. Nonetheless, by drawing on theory, simulations, and five case studies, a few general findings with important policy implications can be derived.

1. By and large, economic distortions taking place at the point where the benefit is paid or the point where the tax is levied will depend on the size of the transfer. A transfer that represents 15 percent of economywide average earnings (as in Egypt) is likely to have fewer impacts on behaviors and require, other things being equal, a lower level of taxation than a transfer that represents 42 percent of economywide average earnings (as in Brazil). A transfer that is close to or equal to the minimum wage might also have more important effects on work incentives.

2. There is an unavoidable trade-off between low EMTRs (to contain distortions in the labor market); the number of people receiving transfers; and the cost of the program, which determines the need for other, explicit, distortionary taxes. This trade-off suggests the existence of an "optimal" EMTR schedule. Although, in practice, trying to identify this optimum can be an elusive task, one can at least be confident that it is unlikely to involve zero targeting. Thus, a targeted transfer would be a superior option to a universal transfer. The choice of income base for the test is another policy question, and similar arguments would indicate that a broader measure of income may be better than only pension income. Successes with the design and implementation of proxy means tests (PMTs) for conditional cash transfers (CTTs) suggest that targeted retirement income transfers could be implemented in most countries (see chapter 12 in this volume).

3. Beyond the effects of retirement income transfers on the supply of labor, there can be effects on the choice between formal and informal sector work. As discussed in the case of Chile, the claw-back rate (and the level of the benefit) can influence contribution densities and therefore the effective coverage of the contributory system. Policy makers should avoid designs in which the total pension (contributory plus noncontributory) paid by the public system does not increase as a function of contributions or in which the transfer abruptly drops to zero above a certain income level. Consistent with the previous message, EMRTs below 100 percent are to be preferred.

4. There is strong evidence that the income effect from the retirement transfers influences decisions about retirement. The case studies of Brazil and Spain showed that by raising the opportunity cost of waiting to retire, retirement income transfers can induce increased early retirement. The eligibility age for the transfer therefore becomes a key policy variable. This variable, along with the level of the transfer, will have the highest impact on the cost of the program. A critical feature of a sustainable design is thus to index the eligibility age with changes in life expectancy.

5. The pure labor supply effects (hours worked) of retirement income transfers are more controversial. The Brazil and U.S. case studies showed that transfers can reduce labor supply, particularly in the ages close to retirement. In Brazil the reduction in labor supply takes place even if the program does not have strings attached (i.e., there is a pure income effect). The South African case showed, however, that there are also indirect effects that need to be taken into account. Although the social pension there does reduce labor supply in the eligible population, it facilitates job search efforts by other prime-age household members. In that case, overall labor supply can increase.

6. The U.S. evidence suggests that retirement income transfers can reduce saving rates. The analysis of the Spanish minimum pension and the simulations presented above

also point in that direction and predict nontrivial effects. In general, however, the effect will depend on the level of the transfer relative to average earnings. Modest transfers focusing on low-income population groups that have a low saving capacity to start with are likely to have very limited macroeconomic effects.

7. Matching contributions, although still in the experimental design stage, appear to be promising instruments for ensuring a minimum level of income during old age and also for stimulating compliance and reducing informality. Other things being equal, our simulations suggest that matching contributions can provide better incentives to enroll and contribute among population groups with some saving capacity than do minimum pension guarantees, unless the latter are conditioned on contribution densities—in which case the effects would be similar. Matching contributions cannot substitute for noncontributory pensions but could be an important complement to them, particularly by giving individuals with limited saving capacity incentives to enroll and contribute. The results even suggest that matching contributions could replace minimum pension guarantees in the contributory system. As with the Chilean and Egyptian public pension systems, individuals who contribute would lose part of the flat subsidy that is provided in the absence of contributions, but a higher expected pension (the sum of the contributory and noncontributory portions) would provide incentives to contribute. Individuals could save elsewhere without matching and still preserve part of the subsidy. The matching contribution, however, would provide an additional incentive to save and would also improve compliance. This type of financial incentive is more relevant for middle-income countries (and probably low-income countries) than the tax credits commonly used in OECD countries (see chapter 13 in this volume).

8. The design and implementation of retirement income transfers call for careful analysis and adequate planning and evaluation. It is especially important that the potential impacts of interactions with other programs be considered. Given the set of uncertainties that surround an ex ante evaluation of economic and social impacts, it would be desirable that the implementation of a new program proceed gradually. Countries could start with small pilots that would be expanded only after rigorous evaluation.

Notes

1. Note that this definition separates retirement income transfers, including social pensions, from standard social security except insofar as social security might incorporate a minimum pension, provided independently of contribution history. It also excludes public provision of services, such as long-term care and health, that will likely be important to the elderly.

2. Willmore (2007) offers an alternative but related classification. He divides what he terms "minimum pensions" into universal non-means-tested pensions, residence-based pensions, recovery pensions, and social assistance (Willmore 2007, 27). In countries that do not maintain adequate records of economic activity among their citizens, community-based social assistance, which may simply represent some implicit or explicit risk sharing within a village or other local jurisdiction, may be most effective in expanding coverage.

3. Robalino, Rao, and Sluchynsky (2007) show that basic and minimum pensions can be characterized by the type of claw-back employed. In the case of the classic minimum pension (top-up) the claw-back is set to 1; that is, there is a 100 percent marginal tax on additional pension income. In the case of the basic (universal) pension, the claw-back is equal to zero.

Other distinctions between means testing besides those listed here exist; for example, many means tests exempt the family home, and this provision has impacts on household choice (Sane and Piggott 2008).

4. For a discussion of links between redistribution and incentives, see Robalino et al. (forthcoming b).

5. This idea is most readily captured as the Harberger t-square rule, which stipulates that under simple assumptions, the efficiency cost of a distortionary tax increases with the square of the tax rate.

6. This line of argument was first set forth by Blinder and Rosen (1985). Sefton, van de Ven, and Weale (2008) make the same point in the context of means-tested pensions in the United Kingdom.

7. Depending on the nature of the scheme, this may be guaranteed to all, to all above a certain age, or only to those enrolled in a social security program.

8. The life-cycle model of consumption smoothing may be less relevant in dealing with social pensions than in some other applications, but it is nevertheless the most rigorous analytical framework available.

9. For a formal description of the model, see Robalino et al. (forthcoming a).

10. Piggott and Whalley (2001) show that in a model with an informal sector and self-supply, a broad-based value added tax may be less efficient than a tax on goods alone, if services can be provided in either the formal or the informal sector.

11. The baseline scenario assumes an earnings-related pension system that pays a 3 percent rate of return on contributions—the equivalent of a notional defined contribution (NDC) system with individual accounts revalorized at 3 percent. Wages grow at 3 percent per year, and the real interest rate on savings is 4 percent. The minimum retirement age is 60 years.

12. The model dynamics depend on five main parameters: preferences regarding consumption and leisure; preferences regarding formal versus informal work; attitudes toward risk; the rate of time preference; and the distributions of two exogenous shocks that affect movement into and out of the social security system, independent of individual decisions. The joint distribution of model parameters is derived from Robalino et al. (forthcoming a) and is estimated for Brazil. The various transfer programs are analyzed within a subsample of this distribution.

13. Two important social pensions not discussed here are those in Australia and the United Kingdom. The Australian means-tested age pension has received only limited attention but is analyzed by Creedy and Kalb (2006), who, in the context of a larger microsimulation study of tax reform, examine its labor supply impacts. The United Kingdom reformed its means-tested pensions, changing the taper from 100 to 40 percent. Sefton, van de Ven, and Weale (2008) use a dynamic programming approach to analyze the labor supply effects of the change.

14. Our sources for information about the SSI provisions and payments include Social Security Administration, "Supplemental Security Income Home Page," http://www.ssa.gov/ssi/, and "SSI Annual Reports," http://www.ssa.gov/OACT/ssir/SSI07/index.html.

15. For a discussion of the interactions among social insurance programs and their effects on labor supply and savings, see Robalino et al. (forthcoming b).

16. Eligibility requirements for PASIS are as follows: the recipient must be at least age 65; cannot have another pension; must have earnings that are below 50 percent of the minimum pension; and must have per capita family earnings that are below 50 percent of the minimum pension.

For an analysis of the current system and the 2008 reform, see Rofman, Fajnzylber, and Herrera (2008). According to the authors of that study, as of March 2008 the minimum pension guarantee was equivalent to US$222 (US$242 after age 70 and $257 after age 75), and the PASIS program provided old age, disability, or mental deficiency benefits equivalent to US$110 before age 70, US$117 after age 70, and US$128 after age 75.

17. Sources for this discussion include HelpAge International, "Social Pensions in South Africa," http://www.helpage.org/Researchandpolicy/PensionWatch/SouthAfrica; South Africa, Department of Social Development, http://www.dsd.gov.za/dynamic/dynamicXML.aspx?pageid=472.

18. This task is undertaken with the help of a life-cycle model with an endogenous retirement decision and a prohibition on borrowing from future pension income. The model is used as the data-generating process in a structural maximum likelihood estimation carried out over a unique, very large sample of labor records obtained from the Spanish Social Security Administration (HLSS).

19. The welfare effect is assessed by computing a compensated equivalent variation that keeps constant the average generosity of the system, in terms of its implicit internal rate of return. See Piggott, Robalino, and Jimenez-Martin (forthcoming) for a formal description of the methodology.

20. In the calculations, the contribution rate is reduced so that the average internal rate of return paid by the system remains unchanged after eliminating the minimum pension.

21. A new social security law has been drafted and is expected to be submitted to the parliament before the end of 2009.

22. The model decomposes the labor force into various occupational groups, including civil servants, self-employed persons, wage earners in the formal sector, and informal wage earners. Within each category, workers are classified by age, gender, and level of income. Costs are estimated for each subgroup separately and are then aggregated. Members of each occupational category face different transition probabilities for moving into and out of social security. For a detailed description of the model, see Di Filippo and Robalino (forthcoming).

References

Ardington, Cally, Anne Case, and Victoria Hosegood. 2007. "Labor Supply Responses to Large Social Transfers: Longitudinal Evidence from South Africa." NBER Working Paper 13442, National Bureau of Economic Research, Cambridge, MA.

Atkinson, Anthony B., and John Micklewright. 1991. "Unemployment Compensation and Labor Market Transitions: A Critical Review." *Journal of Economic Literature* 29 (4, December): 1679–1727

Atkinson, T., F. Bourguignon, C. O'Donoghue, H. Sutherland, and F. Utili. 2002. "Microsimulation of Social Policy in the European Union: Case Study of a European Minimum Pension." *Economica*, n.s., 69 (274, May): 229–43.

Berstein, Solange, Guillermo Larrain, and Ariel Pino. 2006. "Chilean Pension Reform: Coverage Facts and Policy Alternatives." *Economia* 6 (2): 227–79.

Bertrand, Marianne, Sendhil Mullainathan, and Douglas Miller. 2003. "Public Policy and Extended Families: Evidence from Pensions in South Africa." *World Bank Economic Review* 17 (1): 27–50.

Blinder, Alan, and Harvey Rosen. 1985. "Notches." *American Economic Review* 75 (4, September): 736–47.

Blondäl, S., and S. Scarpetta. 1998. "The Retirement Decision in OECD Countries." Working Paper 20, Economics Department, Organisation for Economic Co-operation and Development, Paris.

Boldrin, M., M. Jiménez-Martín, and F. Peracchi. 2004. "Micromodeling of Social Security and Retirement in Spain." In *Social Security and Retirement around the World: Micro-Estimation*, ed. Jonathan Gruber and David Wise. Chicago: University of Chicago Press for the National Bureau of Economic Research.

Bosh, Mariano, and William Maloney. 2007. "Comparative Analysis of Labor Market Dynamics Using Markov Processes: An Application to Informality." IZA Discussion Paper 3038, Institute for the Study of Labor, Bonn.

de Carvalho Filho, Irineu Evangelista. 2008. "Old-Age Benefits and Retirement Decisions of Rural Elderly in Brazil." *Journal of Development Economics* 86 (1, April): 129–46.

Case, Anne, and Angus Deaton. 1998. "Large Cash Transfers to the Elderly in South Africa." *Economic Journal* 108 (450): 1330–61.

Creedy, John, and Guyonne Kalb. 2006. *Labour Supply and Microsimulation: The Evaluation of Tax Policy Reforms.* Cheltenham, U.K.: Edward Elgar.

Di Filippo Mario, and David Robalino. Forthcoming. "A Stochastic Model to Assess the Fiscal Impact of Retirement Income Transfers." Technical Note, Human Development Network, Social Protection (HDNSP), World Bank, Washington, DC.

Gruber, Jonathan, and David Wise, eds. 1999. *Social Security and Retirement around the World.* Chicago: University of Chicago Press for the National Bureau of Economic Research.

Jiménez-Martin, S., and A. R. Sánchez-Martín. 2006. "An Evaluation of the Life-Cycle Effects of Minimum Pension on Retirement Behavior: Extended Version." *Journal of Applied Econometrics.*

———. 2007. "An Evaluation of the Life-Cycle Effects of Minimum Pensions on Retirement Behaviour." *Journal of Applied Econometrics* 22: 923–50.

Mirrlees, J. 1971. "An Exploration in the Theory of Optimum Income Taxation." *Review of Economic Studies* 38: 175–208.

Moffitt, Robert. 1992. "Incentive Effects of the U.S. Welfare System: A Review." *Journal of Economic Literature* 30 (1): 1–61.

Neumark, D., and E. Powers. 1998. "The Effect of Means-Tested Income Support for the Elderly on Pre-Retirement Saving: Evidence from the SSI Program in the US." *Journal of Public Economics* 68: 181–206.

———. 2000. "Welfare for the Elderly: The Effects of SSI on Pre-Retirement Labor Supply." *Journal of Public Economics* 78: 51–80.

OECD (Organisation for Economic Co-operation and Development). 2005. *Pensions at a Glance: Public Policies across OECD Countries.* Paris: OECD.

Piggott, John, and John Whalley. 2001. "VAT Base Broadening, the Informal Sector, and Self Supply." *American Economic Review* 91 (4, September): 1084–94.

Piggott, John, David Robalino, and Sergi Jimenez-Martin. Forthcoming. "Incentive Effects of Retirement Income Transfers." Social Protection Discussion Papers, World Bank, Washington, DC.

Poblete, Dante. 2005. "Grado de focalización óptimo de las pensiones no contributivas en el Tercer Mundo." Tesis de economía, Instituto de Economía, Pontificia Universidad Católica de Chile, Santiago.

Posel, Dorrit, James A. Fairburn, and Frances Lund. 2006. "Labour Migration and Households: A Reconsideration of the Effects of the Social Pension on Labour Supply in South Africa." *Economic Modelling* 23: 836–53.

Robalino, David, and Eduardo Zylberstajn. 2009. "Labor Markets in Latin America: Structure, Dynamics and Implications for the Design of Social Protection Policies." Human Development Department, Latin America and Caribbean Region, World Bank, Washington, DC.

Robalino, David, Gudivada Venkateswara Rao, and Oleksiy Sluchynsky. 2007. "Preventing Poverty among the Elderly in MENA Countries: Role and Optimal Design of Old-Age Subsidies." World Bank, Washington DC.

Robalino David, Eduardo Zylberstajn, Helio Zylberstajn, and Luis Eduardo Afonso. Forthcoming a. "An Ex-Ante Evaluation of the Impact of Social Insurance Policies on Labor Supply in Brazil: The Case for Explicit over Implicit Redistribution." Social Protection Discussion Papers, World Bank. Washington, DC.

Robalino David, Andrew Mason, Helena Ribe, and Ian Walker. Forthcoming b. "The Future of Social Protection in LAC: Extending Coverage to All by Adapting Programs to Labor Markets and Rethinking the Allocation and Financing of Subsidies." World Bank, Washington, DC.

Rofman Rafael, Eduardo Fajnzylber, and German Herrera. 2008. "Reforming the Pension Reforms: The Recent Initiatives and Actions on Pensions in Argentina and Chile." Pension Reform Primer Series, World Bank, Washington, DC.

Rust, John, and Christopher Phelan. 1997. "How Social Security and Medicare Affect Retirement Behavior in a World of Incomplete Markets." *Econometrica* 65 (4): 781–831.

Samwick A. 1998. "New Evidence on Pensions, Social Security and the Timing of Retirement." *Journal of Public Economics* 70: 207–36.

Sane, Renuka and John Piggott. 2008. "Does the Owner-Occupier Exemption from the Pensions Means Test Affect Housing Choice of the Elderly? Evidence from Australia." Social Science Research Network. http://ssrn.com/abstract=1276854.

Sefton, James, Justin van de Ven, and Martin Weale. 2008. "Means Testing Retirement Benefits: Fostering Equity or Discouraging Savings." *Economic Journal* 118 (528, April): 556–90.

Stock, James H., and David A. Wise. 1990. "Pensions, the Option Value of Work, and Retirement." *Econometrica* 58 (5, September): 1151–80.

Valdés-Prieto, Salvador. 2008. "A Theory of Contribution Density and Implications for Pension Design." Social Protection Discussion Paper 0828, Pension Reform Primer Series, World Bank, Washington, DC.

Willmore, Larry. 2007. "Universal Pensions for Developing Countries." *World Development* 35 (1): 24–51.

World Bank. 2006. "Egypt: Improving the Welfare of Future Generations through Pension Reform." Human Development Department, Middle East and North Africa Region, World Bank, Washington, DC.

———. Forthcoming. "Brazil. Social Insurance and Labor Supply: Assessing Incentives and Redistribution." Draft Technical Report, Human Development Department, Latin America and Caribbean Region, World Bank, Washington, DC.

CHAPTER 11

Financing Social Pensions

Alain Jousten

Social pensions are a key tool in the fight against poverty among the elderly and should be an integral part of poverty alleviation strategies. Their benefits, however, have to be weighed against their direct costs and their effects on saving and labor supply. The short-term fiscal costs of social pensions can reach 1 to 2 percent of gross domestic product (GDP), and thus the overall budgetary implications of the schemes have to be kept in mind. A government has two main levers for financing programs: raising additional government revenues, and optimizing public spending. Tax revenues in middle- and low-income countries have remained flat over the past 25 years, however, partly because of trade liberalization, and the range of tax instruments available to these countries is limited. Rationalization of spending is therefore an important complementary policy for financing social pensions. For middle- and high-income countries, these two strategies can be a feasible way of financing social pensions, but for some low-income countries, social pension programs may not yet be within reach. Such initiatives would involve spending a substantial fraction of government resources on income security for the old, in direct competition with spending on human and economic development. Donor financing can help catalyze reform but is not a viable source of long-term funding, if only because of the recurrent nature of spending needs. In the longer run, domestic financing on the revenue or the expenditure side will inevitably need to be secured.

Social pensions—noncontributory cash transfers to older persons—are moving to center stage in the old-age income security debate. To the surprise of some observers, this holds true in both the developed and the developing worlds. One notable and much discussed recent example is the major reform of the Chilean retirement income system in March 2008, which includes the introduction of a new guaranteed solidarity pension for older (low-income) retirees.[1]

At first, it might appear surprising that policy makers in countries across the income and development spectrum are using the same policy tool, social pensions. A closer look, however, makes it obvious why this is and should be the case. All countries share a common interest in improving the social and economic situation of the elderly. Social pensions are a key policy tool in this respect, as they can be used to alleviate old-age poverty and help reduce inequality both among the elderly and between the elderly and other groups in the population—in particular, the working-age population. In the developed world, social pensions often act as a complement to the predominant contributory pension schemes that are in place, providing a minimum safety net for the elderly. In developing countries, social pensions usually have the policy objective of ensuring that elderly citizens do not suffer from deprivation and poverty, particularly given the lack of coverage of a large fraction of the population by any type of contributory pension program.

This chapter focuses on the effects of social pensions on public finances. In the next sections we examine social pensions in the context of other social assistance and insurance programs and explore the government's financing options for social pension programs. The discussion is organized around two broad topics: public expenditure and revenues. The final section summarizes key conclusions.

Conceptual Framework

The direct budgetary cost of a social pension program depends heavily on the precise details of the program, but also on the characteristics of any other programs that are accessible to the elderly poor. Indeed, it is impossible to discuss the financing (and functioning) of social pensions without a reference to contributory schemes, as well as other general social insurance and assistance programs.[2] The interactions are numerous, and some prominent ones—such as impacts on labor supply and demand and on private saving—are addressed in other chapters of the book. We limit our discussion to elements that affect the financing of social pensions. These are grouped in two categories: mechanical and behavioral. In contrast to behavioral effects, mechanical ones result purely from the institutional setting of the country and do not involve any endogenous behavioral response by either individuals or firms.

MECHANICAL EFFECTS

First, a purely mechanical financing effect arises from the degree of complementarity of social pensions with the overall legislative and regulatory framework. The magnitude of the social pension system (that is, whether the system is conceived as a sizeable element or as a marginal tool) and the degree of integration of the various public and private sector programs (that is, whether the benefit entitlements are cumulative or mutually exclusive) are important determinants of the scheme's direct cost.

The direct and narrowly defined budgetary cost of the social pension program may be lower in the presence of other programs or schemes than in their absence, but this does not imply that the overall fiscal cost of the social pension is lower. In fact, in the absence of any behavioral response, part of the cost of ensuring a minimum level of resources to the elderly population is simply shifted and is borne by a different budgetary position—or possibly even the private sector—without affecting social aggregate costs.[3] For example, a minimum pension guarantee in the form of a top-up to a public contributory scheme entails a significantly lower direct budgetary cost than a social pension that gives a basic income guarantee to all individuals, but the aggregate fiscal cost is not affected.

Second, the coverage of the various schemes matters. Although social pensions try to ensure that every older citizen or resident receives a minimum level of resources, coverage is not necessarily the paramount goal of contributory old-age pension and savings arrangements.[4] For example, contributory programs in developing countries are often restricted to a narrow subgroup of the population composed of civil servants and formal private sector wage earners, yet experience from many developed countries with quasi-universal contributory pension schemes illustrates that the distinction, as measured by coverage, between social and contributory pensions may be less stark in practice.[5] Thus, coverage of and participation in the compulsory contributory systems (public and private); the scope of other voluntary arrangements such as individual savings; and overall income distribution in the economy and among the elderly are all important factors influencing the budgetary and social cost of a social pension scheme. Eligibility ages under the various pension schemes play a similar role. These explicit policy parameters have a direct influence on the coverage and hence on the budgetary and social costs of the various programs.

Third, the benefit rules and the eligibility criteria heavily influence the level and time pattern of fiscal costs. The level of financial cost can, for example, be affected by rules regarding targeting of social benefits through means testing or income testing. The timing of the fiscal costs of a social pension can also be influenced by strategically choosing a specific type of scheme.[6] For example, by opting for a system of ex post redistribution through the pension channel, rather than ex ante redistribution based on matched or subsidized contributions, fiscal costs are shifted into the future.

ENDOGENOUS EFFECTS

Budgetary costs resulting from endogenous behavioral adjustments are an important component of total fiscal and social costs and can by no means be neglected as marginal.[7] Different types of effects can be identified. Here, we discuss the most important.

1. Direct short-run effects result when people endogenously move out of other programs into social pensions. This changes the budgetary allocation among government departments, social programs, and coverage of private and public sector schemes. Insofar as all these programs are administratively part of the same level of government, these short-run effects will be rather limited because some offsetting will take place. The situation is more complicated when different levels of government or the private sector are involved. In such cases, issues relating to fiscal federalism and decentralization of functions arise and may induce unexpected and unintended redistributive consequences between regions and private entities in a country.

2. More important, medium- and long-run effects are likely to occur, negatively affecting the functioning of public and private contributory systems. For example, the introduction of a minimum social pension in a country with a Bismarckian system contributes to a weakening of the link between contributions and benefits. Individual and aggregate saving incentives may suffer. One of the most striking real-world examples of the latter effect has been the introduction of the U.K. pension credit regime in the early 2000s. This program introduced a minimum income guarantee for low-income households and was designed to complement the private pension income of older residents. Disney and Emmerson (2005) show that one of the unintended results of the reform was a large (retirement) saving disincentive, ultimately leading to much higher entitlement probabilities and amounts than originally anticipated, with large projected fiscal costs once these low savers start to retire.

3. The introduction of a social pension may well contribute to undermining the incentives for formalization of work relationships, particularly in the developing world. Social pensions reduce the cost of remaining in informality by lowering the risk of poverty in old age; hence, they diminish the medium- to long-term incentives for formalization.

4. People are likely to rely less on intrafamily support, and this may have a substantial effect on the evolution of family structures and living arrangements over time. Kotlikoff and Spivak (1981) show how families can protect against the risk of longevity

by providing implicit annuity contracts for the members. This is in line with the observation that families have historically provided the main type of old-age income support. In developed countries, where formal old-age income systems exist, that role has been taken over by social programs that have progressively shifted the risk to the public sector, with the attached budgetary costs and consequences. In developing countries, families still play a predominant role in providing income support, although major changes are occurring in the face of demographic and external shocks such as HIV/AIDS.

5. Indirect or second-round effects may reinforce the endogenous behavioral responses described above. Those individuals and firms that bear the fiscal burden of the social pension scheme through increased levels of taxation are likely to adjust their behavior in reaction to the changed incentives generated by the overall tax benefit system. It should be kept in mind that the key concept is not so much who pays the tax but, rather, who supports the economic cost of the increased tax burden through lower after-tax producer prices or higher tax-inclusive consumer prices. A deadweight loss and tax incidence analysis is required to fully assess the budgetary and welfare impact of a social pension scheme on the various private and public sector actors.

Public Finance

When considering the introduction or expansion of a program, the fiscal cost of the measure has to be taken into account. In light of the above discussion regarding the scope of short- and long-term budgetary needs and the long-term overall fiscal implications, we now turn to an examination of the alternatives that policy makers face with regard to the financing of a social pension program. In doing so, it is important to realize great heterogeneity among countries in levels and composition of revenue.

Fundamentally, the issue is one of creating fiscal space for accommodating the social pension expenditures. This objective can be achieved in a number of ways. In the short run, fiscal space can be generated by increasing government revenues, by rationalizing other public expenditures, by borrowing, and by using grants from the outside world. These alternatives are discussed in turn below. In an intertemporal sense, given that all borrowing enters the intertemporal budget constraint, it will ultimately have to be paid back by means of reduced expenditures or increased future revenues (and grants). Therefore, sound macroeconomic policies are an important ingredient in ensuring long-term fiscal sustainability.

RAISING REVENUES

Among the different forms of financing, raising additional revenues—primarily through taxes—clearly stands out as one of the most frequently envisaged tools when a government faces additional spending.

Although overall spending on social pension programs may be considered modest in absolute terms—some assessments put the cost of a social pension program at a mere 1 to 2 percent of gross domestic product (GDP)—such levels of increased own revenue may still prove elusive for some countries (see Pal et al. 2005). This is particularly so for countries at the low end of the income spectrum. Keen and Mansour (2008) provide an illustration of these limitations in their study of recent tax trends in Sub-Saharan Africa.

FIGURE 11.1 **Tax trends in Sub-Saharan Africa, by income group, 1980–2005**

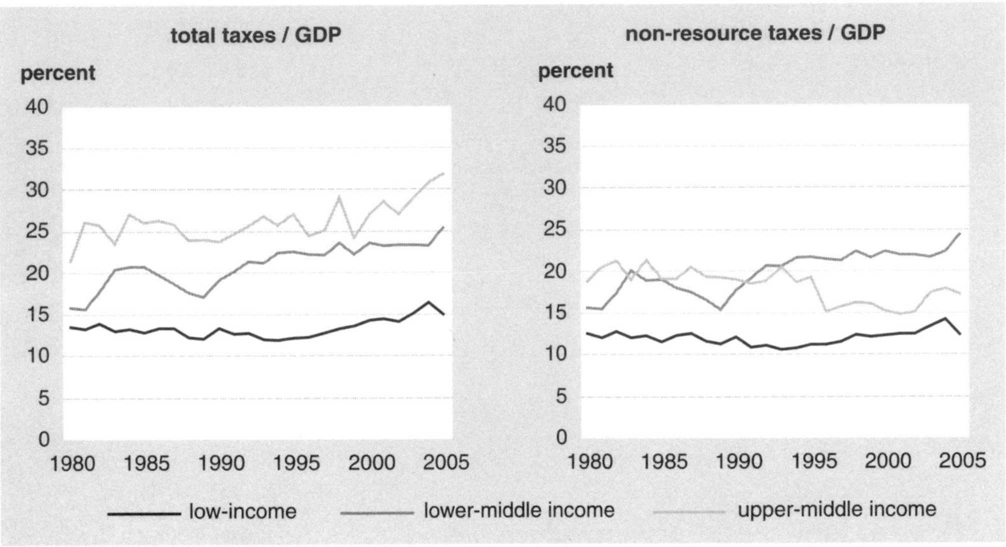

SOURCE: Keen and Mansour 2008.

NOTE: GDP, gross domestic product.

Figure 11.1 documents the relatively low tax-to-GDP ratios for this group of countries over the last 25 years. (Taxes are defined as central government tax revenue; social contributions are not included.) The left-hand panel provides an overview of the aggregate tax-to-GDP ratio for these countries, which are grouped by income level. The right-hand panel reports the same tax ratio but with tax revenues derived from the natural resource sector excluded.

The data in figure 11.1 have interesting implications for social pension financing. First, tax ratios in low-income countries have remained flat, at a rather low level of 12–15 percent of GDP, over the last 25 years. This persistence is all the more striking because numerous countries have attempted to improve their tax revenue performance through administrative reforms and tax policy measures. The figure also reveals that growth of the average tax ratio in middle-income countries has not necessarily been broadly based. This is particularly true for upper-middle-income countries, where the increase in the tax ratio has mostly been driven by tax revenues related to the natural resource sector.

A secular downward trend in trade tax revenue (customs and duties on imports and exports) in the overall revenue mix has been occurring in countries around the world. The trend is likely to be further reinforced by ongoing trade liberalization on a multilateral level (through the World Trade Organization, or WTO), leading to lower customs barriers. Similarly, regional trade agreements and the conclusion of Economic Partnership Agreements with the European Union will exert sustained downward pressure on trade tax revenues. These tendencies are likely to have a particularly strong impact on less developed countries, such as those in Sub-Saharan Africa, where trade taxes still represent a much larger fraction of total revenues than in the developed world (figure 11.2). Another feature illustrated by the figure is the increasing role of indirect taxes, specifically the value added tax (VAT), in the government's revenue mix. Indeed, the introduction of a VAT system,

FIGURE 11.2 **Main components of the tax/GDP ratio in Sub-Saharan African countries, 1980–2005**

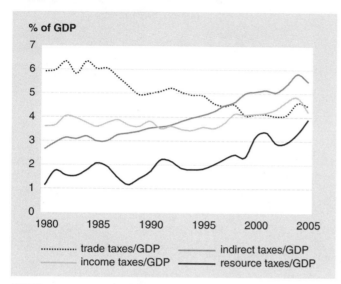

SOURCE: Keen and Mansour 2008.

NOTE: GDP, gross domestic product.

complemented by excise duties, has often been used as a potent domestic revenue alternative in the face of the trend toward lower trade taxes.

Two further trends in Sub-Saharan Africa can be inferred from figure 11.2. First, taxes paid by the natural resource sector play an increasing role in tax revenues but entail problems related to resource depletion and the volatility of the tax base.[8] Second, income tax revenues have remained at a rather constant level, usually driven by a highly progressive personal income tax schedule and a high corporate income tax rate applied to a narrow tax base. This is unlikely to be a steady-state situation: Norregaard and Khan (2007) document and discuss the recent trends in Eastern Europe and other parts of the world toward lower corporate income tax rates, as documented in figure 11.3.[9] This international rate competition represents a bigger revenue challenge for low-income countries than for high-income countries, given their greater reliance on corporate income tax as opposed to personal income tax revenues.

In light of the above discussion, what are the effective tax policy tools that a government can use to generate additional revenues for financing a social pension program? Two types of solutions, both pertaining to indirect taxation, stand out.[10] One strategy is to increase indirect tax financing by broadening the tax base of the VAT through a rationalization of exemptions and a reduction of reliance on reduced tax rates. By earmarking the proceeds for the social protection programs, the measure would prevent further increases in the level of payroll taxation. A positive side effect of this type of policy is that it permits simplification of operational procedures and hence facilitates administrative efficiency in the VAT field. But the distributional impact of any such base-broadening measure is theoretically unclear and needs to be carefully evaluated in a country-specific context.[11] Another strategy is to increase the VAT rate or to introduce a separate, supplementary VAT-like instrument to finance the growing cost of social protection expenditures. The basic idea, which has recently attracted much attention in Europe, is straightforward: make product and service imports and other factors of production, such as owners of capital, contribute to the financing of the social protection system. Although this logic might at first sight seem attractive, its overall effect on growth and employment is unclear, both from a theoretical and from an empirical point of view.[12] Notwithstanding this uncertainty, the effect of any kind of indirect tax financing on the integrity of the budgetary

FIGURE 11.3 **Average top corporate interest rate, by country group, 1993–2007**

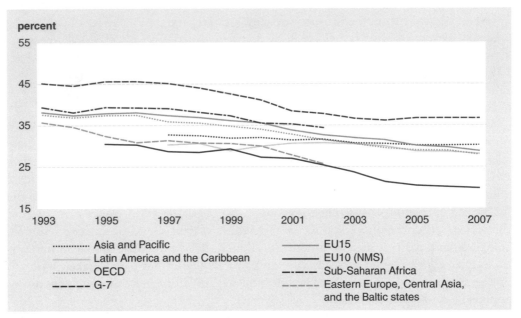

SOURCE: KPMG, Corporate Tax Survey 2007; Norregaard and Khan (2007).

NOTE: OECD, Organisation for Economic Co-operation and Development. EU10 refers to 10 countries admitted to the European Union in 2004. EU15 refers to the 15 countries of the European Union before the 2004 expansion. G-7 refers to the Group of Seven (major industrial countries): Canada, France, Germany, Italy, Japan, the United Kingdom, and the United States.

process itself is clearly negative. The increasing reliance on earmarked tax financing affects the structural and conceptual integrity of the budgetary process, with its basic principles of budgetary unity and fungibility among different types of resources and expenditures.

OPTIMIZING EXPENDITURES

The conceptual underpinning for the strategy of optimizing expenditures is simple: budgetary resources should be spent in the socially most efficient way possible, on those goods and services that generate the largest social benefit. Technically, this implies that at an allocative optimum, the marginal social benefit of any spending should be larger than or equal to the marginal cost of public funds.[13] Social pension programs are no exception to the rule.

This idea has an immediate policy implication for governments that are introducing or scaling up social pensions. They should subject current public spending programs to an efficiency test and evaluate whether there is room for optimizing expenditures to free up budgetary margins.

A first approach is to consider reprioritizing expenditures to minimize unproductive spending and redirecting the funds toward a social pension program. Frequently cited candidates for cuts are subsidies to loss-making enterprises, as well as military spending. Streamlining other types of social spending might also be desirable in some specific country contexts. This could particularly be the case for spending on civil servant or formal private sector pension plans, where these schemes are operating with large systemic deficits or on an unsustainable fiscal path. Indeed, depending on the situation, it could be argued that such social insurance schemes channel important current and future budgetary resources away from the broader population of taxpayers into a system benefiting a relatively narrow group of beneficiaries. By doing so, the schemes could actually generate a regressive overall tax benefit system, which might run counter to societal objectives. Clearly, any such rationalization of expenditures would need to be accompanied by a thorough analysis of the incidence of the current system and the distributional impact of a reform of the system.

A second approach would consist of improvements in the productive efficiency of public spending through a better use of resources to attain a better outcome. Again, any such reallocations would need to be preceded by a thorough analysis of the productive efficiency of the current system. There has been a very active literature in the field of efficiency frontier analysis, applying the concept of a productive efficiency frontier to the health and education sectors. The idea is to provide a relative performance evaluation of the various producers in a given sector to reveal how their use of productive resources compares with the best-practice production frontier derived from the sample of observations. Such benchmarking serves as a useful information point for policy makers trying to optimize resource utilization. (See Herrera and Pang 2005 for a more thorough discussion applied to developing countries.)

It is useful to focus on an often-cited means of attaining additional budgetary resources and more efficient resource utilization: the decentralization of policies, or the deconcentration of their administration. Clearly, delivery of the social pension may be improved through a decentralization strategy because the program is brought closer to the people. This can lead to important efficiency gains and hence to implicit budgetary savings that may facilitate the financing of the program. Decentralization, however, can also lead to inefficiencies in the field of social pensions, particularly in the presence of a large national contributory (social insurance) system. In that case, implicit costs arising from administrative duplication and overlapping coverage may lead to a substantial increase in implicit and explicit budgetary costs. Hence, no clear recommendation for decentralization can be formulated, and the case has to be evaluated in view of each country's institutional background.

EXTERNAL GRANTS

For many developing countries, securing external grants to finance expenditures is a real alternative to domestic financing, particularly when donors are willing to support domestic budgets (see Asher 2005). This is all the more so with respect to expenditures that help countries in their efforts to achieve the United Nations Millennium Development Goals (MDGs).

In the case of a social pension scheme, such external financing has to be seen against the backdrop of the recurrent expenditure stream that a social pension system generates. It is unlikely that any foreign donor can credibly commit to financing a long-term public expenditure program, even in a low-income country, particularly in light of the numerous interactions with other public spending programs. Instead, a key positive role that grant money can play is to act as a catalyst for launching a social pension scheme. The main drawback of this type of social pension financing, from a pure public finance perspective, is that follow-up recurrent costs will have to be borne by the domestic revenue sources and will sooner or later have to compete for scarce domestic fiscal resources.

Conclusions

Social pensions are a key tool in the fight against poverty among the elderly and, as such, should become an integral part of poverty alleviation strategies. The benefits of any policy of this kind, however, have to be compared with its costs, especially for the public sector. The direct costs of social pensions will depend heavily on the general social insurance and assistance landscape in the country because these programs interact with other programs and systems and generate mechanical and behavioral responses. Short-term costs rapidly become substantial; even in best-case scenarios, they reach 1 to 2 percent of GDP. Although these static fiscal costs may still be considered modest, the overall budgetary implications, both current and future, have to be kept in mind. This is a particularly important issue in low-income countries such as those in Sub-Saharan Africa where the average tax-to-GDP ratio is barely 15 percent and in some cases is closer to 10 percent.

On the financing side, any government has two broad levers at hand: raising additional government revenues, and optimizing overall public spending. Raising additional government revenues, particularly through indirect taxes, is a likely component of any financing strategy. The outcomes of any such measure, however, have to be cast against the backdrop of past, current, and future revenue collection performance. In light of the ongoing international and regional trade liberalization, as well as the numerous tax incentives granted to new investments in many countries, a large array of revenue needs will have to be satisfied by an ever more limited number of tax instruments. These revenue needs include social pensions but are clearly not limited to them. The rationalization of spending is thus an important complementary policy for financing social pensions. By evaluating the relative merits of public expenditure programs and optimizing the resource utilization of each program, it is possible to unleash significant budgetary resources.

To sum up, for middle- and high-income countries, the above strategies can represent a potent and feasible way of financing a social pension program. For some low-income countries, social pension programs may not (yet) be within reach. Even in best-case scenarios, such programs would involve spending a substantial fraction of government resources on income security for the old, in direct competition with other (more) urgent spending on human and economic development for the population at large—in education, primary health care, and so on. In those cases even donor financing is not a viable alternative in the long run, if only because of the recurrent nature of spending needs. External support can, however, help catalyze reform. In the longer run, domestic financing on the revenue or the expenditure side will inevitably need to be secured.

Notes

1. The Chilean legislation to amend the social security system is Law 20,255 published on March 17, 2008, in the *Official Gazette*.
2. For the purposes of this chapter, we define the term "social insurance" to include civil servant pension schemes, even when there are no contribution payments in a strict sense.

3. For simplicity, the above argument abstracts from potential differences in the efficiency of social pension provision between a pure social pension scheme and a mixed social pension and assistance scheme.

4. Social assistance programs in the European Union are designed on the basis of residence only, whereas contributory social insurance programs rely on a place-of-work reference.

5. This narrow coverage raises a set of distributional and equity considerations, particularly if the contributory system is on an unsustainable intertemporal path.

6. For a summary of the different types of social pension schemes, see chapter 1 in this volume.

7. For a broader discussion of incentives and behavioral adjustment, see chapter 10 in this volume.

8. Taxes do not constitute the only type of benefit to the public budget generated by the natural resource sector. Others include production-sharing agreements and infrastructure expenditures financed by mining and oil companies.

9. The downward trend in corporate income tax rates is often accompanied by a trend toward a lower and flatter personal income tax schedule. Both tendencies are likely to affect the overall degree of redistribution of the tax system, with the sign and magnitude of the change depending heavily on the country-specific situation.

10. In the text we focus on the VAT as the key policy instrument. A similar case can be made for excise duties.

11. Although it has repeatedly been shown that the VAT is often a regressive tax in developed countries (see European Union 2007; Warren 2008), the inverse may well hold true in numerous developing countries; see O'Donnell et al. (2008).

12. Besson (2007) provides a good survey of the efficiency and distributional arguments in the context of the 2007 French debate on a shift toward a social VAT.

13. Notice that this condition implies that for sufficiently high marginal costs of public funds, a zero level of spending on certain programs could be optimal.

References

Asher, M. G. 2005. "Mobilizing Non-Conventional Budgetary Resources in Asia in the 21st Century." *Journal of Asian Economics* 16: 947–55.

Besson, E. 2007. "TVA sociale." Secrétariat d'état chargé de la prospective et de l'évaluation des politiques publiques, Paris. http://www.premier-ministre.gouv.fr/IMG/pdf/TVA_sociale_rapport_remis_par_Eric_Besson.pdf.

Disney, R., and C. Emmerson. 2005. "Public Pension Reform in the United Kingdom: What Effect on the Financial Well-Being of Current and Future Pensioners?" *Fiscal Studies* 26 (1): 55–81.

European Union. 2007. "Study on Reduced VAT Applied to Goods and Services in the Member States of the European Union." Final report prepared by Copenhagen Economics for Taxation and Customs Union Directorate General, European Union, Brussels.

Herrera, S., and G. Pang. 2005. "Efficiency of Public Spending in Developing Countries: An Efficiency Frontier Approach." Policy Research Working Paper 3645, World Bank, Washington, DC.

International Tax Dialogue. 2005. "The Value Added Tax: Experiences and Issues." Background Paper, International Tax Dialogue. www.itdweb.org.

Keen, M., and M. Mansour. 2008. "Revenue Mobilization in Sub-Saharan Africa: Key Challenges from Globalization." International Monetary Fund, Washington, DC.

Kotlikoff, L., and A. Spivak. 1981. "The Family as an Incomplete Annuities Market." *Journal of Political Economy* 89 (2): 372–91.

Norregaard, J., and T. Khan. 2007. "Tax Policy: Recent Trends and Coming Challenges." IMF Working Paper 07/274, International Monetary Fund, Washington, DC.

Pal, K., C. Behrendt, F. Léger, M. Cichon, and K. Hagemejer. 2005. "Can Low-Income Countries Afford Basic Social Protection? First Results of a Modelling Exercise." Issues in Social Protection Series, Discussion Paper 13, Social Security Department, International Labour Office, Geneva.

O'Donnell, Owen, Eddy van Doorslaer, Ravi P. Rannan-Eliya, Aparnaa Somanathan, Shiva Raj Adhikari, Baktygul Akkazieva, Deni Harbianto, Charu C. Garg, Piya Hanvoravongchai, Alejandro N. Herrin, Mohammed N. Huq, Shamsia Ibragimova, Anup Karan, Soon-man Kwon, Gabriel M. Leung, Jui-fen Rachel Lu, Yasushi Ohkusa, Badri Raj Pande, Rachel Racelis, Keith Tin, Kanjana Tisayaticom, Laksono Trisnantoro, Quan Wan, Bong-Min Yang, and Yuxin Zhao. 2008. "Who Pays for Health Care in Asia?" *Journal of Health Economics* 27 (2, March): 460–75.

Warren, N. 2008. "A Review of Studies on the Distributional Impact of Consumption Taxes in OECD Countries." OECD Social, Employment and Migration Working Paper 64, Organisation for Economic Co-operation and Development, Paris.

CHAPTER 12

Defining Eligibility for Social Pensions: A View from a Social Assistance Perspective

Margaret Grosh and Phillippe G. Leite

Social pensions, as noncontributory transfers to the elderly, fall within the conceptual window of social assistance. Fiscal constraints and the tradeoffs between wide coverage and adequate benefit will often, particularly in poor countries, imply the need for a targeted social pension. If a targeting system is to be devised, there is no *prima facie* case for a social pension system to be run separately from a general needs-based social assistance program. Integration will lower administrative costs and guard against unequal treatment of different groups at the same welfare level. The general lessons of targeting (the need for program-specific decisions about the degree of targeting sought, appropriate instruments, and so on) apply to social pensions. Our examination of options for proxy means-tests formulas shows that they do not discriminate against the elderly. With some extra attention to the elderly (by adding elderly-related variables to the formulas, or by estimating the formulas separately for households with and without elderly members, or both), their performance can be further improved.

A country's social pension policy involves both the pension system and the social assistance system (that is, noncontributory transfers). Most of this volume has discussed issues with the pension system. This chapter focuses on the interactions between social pensions and social assistance policies. It addresses two questions: (1) Should the elderly be protected from poverty by a freestanding social pension program, or should they be included in a more general social assistance program? (2) When social pension programs are implemented, how would different targeting mechanisms affect the likelihood of reaching the intended beneficiaries, the impact of the transfer on poverty rates of poor households and the elderly, and the cost-effectiveness of public spending?

The next section deals with the first policy question, concerning social pensions versus general safety nets. Next, issues related to the design of universal and targeted systems and their fiscal implications are examined. The potential impacts of alternative forms of social pensions on poverty rates, exclusion errors, and cost-effectiveness indicators are then explored, using household survey data for the Kyrgyz Republic, Niger, Panama, and the Republic of Yemen. The data used in the analysis and the poverty situation of the elderly are described, after which microsimulations of the coverage, incidence, and cost-effectiveness ratios of a universal social pension program scheme and of some targeted social pension schemes are presented. The last two sections contain the principal findings of the analysis and the main conclusions of the chapter.

Are Special Programs for the Elderly Poor Needed?

The first step in formulating social assistance policy should be a diagnostic of poverty and vulnerability (see Grosh et al. 2008). How many elderly persons are poor or at risk of poverty? What are their characteristics? What are the causes of their poverty and vulnerability? In this chapter we argue that social pension policy should not axiomatically take the view that the elderly who are not covered by contributory pension schemes or have not contributed enough to earn a minimum pension are vulnerable. A rigorous economic analysis is needed to probe the situation of the elderly further before giving them high priority. How poor are the elderly vis-à-vis other groups? Is the common lifetime income path of reliance on one's own or one's partner's wage earnings suddenly eliminated by retirement, with no replacement via a pension? Do the elderly sharply withdraw from productivity and earnings as in formal sector retirement, or do they continue their economic activities, possibly at diminishing levels or with diminishing earnings? Do they live alone, or in families with other earners? Do families pool income across members of different ages?

The answers to such questions are country specific and can vary by groups of elderly; they may differ between those who had formal sector employment and those who did not, between those employed in agriculture and in other sectors, and perhaps by ethnicity if that affects household structure.

The diagnostic of poverty and vulnerability should include not only the elderly but also other groups that may be in need of assistance. Even where the elderly are poorer than average, there are many poor who are not elderly, and there are elderly persons who are not poor. Comparisons of rates of poverty among the elderly show that in many countries they are a bit poorer than average but that this is not universally the case (see chapters 1 and 3; also see, for example, Schwarz, 2003 and Kakwani and Subbarao, 2005). That finding is echoed in the four countries examined here.

Social pension programs need to fit well into the overall picture of social assistance in each particular country. Are there other programs that serve other groups? If not, then a social pension, especially a universal one, violates the principle of horizontal equity by implying that the elderly are somehow more worthy of support than other needy groups, such as poor children, persons with disabilities, working families with low earnings, and so on. This issue will be especially severe in lower-income countries, where social assistance is, in general, most lacking. These are often also the countries in which contributory pensions are least common, the coverage gap is largest, and social pensions are thus of most interest.

In countries that have other programs for other groups, the issue of horizontal inequity may be less important, but it does not vanish, as separate programs are rarely fully equal. The question of efficiency arises: should income support be provided through a social pension, or through the inclusion of the elderly in other social assistance programs? Some of the pros and cons of various options are summarized in table 12.1. Having a single system offers obvious administrative advantages for targeting, payments, monitoring and evaluation, and so on. Furthermore, when groups are integrated into a single program, the issue of who is more worthy of support is avoided. Thus, in view of the criteria of horizontal equity or administrative efficiency, the integration of the poor elderly into a poverty-targeted social assistance program is the preferred option.

Integration of the elderly into social assistance is, of course, always done implicitly in general needs-based programs, and it is even done in four of the best-known conditional

TABLE 12.1 **Options for providing income support to the elderly**

Principal advantages	Principal disadvantages
Contributory pension	
• Unified pension policy • Lifetime income smoothing	• Low coverage; does not increase enough to solve problem • Will not provide adequate support to lifetime poor, those with incomplete employment history, or informal sector workers who prefer not to contribute • Difficulties with collection and recordkeeping
Universal social pension	
• Apparent simplicity: no affiliation, contribution, or targeting issues • Labor disincentives not a big issue for direct beneficiaries • Potentially high political support	• Potential high fiscal cost • Implicit issue of whether elderly are the most or the only deserving in the society • Most money directed to nonpoor because most elderly live in nonpoor households
Targeted social pension	
• Radical reduction in fiscal cost • Potential for reduced horizontal inequity with other groups • Political support usually high	• Targeting system required
Inclusion of elderly in poverty-targeted general social assistance program	
• Minimization of administrative costs, duplication of functions avoided • Issues of one group being more worthy of support than another avoided • Social security administration able to stay service oriented rather than become gatekeepers	• Stigma possibly greater if support called social assistance rather than a pension • Receipt of family-based social assistance not suited to empowering the elderly within the household the way receipt of an individual-specific pension might • Political support for social assistance often less than political support for pensions

SOURCE: Authors' elaboration.

cash transfer programs—those in Brazil, Ecuador, Jamaica, and Mexico—which are usually thought of as serving only children. There are ways to explicitly modify the broader social assistance programs to ensure that the elderly are well served, through adjustments to eligibility rules, the determination of benefits, or other program requirements. The eligibility threshold for Bulgaria's guaranteed minimum income program is adjusted depending on family characteristics and is higher for families with elderly members. In Jamaica's PATH program (a conditional cash transfer), the formula for the proxy means test was adjusted to lower the weight given to housing assets in order to allow significant numbers of elderly living alone to participate. The elderly receive their full payment even if children in the household default on the conditions pertinent to them and fail to qualify for their own benefits. In the U.S. food stamp program, the recertification period is longer for households headed by elderly than for other households, since the labor earnings of the elderly are less likely to change. In Romania's guaranteed minimum income program, the elderly are exempt from the public service requirement.

Universal versus Targeted Social Pensions

A second pervasive concern in social assistance is the fiscal constraint. This issue implies careful scrutiny of both opportunity costs and cost-effectiveness (see also chapters 10 and 11 in this volume). Various authors have calculated the fiscal costs of universal pensions, most often for Sub-Saharan Africa, where both contributory pension schemes and the more general safety nets that might provide alternatives are least developed. Schwarz (2003) calculates the cost of providing US$1 per day to all those over age 65 in 40 Sub-Saharan African countries and comes up with estimates ranging from 0.1 percent of gross domestic product (GDP) in the Seychelles to 10.6 percent of GDP in Ethiopia. Confining the pension to those older than age 75 reduces costs somewhat—for example, to 3.0 percent in Ethiopia. Kakwani and Subbarao (2005) simulate the impact of a transfer calibrated to be 70 percent of the country-specific poverty line to all those older than age 65 in 15 Sub-Saharan African countries and find that the costs range from 0.7 percent of GDP in Madagascar to 2.4 percent of GDP in Ethiopia. These costs are large in relation

---

BOX 12.1 Universalism versus targeting for social pensions

Targeting is a hugely controversial topic. It is considered anathema by some and a panacea by others. As with many divisive topics, the most sensible view is probably somewhere in between.

In relation to social protection, the universalist approach proposes that all citizens of a nation receive the same state-provided benefits. Targeting would have state-provided benefits differ according to individual circumstances. Proponents of both approaches understand that in most developing countries, current budgets do not allow a meaningful provision of transfers to all citizens and that targeting experience is far from uniformly excellent. There are two glasses of milk, each of them half empty and half full; the two camps differ about which they perceive can be filled.

Universalists are optimistic that the social unity resulting from a uniform provision of benefits will garner a sufficient budget (nationally financed in middle-income countries and donor assisted in low-income countries) to provide meaningful protection. They believe that experience with targeting as a way of increasing the efficiency of redistributive spending has been unsatisfactory to date, uninspiring as a reason for hope in the future, and detrimental to efforts to increase the budget.

Targeters have a more optimistic assessment of targeting experience and are hopeful that bad experiences can be replaced by good experiences and that perhaps the good experiences can be improved. Targeters' pessimism concerns budgets; they see both political and technical obstacles to budgets' becoming sufficient to provide meaningful universal benefits.

In reality, the distinction between the approaches is not absolute. Even the European welfare states that have gone the furthest in universal provision of child allowances, education, and health insurance and have extensive minimum wage laws, labor market activation, pension coverage, and the like have last-resort needs-based programs that are tightly targeted.

SOURCE: Grosh et al. (2008), box 4.2.

to expenditures on social assistance as a whole. In most developing countries, social assistance expenditures amount to only 1–2 percent of GDP for all programs and are markedly less in some countries, although in a few poor countries with large donor support for social assistance, it can be more (Weigand and Grosh 2008). In most of these countries the safety net is far from complete, as measured by coverage or the adequacy of benefit levels.

The costs of universal social pensions are daunting. Some social policy analysts see them as suggesting a need to enlarge social assistance budgets significantly, while to others they imply the need for targeting (see box 12.1).

If targeting is chosen, there are several implications. First a targeting mechanism must be selected. There are several choices available (see table 12.2), but the categorical options

TABLE 12.2 **Options for targeting social pensions**

Principal advantages	Principal disadvantages
By age	
• Administratively simple • High age threshold, such as 75 or 80, can limit numbers substantially	• Inaccurate; elderly are not always poor or the only poor • Because the poor die younger on average, high age threshold concentrates benefits on those who have been well off for most of their lives
By household structure (benefiting only households with only elderly, or elderly and children in "missing generation" households)	
• Household structure easier to observe than income • Limits benefits substantially because such households may constitute only 1–2 percent of all households	• Inaccurate; many elderly living alone are those who can afford to, rather than those who have no family • Worrisome incentive for families to have their elderly live alone rather than absorb them into households with earners and caregivers
Community-based methods (determination by local officials or committees of who in community needs assistance)	
• In most such schemes, elderly often included as a priority group • Relatively little administrative apparatus needed	• Possible costs to community cohesion not well understood • Accuracy not well known
Means testing	
• Usually the most accurate • Relies on an excellent measure of household welfare	• Requires the most administrative apparatus • Welfare hard to verify by the authorities that run the program • May discourage work, since targeting is directly on welfare
Proxy means testing	
• Usually provides fairly good individual-level targeting of program • Based on poverty status using a relatively small amount of information	• Requires the most administrative apparatus • Requires staff with computer training skills and moderate to high levels of information and technology • Formula can be insensitive to quick changes in household welfare or disposable income • Sensitive to selection of variables

SOURCE: Authors' elaboration.

(age, household structure, and so on) are not very accurate, which strongly implies that use of a more sophisticated mechanism (community-based methods, proxy means testing, or means testing) will be desirable when the administrative capacity exists or can be built.

Fortunately a great deal is already known about the pros, cons, and requirements of targeting systems for the general population. (See table 12.1; also see, for example, Coady, Grosh, and Hoddinott 2004; Castañeda and Lindert 2005; Grosh et al. 2008.) Nonetheless, it is important to check whether the methods used for targeting the generally poor population work equally well for the elderly population. Below, we look in depth at proxy means testing (see box 12.2), one of the most commonly chosen and fastest-growing targeting methods, and consider how well it works for the elderly. We also compare simulated means tests.

Data for Assessing the Impact of Social Pensions on Poverty

The empirical analysis that follows is based on recent national representative household surveys for four countries: the Kyrgyz Republic, Niger, Panama, and the Republic of Yemen. Box 12.3 summarizes the data sources and the basic definitions of variables such as welfare, the poverty line, and targeting errors.

The Kyrgyz Republic, Niger, and the Republic of Yemen are poor, but their intensity of poverty differs. Panama is a middle-income country with an income per capita 20 times that of Niger and 10 times that of the Kyrgyz Republic. Income inequality is low to moderate in each of these countries (table 12.3), which makes targeting somewhat more

---

BOX 12.2 **Proxy means tests**

Proxy means tests (PMTs) are a common targeting tool that offers an alternative to means tests. Their popularity has exploded in the last 20 years. Chile pioneered the practice in 1980, and proxy means testing is now used in many Latin American countries and has spread to countries in every region of the world.

Quantifying and verifying the incomes of workers in the informal sector, household enterprises, and small farming is difficult. The premise of proxy means testing is that household welfare can be fairly accurately predicted on the basis of a rather small number of easily measured and often easily verified indicators (or proxies). Application forms typically contain two or three dozen questions concerning household demographics and the education of household members; perhaps whether members work and what kind of work they do; the location and quality of the household's dwelling; the household's possession of durable goods and livestock, and so on.

The proxy means test is based on a statistical model that simulates (predicts) what would be the household consumption (income) level of the applicant on the basis of observable characteristics. The model is derived using existing representative household survey data that directly measure consumption (income), as well as other household and individual characteristics that are correlated with poverty. (See Castañeda and Lindert 2005 for a further discussion.)

SOURCE: Authors' compilation.

BOX 12.3 **Summary of data sources, definitions, and methods**

DATA

Kyrgyz Republic: Household Budget Survey (KIHBS), 2005

Panama: Encuesta de condiciones de vida (ECV), 2002–3

Niger: Questionnaire des indicateurs de base du bien-être (QUIBB), 2005

Republic of Yemen: Household Budget Survey (YHBS), 2005–6

WELFARE MEASURE

The welfare measure is household per capita consumption for all four countries, gross of receipt of any social transfers and pensions.

POVERTY LINES

Poverty lines are set to include 20 percent of the population on the basis of household per capita consumption distribution.

ELDERLY

Elderly persons are men and women age 65 or older.

TARGETING ERRORS

Exclusion error is calculated as the ratio of poor households predicted as nonpoor to the total number of poor households.

Inclusion error is calculated as the ratio of nonpoor households predicted as poor to the total number of nonpoor households.

COST-BENEFIT RATIO

The cost-benefit ratio is the reduction of the poverty gap for each U.S. dollar spent in the program.

TABLE 12.3 **Basic social indicators, Kyrgyz Republic, Niger, Panama, and the Republic of Yemen**

Indicator	Kyrgyz Republic	Niger	Panama	Yemen, Republic of
Population (millions)[a]	5.1	14.4	3.3	20.1
Rural population (percent)[b]	63	83	39	73
GDP (billions of current U.S. dollars)[a]	2.8	3.7	17.1	19.1
Gross national income per capita (current U.S. dollars)[a]	500	270	5000	760
Life expectancy at birth (years)[a]	68	56	75	62
Primary school enrollment (percent net)[a]	86	43	98	75
Population age 65+ (percent of total population)[a]	6	3	6	2
Pension coverage	42	2	70	10
Poverty level (percent)[b]				
FGT(0)	58.1	62.1	37.1	36.5
FGT(1)	22.7	24.1	15.3	10.2
FGT(2)	11.9	12.3	8.7	4.1
Inequality[b]				
Gini index	0.29	0.44	0.47	0.39
P90/P10	3.4	5.7	10.4	4.4

SOURCE: See box 12.3 for country sources. For pension coverage, World Bank, Human Development Anchor, Nutrition and Social Protections Group, Pensions Database.

NOTE: FGT refers to Foster-Greer-Thorbecke family of poverty measures; P90/P10 refers to the 90th and 10th percentiles.

a. World Bank, reference year 2006.

b. Computed on household per capita consumption and national poverty lines.

difficult than in high-inequality countries. Each country has some social assistance and contributory pensions. None currently provide social pensions. Although there is a substantial variation in coverage (measured as active members as a share of the labor force), all countries exhibit substantial coverage gaps (table 12.4). Panama has the highest level, 70 percent, followed by the Kyrgyz Republic, with 42 percent. In Niger and the Republic of Yemen, less than 10 percent of the population is covered by pensions.

Poverty Analysis

A very abbreviated version of the fuller poverty and vulnerability analysis that would be included in a social assistance assessment is enough to shed light on issues of interest pertinent to the design of social pension programs. The patterns of poverty and household structure vary somewhat by country, but there are a number of commonalities (figure 12.1).

Most elderly persons live in households with working-age adults. In the Republic of Yemen only 6 percent of the elderly live without such support; in Niger the share is only 10 percent. Households anchored by the elderly are more common in the Kyrgyz Republic and in Panama. In both countries almost a third of the elderly population lives

TABLE 12.4 **Basic social protection programs, Kyrgyz Republic, Niger, Panama, and the Republic of Yemen**

Country	Social insurance coverage	Social insurance expenditures as a percent of GDP	Social assistance coverage	Social assistance expenditures as a percent of GDP
Kyrgyz Republic	Pensions; maternity benefits; work injury benefits; unemployment benefits	5.1	Family allowances (monthly benefits) for disadvantaged population (children, elderly, and disabled)	0.7
Niger[a]	Pensions; maternity benefits; work injury benefits; health insurance	1.01	Food-for-work program; general food aid; cash-for-work program	—
Panama	Pensions; maternity benefits; work injury benefits; health insurance; unemployment benefits	5	Cash transfers; school feeding; subsidies	1.7
Yemen, Republic of	Pensions; maternity benefits for public sector employees; work injury benefits	0.9	Social welfare fund; social fund for development; petroleum subsidies; public transfers (income assistance for martyrs' families, agriculture, fishing, etc.)	1

SOURCE: For social insurance and social assistance programs as percent of GDP, Weigard and Grosh (2008). For Kyrgyz Republic, SSA (2002–3); World Bank (2003). For Niger, SSA (2003a); World Bank (2008). For Panama, SSA (2003b); World Bank (2002a). For Republic of Yemen, SSA (2002); World Bank (2002b).

NOTE: —, not available. GDP, gross domestic product.

a. Social protection programs in Niger (70 percent of total safety net expenditures) are mainly focused on the food crisis.

FIGURE 12.1 **Poverty levels and household composition, Kyrgyz Republic, Niger, Panama, and the Republic of Yemen**

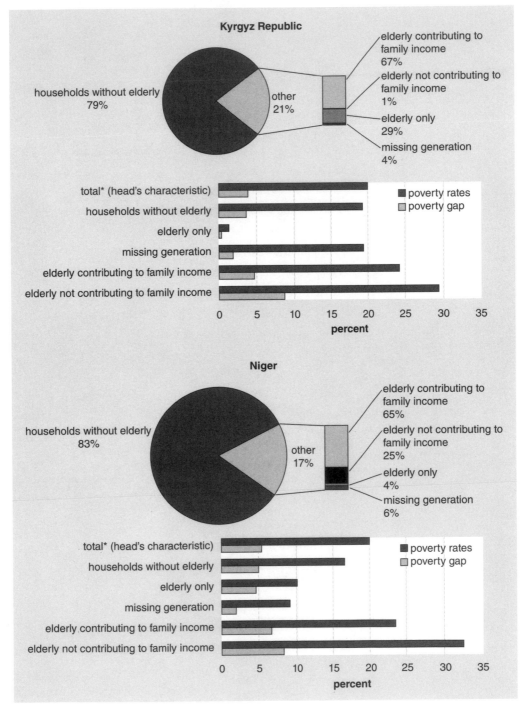

continued

FIGURE 12.1 (continued) **Poverty levels and household composition, Kyrgyz Republic, Niger, Panama, and the Republic of Yemen**

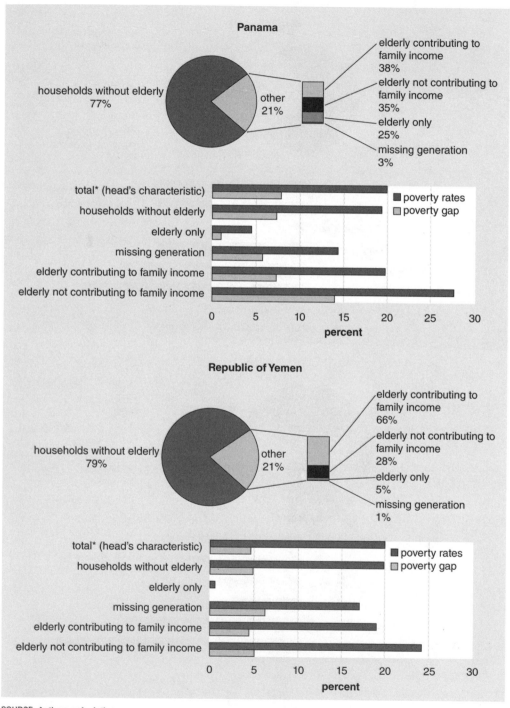

SOURCE: Authors calculations.

in households without working-age adults. In the poorer countries with less formal labor markets, about two-thirds of elderly members contribute income to the household; in Panama only a third does.

About one in five households includes an elderly member. The differences in poverty rates between households that contain elderly persons (mixed households) and those that do not are variable. If we regard as poor the 20 percent poorest from the household consumption distribution, households with elderly members in the Kyrgyz Republic and Panama are somewhat poorer than households without. The difference in degree of poverty between households with and without elderly members is more marked in Niger but not as much in the Republic of Yemen. The highest poverty rates are found in households with elderly members who do not contribute to household income. In the four countries of this study, poverty rates are indeed worrisomely high in such households, but that category accounts for only a quarter to a third of households with elderly members and for less than 10 percent of all households. Kakwani and Subbarao (2005) show that in 11 out of 15 countries that they studied in Sub-Saharan Africa, households with elderly members (whether contributing to household income or not) have poverty levels higher than the national average, and in 9 out of 11 the difference was statistically significant.

Missing-generation households (composed of elderly household heads and children but no prime-age adults) are of particular salience in policy discussions about social pensions—although they are not very numerous, especially in countries that do not have severe HIV epidemics. In Panama missing-generation households represent 0.6 percent of the total number of households; in Niger the share is 1 percent. In the Kyrgyz Republic and in the Republic of Yemen poverty rates (headcounts) for these households are about the same as for all households. In Panama the rates are much lower, at about 5 percentage points below the national average, and in Niger they are more than 10 points below the average.

Some similar findings emerge in other countries in the Middle East and North Africa and in Sub-Saharan Africa (see chapter 3 in this volume). The average or low level of poverty in missing-generation households contrasts with the popular impression of destitution of these households. A look at the higher-order measures of the poverty gap, which measure the distance of actual consumption or income from the poverty line, reflecting the depth of poverty, helps in better understanding the situation. The poverty gap for missing-generation households is higher than or close to the average for all households in all four countries, despite their lower-than-average poverty headcount rates. The low or average headcounts imply that elderly persons living in households without working-age adults are mostly those who can afford it, but the higher poverty gap indicates that there is a subset of missing-generation households that are very poor indeed. Again, although these households are not numerous, they are of salient policy concern—the figurative "poster case" for social pensions.

In the poverty analysis we assume that households pool income and that there are no economies of equivalence or scale. These assumptions may not be valid and in fact are probably not completely accurate, so it is worthwhile considering them for a moment.

We are forced to the income-pooling assumption because, as is true of almost all consumption data sets, those we use do not contain individual-specific consumption for most items. Thus, we have aggregate, not individual-specific, measures of consumption. There is a large literature on intrahousehold allocation between men and women, and girls and boys, showing that income is not completely pooled (see, for instance, Haddad, Hoddinott, and Alderman 1997; Quisumbing and Maluccio 2000), but there is much less literature on intrahousehold income allocation from others to the elderly. (Case and Deaton 1998 and Duflo 2003 show that the elderly share their social pensions for the benefit of children.) A hypothesis common in discussions of social pensions, but as yet little substantiated because of the same data problems we face, is that the elderly will be discriminated against. If this were true, our poverty findings would underestimate poverty among the elderly living as part of larger households (see also the discussion in chapter 3 in this volume).

The size and age structure of households may affect whether households with the same consumption level per capita live equally well. There may be economies of scale; it may cost as much to boil a pot of rice, provide a television set, or heat a house for one person as for three or six people. And not all members may need the same things to be equally well off: children need fewer calories from food than adults, prime-age adults need less health care than elderly persons or children, the elderly need no school fees or textbooks, and so on. The conceptual importance of equivalence scales and economies of scale is recognized in the economics literature, but there is no agreement on the magnitude of adjustments, and results may be sensitive to those adjustments (see Lanjouw, Milanovic, and Paternostro 1998; Deaton and Zaidi 2002). We therefore follow typical practice and continue using simple household per capita consumption or income as our measure of welfare, while recognizing the shortcomings of these indicators.

To the extent that there are economies of scale, our findings that the elderly living alone are less poor than others would be somewhat tempered, but given the magnitude of the effects we find, they are unlikely to be reversed. Predicting the bias implied in not using equivalence scales is trickier and depends on the welfare level, consumption patterns, and patterns of provision of public services in the various countries. In Niger food is a very large share of consumption; children need fewer calories than adults, and, in addition, health services are rarely used, so children may be less expensive to maintain than adults. Not using adult equivalence scales might have biased the results in a way that would make households with children look relatively poor and those without children relatively less poor than if equivalence scales had been used. The bias is probably less in Panama, where food is a lower share of the consumption basket and the elderly receive more medical care, some purchased from private providers. But although we use the simplification of household per capita income, our main findings are comparable to those of other papers on the subject that use calorie-based equivalence scales and a coefficient for economies of scale, as Kakwani and Subbarao (2005) do.

Simulating the Impact of Universal and Targeted Social Pensions on Poverty Rates

To help understand how choices about targeting affect the outcomes of social pension programs, we simulate the impacts of three types of scheme: universal coverage among the elderly, a means test, and a proxy means test. In all scenarios, the potential beneficiaries are the elderly, age 65 and older.

For the *universal social pension* scheme, all persons over age 65 are considered eligible to participate. From figure 12.1 we estimate that about 20 percent of households in all four countries contain at least one elderly person. The elderly population represents about 6 to 7 percent of the population in the Kyrgyz Republic (321,000 persons) and Panama (210,000) and about 2 to 3 percent in Niger (355,000) and the Republic of Yemen (688,000).

For the pure *means test,* household per capita income is used as the welfare measure in all four countries. Income definitions are different, but all the countries take into account nonmonetary and agricultural production income. For this method, the elderly living in the poorest 20 percent of households according to this welfare measure are considered eligible to participate in the targeted social pension program. This scheme yields a lower number of participants than the universal program and thus either a higher unit benefit for a fixed budget or the possibility of lower cost if the transfer size is fixed. Means tests in countries with high informality, however, are notoriously inaccurate. It can be difficult for individuals to disentangle the net earnings of their various enterprises or to arrive at a sound yearly total for intermittent earnings. Since these earnings cannot be easily verified by the social welfare agency, there is scope for undetected underreporting. This scenario is perhaps not the one most likely to be accurate, but it is included here for completeness' sake and because unverified or partially verified means tests are in fact used in a number of developing countries, including the Kyrgyz Republic.

For the *proxy means test* (PMT), first a basic proxy means test formula such as is used in many social assistance programs is considered; then variations in how the proxy means-testing formulas might be derived are examined to ensure that the situation of the elderly is as well represented as possible.[1] The tests are defined as follows:

- PMT 1 is a generic or baseline formula, using the standard sorts of variables and techniques common in the field.
- PMT 2 uses formulas calculated separately for households with and without elderly persons. This could improve the accuracy of prediction if, for example, the relationship of assets and welfare is different for the elderly and for the nonelderly, as might be the case if the elderly had accreted good housing over their lifetime and were enjoying its benefits but had relatively low income compared with younger homeowners.
- PMT 3 uses a single formula with augmented information about the presence, number, and contribution of the elderly in the household, as well as household structure, to capture as much as possible the diverse ways in which the elderly may contribute to or burden a household.
- PMT 4 employs both the augmented information set and separate formulas for households that do and do not contain elderly persons.

Further details on the calculation of the proxy means test are provided in annex A.

In the simulations we use two different approaches to allocate the budget. In the first case, the social pension budget is fixed and is equally divided among potential beneficiaries selected by each targeting approach. The size of the transfer is endogenous and varies from scenario to scenario with the number eligible. The budget is fixed at 0.5 percent of GDP for all four countries. This is low in comparison with some such simulations.[2] It is, however, consistent with the notion that total social assistance expenditures commonly range between 1 and 2 percent of GDP and sometimes less, and that social pensions would not be the only program in the country.

In the second case, we fix the level of the transfer, and the budget becomes endogenous. The benefit level is set at 20 percent of the country's average household per capita consumption to better analyze the cost-effectiveness of each simulated scenario. This fixed benefit is higher (or smaller) than the simulated benefit under the fixed-budget scheme for the universal (or the targeted) program. Looking at the impact on the budget, under the universal social pension scheme the fixed-transfer scenario would raise expenditures on social pensions from 0.5 percent of GDP for all four countries to 1.25 percent in the Kyrgyz Republic, 0.6 percent in Niger, 1.41 percent in Panama, and 0.7 percent in the Republic of Yemen. But the overall budget for all the targeted scenarios would be less than 0.5 percent of GDP (0.1 to 0.2 percent of GDP, depending on the country and targeting method), given a smaller benefit size per beneficiary.

To compare policy simulations, we look at several outcome indicators: coverage, generosity, fiscal cost, errors of inclusion and exclusion, and effects on the poverty head-count, the poverty gap, and the severity of poverty (i.e., the Foster-Greer-Thorbecke family of poverty measures). As an indicator of cost-effectiveness, we examine the reduction in the poverty gap (in local currency units) for each local currency unit spent.

Findings

If a social pension were to be universal in these countries, it would be mildly progressive in its targeting because households with elderly members are somewhat poorer than average, but a substantial share of the benefits would go to the nonpoor because many of the elderly live in households that are not poor. In all the countries, more than 80 percent of the elderly population lives in nonpoor households. In the Kyrgyz Republic, 85.4 percent of about 300,000 elderly persons are nonpoor; the shares are 80.2 percent in Niger (out of 355,000 elderly population), 88 percent in Panama (out of 99,000), and 83.4 percent in the Republic of Yemen (out of 688,000). Moreover, the universal social pension would address only a part of overall poverty, as an important share of poor households has no elderly members; this is the case for 79 percent of poor households in the Kyrgyz Republic, 78 percent in Niger, 79 percent in Panama, and 80 percent in the Republic of Yemen.

As ever, targeting induces exclusion errors and reduces inclusion errors. When the target group is set to the poorest 20 percent of the population (based on household consumption per capita), as many as 40 percent of these may be excluded, although the exclusions occur most often around the threshold of eligibility. Coverage in the poorest decile is quite high, with only around 10 percent of this group excluded in the Kyrgyz Republic, Panama, and the Republic of Yemen. Errors of exclusion are higher in Niger, the poorest country in the sample. Inclusion errors are low, with only 5 to 20 percent of those households predicted to be poor not actually being poor. Again, performance is substantially better in Panama than among the poorer countries and is worst in Niger—as expected, given the lack of precision obtained with the proxy means test model there, and in keeping with the general experience that it is more difficult to target narrowly in countries with very low incomes.[3]

The erroneous exclusion of poor households from a program is troubling. Is the reduction in errors of inclusion sufficient to justify the exclusions? Figure 12.2 provides a visual portrayal of the distribution of coverage. There are three important things to note:

- The elderly are not excluded more often than the nonelderly; indeed, in some cases they are excluded less often. Thus, concerns that the proxy means test

FIGURE 12.2 **Coverage rate when proxy means test used for targeting, Kyrgyz Republic, Niger, Panama, and the Republic of Yemen**

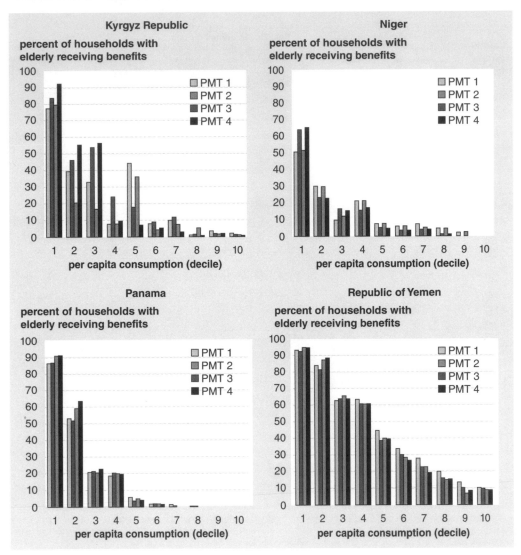

SOURCE: Authors calculations.

formula might not work as well for the elderly as for the general population are not supported, at least for the countries studied and for the elderly as a whole.

• Extra attention to issues pertinent to the elderly in the definition of the proxy means test formulas—through augmenting information (PMT 3) or through estimating the formulas separately (PMT 2), or both (PMT 4)—improve performance with respect to the elderly and do not harm it for the nonelderly. These are nearly costless improvements to targeting.

TABLE 12.5 **Inclusion and exclusion errors from simulated proxy means tests (PMTs), poorest 20 percent of population, Kyrgyz Republic, Niger, Panama, and the Republic of Yemen** (percent)

Country and PMT formulas	Households with elderly		Households without elderly		All households	
	Exclusion error	Inclusion error	Exclusion error	Inclusion error	Exclusion error	Inclusion error
Kyrgyz Republic						
PMT 1	39.5	16.0	41.0	8.9	40.6	10.3
PMT 2	33.0	18.0	43.2	8.2	40.9	10.1
PMT 3	33.4	11.5	40.2	9.4	38.7	9.8
PMT 4	24.0	13.5	39.5	8.1	36.0	9.2
Niger						
PMT 1	38.0	19.0	53.5	10.8	49.4	12.3
PMT 2	28.7	16.0	52.3	10.5	46.1	11.5
PMT 3	38.2	18.9	53.6	10.9	49.6	12.4
PMT 4	29.9	16.7	52.3	10.4	46.4	11.6
Panama						
PMT 1	29.3	5.3	23.6	7.1	24.8	6.8
PMT 2	29.7	5.1	22.6	6.9	24.0	6.5
PMT 3	24.1	4.8	22.1	6.5	22.5	6.1
PMT 4	22.0	5.2	22.6	6.4	22.5	6.2
Yemen, Republic of						
PMT 1	44.6	14.5	50.3	11.6	48.9	12.3
PMT 2	42.6	10.9	47.9	12.0	46.7	11.7
PMT 3	42.7	12.5	45.8	10.9	45.1	11.3
PMT 4	37.9	10.9	45.8	11.0	43.9	11.0

SOURCE: Authors' calculations.

NOTE: Errors are defined under household per capita consumption and the targeting method for households with elderly. For the proxy means test, the poor population is always classified according to per capita consumption, and potential beneficiaries according to household predicted per capita consumption. PMT formulas are defined as follows: PMT 1 is a generic or baseline formula; PMT 2 uses formulas calculated separately for households with and without elderly persons; PMT 3 uses a single formula with augmented information about the presence, number, and contribution of the elderly in the household, as well as household structure; PMT 4 employs both the augmented information set and separate formulas for households that do and do not contain elderly persons. See the text for further discussion.

- Exclusion and inclusion errors for households with elderly members remain relatively stable for both calibrated models, but the separated estimation (PMT 4) reduces exclusion errors of households with elderly members in all countries, despite a small increase in inclusion errors in the Kyrgyz Republic and in Panama (table 12.5).

Table 12.6 summarizes the results for the case of a fixed budget. The key findings of the policy simulation can be summarized as follows:

- Naturally, with a fixed budget, the generosity of simulated programs varies according to the number of beneficiaries selected. The magnitude of the difference is, however, quite large, with transfers for universal social pensions representing between a tenth and a third of that possible with the targeted options.

- Because of its smaller transfer size, the universal social pension has less effect on poverty.

- The universal social pension has the lowest cost-effectiveness ratio, since in all four countries the great majority of elderly is not poor.

- The PMT formulas have the greatest impact on poverty, for all measures of poverty, and the greatest cost-effectiveness ratio.

- Separate estimation of the model for households with and without elderly members increases cost-effectiveness in all countries except the Kyrgyz Republic. (Compare the results for PMT 1 and PMT 2, or for PMT 3 and PMT 4.)

- The calibration of the proxy means test formulas toward the elderly population improves targeting for all countries except Niger. (Compare the results for PMT 1 and PMT 3, or for PMT 2 and PMT 4.)

- Overall, the proxy means test formula can generate higher impacts on poverty reduction and improve the cost-effectiveness ratio by calibrating the model toward the elderly or by estimating the model separately for households with elderly members.

The results with a fixed transfer amount are summarized in table 12.7. The main messages of the policy simulations are as follows:

- The cost of the program increases to more than 0.5 percent of GDP in all countries without having any impact on cost-benefit ratios compared with the fixed-budget case.

- The cost of the program falls to less than 0.2 percent of GDP for all targeted programs, and this fixed benefit even increases the cost-benefit ratio compared with the fixed-budget case.

- The universal social pension has a higher effect on headcount poverty because there are no exclusion errors and, with the fixed benefit, the budget is higher. As with a lower and fixed budget, however, the program has the lowest cost-effectiveness ratio because in all four countries studied, the great majority of elderly people are not poor.

- Despite the much higher budget for the universal social pension, the impacts on the poverty gap and on the severity of poverty of the targeted options come close to those for the universal social pension, as a result of higher cost-effectiveness.

- The proxy means tests formulas produce better results than the means test for all measures of poverty in all four countries. Differences are particularly important for the poverty gap and the severity of poverty.

- As in the case of the fixed budget, the proxy means test formulas can have a higher impact on poverty reduction and generate a higher cost-effectiveness ratio by calibrating the model toward the elderly or by estimating the model separately for households with elderly members.

TABLE 12.6 **Simulated results of alternate policies: fixed cost, Kyrgyz Republic, Niger, Panama, and the Republic of Yemen**

	Annual cost (LCU)	Number of beneficiaries	Transfer per beneficiary	Average per capita consumption of families with beneficiaries	ΔFGT(0) (percent)[a]	ΔFGT(1) (percent)[a]	ΔFGT(2) (percent)[a]	Correlation[b]	Cost-benefit ratio[c]
Kyrgyz Republic (potential beneficiaries 46,946)									
Universal Social Pensions	3,913.3	321,247	1,015	14,695	1.6%	3.2%	4.9%		0.14
Means test	3,913.3	33,530	9,726	8,204	3.6%	7.9%	9.4%	0.561	0.34
PMT 1	3,913.3	46,177	7,062	8,473	3.8%	10.6%	14.7%	0.686	0.46
PMT 2	3,913.3	53,391	6,108	8,153	4.3%	10.2%	14.2%	0.738	0.44
PMT 3	3,913.3	43,039	7,577	7,500	5.0%	12.2%	16.0%	0.697	0.52
PMT 4	3,913.3	51,934	6,279	7,399	6.1%	11.9%	15.7%	0.809	0.51
Niger (potential beneficiaries 70,473)									
Universal Social Pensions	7,439.5	355,409	1,744	11,570	3.0%	4.1%	5.2%		0.18
Means test	7,439.5	55,624	11,145	8,601	2.4%	6.0%	7.8%	0.188	0.26
PMT 1	7,439.5	61,738	10,042	5,060	4.6%	9.8%	12.1%	0.461	0.43
PMT 2	7,439.5	74,211	8,354	4,646	6.2%	10.0%	12.7%	0.465	0.44
PMT 3	7,439.5	63,094	11,059	8,606	4.8%	9.5%	11.6%	0.462	0.42
PMT 4	7,439.5	75,867	8,172	4,788	6.1%	9.6%	12.3%	0.465	0.42
Panama[d] (potential beneficiaries 24,058)									
Universal Social Pensions	330.7	210,679	131	2,105	2.0%	2.2%	2.7%		0.11
Means test	330.7	28,948	952	632	3.5%	7.6%	10.5%	0.779	0.38
PMT 1	330.7	20,904	1,318	528	5.1%	9.2%	12.8%	0.802	0.46
PMT 2	330.7	19,986	1,379	508	5.4%	9.6%	13.3%	0.809	0.48
PMT 3	330.7	19,130	1,441	453	6.3%	10.7%	14.7%	0.790	0.53
PMT 4	330.7	20,787	1,326	472	5.7%	10.3%	14.0%	0.823	0.51

	Annual cost (LCU)	Number of beneficiaries	Transfer per beneficiary	Average per capita consumption of families with beneficiaries	ΔFGT(0) (percent)[b]	ΔFGT(1) (percent)[a]	ΔFGT(2) (percent)[a]	Correlation[b]	Cost-benefit ratio[c]
Yemen, Republic of (potential beneficiaries 114,552)									
Universal Social Pensions	122,273.5	688,216	14,806	123,641	1.9%	3.4%	4.2%		0.15
Means test	122,273.5	205,038	49,695	136,298	1.7%	3.3%	3.9%	0.099	0.15
PMT 1	122,273.5	117,230	86,919	58,836	5.1%	8.3%	9.7%	0.331	0.37
PMT 2	122,273.5	101,233	100,654	55,754	5.8%	8.9%	10.3%	0.330	0.40
PMT 3	122,273.5	111,396	91,470	55,625	5.2%	9.1%	10.9%	0.818	0.40
PMT 4	122,273.5	109,315	93,212	54,014	5.7%	9.7%	11.6%	0.350	0.44

SOURCE: Authors' compilation; for data sources, see box 12.3.

NOTE: Potential beneficiaries are elderly persons (age 65 or older) living in poor households. The poverty line is equal to the first quintile (Q1) maximum household per capita consumption. Universal social pensions represent a transfer T to all the elderly population (age 65 or older). The means test is defined under household per capita income. PMT 1 is estimated jointly for households with and without elderly members. PMT 2 is estimated separately for households with and without elderly members. PMT 3 is calibrated to capture the elderly population and is estimated jointly for households with and without elderly members. PMT 4 is calibrated to capture the elderly population and is estimated separately for households with and without elderly members.

a. Poverty measures are computed for household per capita consumption, setting elasticity of consumption equal to 1. Only households with elderly members are considered here.

b. For the means test, the correlation between household per capita consumption and household per capita income is used; for the proxy means test, the correlation between household per capita consumption and household predicted per capita consumption is used.

c. Reduction, in U.S. dollars, in the poverty gap for each dollar spent in the program.

d. Cost is set as 0.1 percent of per capita GDP.

TABLE 12.7 **Simulated results of alternate policies: fixed transfer, Kyrgyz Republic, Niger, Panama, and the Republic of Yemen**

	Annual cost (LCU)	Number of beneficiaries	Transfer per beneficiary	Average per capita consumption of families with beneficiaries	ΔFGT(0) (percent)[a]	ΔFGT(1) (percent)[a]	ΔFGT(2) (percent)[a]	Correlation[b]	Cost-benefit ratio[c]
Kyrgyz Republic (potential beneficiaries 46,946)									
Universal Social Pensions	9,811.0	321,247	2,545	14,695	5.5%	7.4%	9.7%		0.13
Means test	1,024.0	33,530	2,545	8,204	0.7%	2.6%	3.8%	0.561	0.43
PMT 1	1,410.3	46,177	2,545	8,473	0.9%	4.3%	7.0%	0.686	0.52
PMT 2	1,630.6	53,391	2,545	8,153	2.8%	4.8%	7.4%	0.738	0.50
PMT 3	1,314.4	43,039	2,545	7,500	1.4%	4.8%	7.4%	0.697	0.62
PMT 4	1,586.1	51,934	2,545	7,399	2.6%	5.5%	8.2%	0.809	0.59
Niger (potential beneficiaries 70,473)									
Universal Social Pensions	8,793.5	355,409	2,062	11,570	3.7%	4.7%	6.0%		0.18
Means test	1,387.0	55,624	2,062	8,601	0.5%	1.4%	2.1%	0.188	0.32
PMT 1	1,527.5	61,738	2,062	5,060	1.0%	2.4%	3.5%	0.461	0.52
PMT 2	1,836.1	74,211	2,062	4,646	1.7%	3.0%	4.2%	0.465	0.53
PMT 3	1,561.1	63,094	2,062	8,606	1.0%	2.5%	3.5%	0.462	0.52
PMT 4	1,877.1	75,867	2,062	4,788	1.7%	2.9%	4.1%	0.465	0.51
Panama (potential beneficiaries 24,058)									
Universal Social Pensions	929.4	210,679	368	2,105	4.5%	5.0%	6.5%		0.09
Means test	127.7	28,948	368	632	1.9%	3.5%	5.2%	0.779	0.45
PMT 1	92.3	20,904	368	528	1.7%	3.2%	5.1%	0.802	0.57
PMT 2	88.2	19,986	368	508	1.6%	3.2%	5.1%	0.809	0.60
PMT 3	84.4	19,130	368	453	1.7%	3.4%	5.4%	0.790	0.66
PMT 4	91.7	20,787	368	472	2.1%	3.5%	5.5%	0.823	0.64

	Annual cost (LCU)	Number of beneficiaries	Transfer per beneficiary	Average per capita consumption of families with beneficiaries	ΔFGT(0) (percent)[a]	ΔFGT(1) (percent)[a]	ΔFGT(2) (percent)[a]	Correlation[b]	Cost-benefit ratio[c]
Yemen, Republic of *(potential beneficiaries 114,552)*									
Universal Social Pensions	167,858.1	688,216	20,325	123,641	2.7%	4.6%	5.6%		0.15
Means test	50,009.6	205,038	20,325	136,298	0.5%	1.5%	2.0%	0.099	0.17
PMT 1	28,592.7	117,230	20,325	58,836	2.4%	2.4%	3.3%	0.331	0.46
PMT 2	24,691.0	101,233	20,325	55,754	1.0%	2.4%	3.2%	0.330	0.53
PMT 3	27,169.9	111,396	20,325	55,625	0.8%	2.5%	3.5%	0.818	0.51
PMT 4	26,662.2	109,315	20,325	54,014	1.1%	2.7%	3.8%	0.350	0.56

SOURCE: Authors; compilation; for data sources, see box 12.3.

NOTE: Potential beneficiaries are elderly persons (age 65 or older) living in poor households. The poverty line is equal to the first quintile (Q1) maximum household per capita consumption. Universal social pensions represent a transfer T to all the elderly population (age 65 or older). The means test is defined under household per capita income. PMT 1 is estimated jointly for households with and without elderly members. PMT 2 is estimated separately for households with and without elderly members. PMT 3 is calibrated to capture the elderly population and is estimated jointly for households with and without elderly members. PMT 4 is calibrated to capture the elderly population and is estimated separately for households with and without elderly members.

a. Poverty measures are computed for household per capita consumption, setting elasticity of consumption equal to 1. Only households with elderly members are considered here.

b. For the means test, the correlation between household per capita consumption and household per capita income is used; for the proxy means test, the correlation between household per capita consumption and household predicted per capita consumption is used.

c. Reduction, in U.S. dollars, in the poverty gap for each dollar spent in the program.

Conclusions

The issues surrounding the targeting of social pensions are not very different than for other aspects of social policy. It is important to consider the situation of the target group by itself and in relation to others and to consider all available options.

Much of the general know-how with respect to targeting systems and proxy means testing for social assistance will carry over to applications in social pension programs, although some specific attention to the elderly in defining the formulas for proxy means tests is useful.

As in the case of the wider social assistance system, targeting choices are situation specific and entail significant errors. Universal pensions reach all the poor, but most resources go to the nonpoor and so the programs are not very cost-effective. In a budget-constrained environment, this means that the benefit level is likely to be so low that the policy cannot provide adequate benefits to the poor it does reach. Targeted social pensions are much more cost-effective per dollar spent, and with fewer beneficiaries they could, for a fixed budget, convey a higher benefit. But they entail some errors of exclusion, the rates of which are quite variable by country.

Considering all the findings and the need for cost-effective programs due to financial constraints, particularly in poor countries, the study considers the universal approach not desirable in many cases. Targeting social pension programs will often be the preferred solution. If a targeting system is to be devised, there is no prima facie case for a social pension system to be run separately from a general needs-based social assistance program. Integration will lower administrative costs and guard against unequal treatment of different groups at the same welfare level.

Finally, our examination of options for proxy means tests formulas shows that in general, they do not discriminate against the elderly. With some extra attention to the elderly (by adding elderly-related variables to the formulas, or by estimating the formulas separately for households with and without elderly members, or both), their performance can be further improved.

Notes

1. Panama uses a proxy means test for its conditional cash transfer program, Red de Oportunidades, and the Republic of Yemen is introducing a proxy means test for targeting its unconditional cash transfer program, the Social Welfare Fund. The calculations shown here are not the exact formulas used in these countries but are respecified to make this analysis as comparable as possible across countries.

2. An example is Silvia Stefanoni, HelpAge International, "Global Social Floor: A Universal Social Pension," www.un.org/esa/socdev/social/documents/side%20events/HelpAgeInt_GlobalSocialFloor.ppt.

3. In annex B it is evident that the Niger sample has very few households containing elderly members. In addition, Niger is a very poor country with a low variance in the income of its population. As a consequence, the precision of the model is affected, and proxy means testing would generate more inclusion and exclusion errors.

References

Case, Anne, and Angus Deaton. 1998. "Large Cash Transfers to the Elderly." *Economic Journal* 108 (45): 1330–61.

Castañeda, Tarsicio, and Kathy Lindert. 2005. "Designing and Implementing Household Targeting Systems: Lessons from Latin America and the United States." Social Protection Discussion Paper 0526, World Bank, Washington, DC.

Coady, D., M. Grosh, and J. Hoddinott. 2004. *Targeting of Transfers in Developing Countries: Review of Lessons and Experience.* Regional and Sectoral Studies. Washington, DC: World Bank.

Deaton, Angus, and S. Zaidi. 2002, "Guidelines for Constructing Consumption Aggregates for Welfare Analysis." Living Standards Measurement Study (LSMS) Working Paper 135, World Bank, Washington, DC.

Duflo, E. 2003. "Grandmothers and Granddaughters: Old Age Pension and Intrahousehold Allocation in South Africa." *World Bank Economic Review* 17 (1): 1–25.

Grosh, M., Carlo del Ninno, Emil Tesliuc, and Azedine Ouerghi. 2008. *For Protection and Promotion: The Design and Implementation of Effective Safety Nets.* Directions in Development Series. Washington, DC: World Bank.

Haddad, L., J. Hoddinott, and H. Alderman. 1997. *Intrahousehold Resource Allocation in Developing Countries: Models, Methods, and Policy.* Baltimore: Johns Hopkins University Press.

ILO (International Labour Organization). 2006."Social Security for All: Investing in Global Social and Economic Development." Issues in Social Protection Discussion Paper 16, ILO, Geneva. http://www.globalaging.org/pension/world/2007/ssforall.pdf.

Kakwani, Nanak, and Kalanidhi Subbarao. 2005. "Aging and Poverty in Africa and the Role of Social Pensions." Social Protection Discussion Paper 0521, World Bank, Washington, DC.

Lanjouw, P., B. Milanovic, and S. Paternostro. 1998. "Poverty and the Economic Transition: How Do Changes in Economies of Scale Affect Poverty Rates for Different Households?" Policy Research Working Paper 2009, World Bank, Washington, DC.

Quisumbing, A., and J. Maluccio. 2000. "Intrahousehold Allocation and Gender Relations: New Empirical Evidence from Four Developing Countries." Food Consumption and Nutrition Division Discussion Paper 84, International Food Policy Research Institute, Washington, DC.

Schwartz, Anita M. 2003. "Old Age Security and Social Pensions." Social Protection Department, World Bank, Washington, DC. http://info.worldbank.org/etools/docs/library/78330/3rd%20 Workshop/Srmafrica/paristwo/pdf/readings/oldage.pdf.

SSA (U.S. Social Security Administration). 2002. "Yemen." 2002. SSA, Washington, DC. http:// www.ssaonline.us/policy/docs/progdesc/ssptw/2002-2003/asia/yemen.pdf.

———. 2002–3. "Kyrgyzstan." SSA, Washington, DC. http://www.ssa.gov/policy/docs/progdesc/ ssptw/2002-2003/asia/kyrgyzstan.html.

———. 2003a. "Niger." SSA, Washington, DC. http://www.ssa.gov/policy/docs/progdesc/ ssptw/2002-2003/africa/niger.pdf.

———. 2003b. "Panama." SSA, Washington, DC. http://www.ssa.gov/policy/docs/progdesc/ ssptw/2002-2003/americas/panama.pdf.

Weigand, Christine, and Margaret Grosh. 2008. "Levels and Patterns of Safety Net Spending in Developing and Transition Countries." Social Protection Discussion Paper 0817, World Bank, Washington, DC.

World Bank. 2002a. "Panama Poverty Assessment: Toward Effective Poverty Reduction." Report 36307-PA, World Bank, Washington, DC.

————. 2002b. *Reducing Vulnerability and Increasing Opportunity: Social Protection in the Middle East and North Africa.* Orientations in Development Series. Washington, DC: World Bank.

————. 2003. "Kyrgyz Republic: Enhancing Pro-Poor Growth." Report 24638-KG, World Bank, Washington, DC.

————. 2008. "Niger: Food Security and Safety Nets." World Bank, Washington, DC.

Annex A: Variable Definitions in Proxy Means Tests

Measure	Definition or method
Dependent variable	Logarithm of household per capita consumption. No adult equivalence scales; health and travel expenses not included
Characteristics of household head	Age, educational level, gender
Household's demographics	Household size, number of children, number of elderly
Household's infrastructure	Type of household, number of rooms, material of outer walls, material of roof, type of toilet, source of water, combustible for cooking, possession of telephone, access to electricity
Variables used to calibrate model for the elderly population	Type of family: no elderly, elderly alone, missing generation, elderly contributing to income and elderly not contributing to income; number of elderly classified as parent of head; number of elderly who contribute to household income; share of elderly
Durable goods	Freezer; washing machine, television set, car, sofa, wardrobe, etc.
Presence of livestock	Cow, sheep, goat, horse, etc.
Source of household income	Autoconsumption, agricultural production, wages in private or public sector, property or equipment rents, public or private pensions and remittances, donations, other
Infrastructure of the region	Distances to hospitals, schools, road, communications services (post offices, telephone)
Regional component	Dummies for region

Annex B: Customizing Proxy Means Tests for the Elderly, Kyrgyz Republic, Niger, Panama, and the Republic of Yemen

Kyrgyz Republic

	# obs	# var	R^2	MSE
Bishkek				
PMT 1	753	25	0.5069	0.090
PMT 2				
hh with elderly	214	30	0.800	0.038
hh without elderly	539	29	0.5327	0.089
PMT 3	753	40	0.6027	0.073
PMT 4				
hh with elderly	214	36	0.869	0.026
hh without elderly	539	37	0.6063	0.073
Urban				
PMT 1	2,141	35	0.5122	0.109
PMT 2				
hh with elderly	416	32	0.742	0.066
hh without elderly	1,725	28	0.509	0.109
PMT 3	2,141	39	0.609	0.088
PMT 4				
hh with elderly	416	53	0.833	0.045
hh without elderly	1,725	46	0.6185	0.084
Rural				
PMT 1	1,849	38	0.545	0.105
PMT 2				
hh with elderly	459	19	0.598	0.100
hh without elderly	1,390	36	0.579	0.096
PMT 3	1,849	38	0.564	0.096
PMT 4				
hh with elderly	459	34	0.747	0.065
hh without elderly	1,390	46	0.6137	0.089

Niger

	# obs	# var	R^2	MSE
Niamey				
PMT 1	776	31	0.693	0.143
PMT 2				
hh with elderly	113	35	0.826	0.068
hh withoutelderly	663	32	0.731	0.135
PMT 3	776	34	0.698	0.142
PMT 4				
hh with elderly	113	38	0.849	0.068
hh without elderly	663	32	0.731	0.130
Urban				
PMT 1	957	43	0.551	0.232
PMT 2				
hh with elderly	154	34	0.664	0.194
hh without elderly	803	39	0.580	0.218
PMT 3	957	48	0.559	0.229
PMT 4				
hh with elderly	154	35	0.679	0.192
hh without elderly	803	39	0.580	0.218
Rural				
PMT 1	4,528	49	0.368	0.283
PMT 2				
hh with elderly	779	35	0.416	0.238
hh without elderly	3,749	40	0.369	0.288
PMT 3	4,528	48	0.368	0.282
PMT 4				
hh with elderly	779	40	0.426	0.236
hh without elderly	3,749	41	0.369	0.288

SOURCE: Authors' calculation; Niger QUIBB 2005; Panama ECV 2002/03; Kyrgyz HBS 2005; Yemen HBS 2005.

Panama

	# obs	# var	R²	MSE
Urban				
PMT 1	3,373	16	0.668	0.185
PMT 2				
hh with elderly	670	17	0.638	0.201
hh without elderly	2,703	17	0.687	0.176
PMT 3	3,373	25	0.701	0.167
PMT 4				
hh with elderly	670	21	0.678	0.176
hh without elderly	2,703	21	0.714	0.160
Rural				
PMT 1	2,521	18	0.607	0.194
PMT 2				
hh with elderly	593	18	0.502	0.235
hh without elderly	1,928	18	0.641	0.181
PMT 3	2,520	25	0.645	0.176
PMT 4				
hh with elderly	592	18	0.591	0.194
hh without elderly	1,928	20	0.667	0.168
Indigenous				
PMT 1	350	13	0.446	0.258
PMT 2				
hh with elderly	74	9	0.412	0.285
hh without elderly	276	13	0.476	0.249
PMT 3	343	18	0.485	0.230
PMT 4				
hh with elderly	71	11	0.572	0.212
hh without elderly	272	12	0.491	0.234

Yemen

	# obs	# var	R²	MSE
South-Urban				
PMT 1	1,532	17	0.387	0.102
PMT 2				
hh with elderly	398	18	0.388	0.100
hh without elderly	1,134	28	0.433	0.098
PMT 3	1,532	35	0.481	0.088
PMT 4				
hh with elderly	398	20	0.468	0.084
hh without elderly	1,134	31	0.510	0.085
South-Rural				
PMT 1	835	20	0.322	0.180
PMT 2				
hh with elderly	267	19	0.385	0.152
hh without elderly	568	19	0.361	0.181
PMT 3	835	26	0.358	0.171
PMT 4				
hh with elderly	267	25	0.417	0.147
hh without elderly	568	23	0.391	0.174
North-Urban				
PMT 1	4,386	32	0.362	0.118
PMT 2				
hh with elderly	803	29	0.383	0.130
hh without elderly	3,583	38	0.370	0.114
PMT 3	4,386	41	0.398	0.112
PMT 4				
hh with elderly	803	47	0.435	0.122
hh without elderly	3,583	43	0.401	0.108
North-Rural				
PMT 1	3,606	37	0.352	0.135
PMT 2				
hh with elderly	767	30	0.371	0.129
hh without elderly	2,839	40	0.359	0.137
PMT 3	3,606	49	0.395	0.127
PMT 4				
hh with elderly	767	44	0.435	0.118
hh without elderly	2,839	50	0.396	0.129

SOURCE: Authors' calculation; Niger QUIBB 2005; Panama ECV 2002/03; Kyrgyz HBS 2005; Yemen HBS 2005.

CHAPTER 13

Matching Defined Contributions: A Way to Increase Pension Coverage

Robert Palacios and David A. Robalino

This chapter introduces matching defined contribution (MDC) schemes as a useful approach for expanding coverage to the informal sector. MDCs are voluntary systems that can be funded or pay-as-you-go. Workers contribute flat rates, as opposed to a share of earnings, and have flexible contribution schedules. To create incentives to enroll, the government matches contributions up to a maximum capital. Matching levels can be set on the basis of reported earnings or proxy means tests. We argue that MDCs can be a better use of fiscal resources for old-age income security than income tax deductions. The main difficulty in implementing the program is to estimate the take-up rate/matching elasticity, which is not known for middle- and low-income countries. Theory and empirical evidence from high-income countries nonetheless suggest that MDCs can have meaningful effects on contribution densities. We thus recommend combining MDCs with social pensions in the context of a long-term policy strategy for expanding coverage and preventing old-age poverty. In essence, poverty among the elderly over the short run would be prevented through social pensions, and for the future elderly through MDCs. This integrated policy approach could significantly reduce the financial burden of population aging without compromising the government's primary policy objective of minimizing poverty in old age.

Social security coverage has remained stubbornly low for decades in low-income countries. It is now widely recognized that traditional social insurance schemes, which depend on payroll tax deductions from formal sector wage earners, cannot be expanded to cover the entire labor force and, in particular, workers who spend most of their active lives in the informal sector.

This chapter argues that a useful approach to expanding pension coverage is a matching defined contribution (MDC) scheme. In essence, this is a defined contribution pension system in which the plan's sponsor, which is likely to be the government, provides an incentive by matching voluntary contributions made by plan members.[1] Several countries have already introduced this type of scheme, but there is little or no evidence on performance to date.

The next three sections review the general characteristics of the informal sector and the rationale for MDCs; present a stylized example of a targeted scheme as applied to India; and discuss the role of financial incentives in generating voluntary take-up and expanding coverage. We then use a simulation model to examine how alternative combinations of MDCs with social pensions affect fiscal costs. The final section offers conclusions.

Informal Sector Environment and MDCs

The informal sector in low-income countries typically comprises more than two-thirds of the work force. In India, for example, more than 90 percent of workers are in the "unorganized" sector. A large proportion of these workers and their families are poor or near poor, and their incomes fluctuate. Most live in rural areas and have less access to public services and shorter life spans than workers in the formal sector. The very poorest are not in a position to save at all, while those who can save have very high discount rates and a strong preference for liquidity. Most have little or no interaction with financial sector institutions. The main form of old age income security for these workers is family support.

Even in the case of middle-income countries, such as Argentina and Brazil, with more integrated formal and informal labor markets, where informal work or self-employment does not necessarily imply lower earnings, contribution densities in mandatory and voluntary defined contribution systems tend to be low (see chapter 2 in Robalino et al., forthcoming). This is particularly true among low-income workers and youths. Moreover, there is empirical evidence that movements into and out of the social security system during the life cycle can only in part be explained by exogenous shocks. In other words, workers often make the conscious choice to engage in informal sector work or self-employment and avoid paying social security contributions (see chapter 10 in this volume; see also Levy 2006; Perry et al. 2007). These choices can be explained by myopia and high discount rates but can also be seen as the result of a rational calculation of costs and benefits. For instance, when the perceived value of the bundle of social insurance benefits is below the contribution rate workers might choose to take informal sector jobs. Similarly, if a high contributory pension implies the loss of an income transfer for old age, individuals might have incentives to reduce contribution densities.

There are several implications for the design of pension systems that cover workers who spend large shares of their active life in the informal sector. First, by the nature of this population, it is not possible (or at least, it is very costly) to enforce on it a mandate to contribute. Clearly, contributions must be voluntary. Second, defined benefit pensions based on regular contributions and on a formula linked to wage histories are not feasible. Third, financial incentives are needed for significant take-up. Fourth, traditional points of contact for contribution collection may not be available. Fifth, transaction costs would have to be minimal, given the size of incomes and contributions. Finally, the payout phase should take into account that the mortality rates of this group can be higher than average, particularly in low-income countries.

The first point, if accepted, leaves only a few options for the design of a contributory pension scheme for this group. One approach, used in Sri Lanka's pension scheme for farmers and fishers, is to specify a table of contributions and payouts in absolute monetary terms (e.g., 200 rupees per month). But the experience of Sri Lanka over the last decade illustrates the problem with this approach; inflation and wage growth have rendered the original table obsolete (Eriyagama and Rannan-Eliya 2003). Although it would be possible to index the amounts, the result would be a more complex system with ever-changing contribution and benefit rules. The use of a single contribution amount for all informal sector workers would also ignore large variations in incomes and affordability. Finally, for this type of formula to be financially sustainable, benefits would need to vary as a function of the retirement age.

Another approach is to establish a proxy wage for a particular occupational group on the basis of survey data (as is done in Tunisia). A fixed rate can then be applied to these workers, and a pseudo–defined benefit scheme can be operated. The problem again is that for the system to be financially sustainable and allow for different contribution rates and different retirement ages, the defined benefit formula would have to be quite complex. Accrual rates would need to be determined that would depend on the level of the contribution rate and life expectancy at retirement. In addition, for certain groups the proxy wage may be a bad approximation of actual incomes. If the proxy wage is overestimated, the resulting contribution rates can be too high for the targeted group and can lead to low take-up rates.

In principle, a defined contribution scheme has several advantages over the other approaches. Specifically, it can allow for flexibility in both the frequency and the level of contributions. It is also portable between sectors and occupations. One application of this portability is rural-urban migration. In countries such as China many workers move from the countryside to cities, spending part of their working lives in one or the other place. Rural MDCs in China could, in principle, be carried to urban areas where there is also a defined contribution scheme. A defined contribution arrangement is also better able to cover workers who switch frequently between jobs and sectors.

There are two important policy challenges related to MDCs. First, disability and death are contingencies normally covered within the scope of traditional pension schemes, and pure defined contribution arrangements would not provide insurance against these important risks. Second, when defined contribution schemes are funded, they entail financial risks that are borne by workers. Depending on local conditions and regulations on investments and the asset management environment, these risks may be substantial.

Nonetheless, there are fairly straightforward ways of dealing with both issues. Many defined contribution schemes incorporate insurance provisions and essentially purchase group insurance policies for disability and life for all of the individual account holders. The premium can be determined in the market on the basis of actuarial statistics for the group and can take into account the use of defined contribution balances to finance the insurance payout. In other words, the insurance covers the difference between what the individual has accumulated in his defined contribution account and the benefit that would be paid (either as a lump sum or as an annuity) in case of death or disability. These ancillary benefits can thus be added in a modular way.[2]

The challenge of mitigating or curtailing investment risk for largely unsophisticated investors can be tackled with several policy levers. First, investment options could be limited in such a way so as to reduce risk and volatility. Of course, a more conservative portfolio would generally result in lower returns. Alternatively, or in combination, guarantees could be offered. This would result in a contingent liability for the government unless some way were found to hedge the risk in the market.[3] Finally, an approach that would bypass the capital markets altogether could be designed along the lines of notional account-type schemes in which the return is based on wage or income growth. Again, this type of system might require that the government step in if the system faces shortfalls, unless automatic balancing mechanisms are in place, as in Sweden (see Robalino and Bodor 2007).

Examples of MDCs that are already in operation include China's rural pension scheme and a new scheme for informal sector workers recently introduced in two Indian states, Rajasthan and Madhya Pradesh. (The state of Andhra Pradesh plans to introduce such a scheme in 2009.) Legislation introducing MDC legislation has been passed in the Dominican Republic, Indonesia, and Vietnam but had not been implemented at the time of writing. The contrast between the MDCs in China and India is particularly interesting. Both involve matching contributions for the defined contribution pension, but in China the government (at the county level) manages the funds and does not invest in the capital markets. In India asset management is contracted out by the state government, and investments are made through the markets, including equity markets. There are no guarantees.

To summarize, the nature of the informal sector in most developing countries makes it impossible to enforce a mandate to contribute to a pension or insurance scheme. Moreover, traditional defined benefit schemes are not feasible because they depend on a well-defined and properly reported wage for the calculation of the benefit. In principle, MDCs are a feasible alternative in that they do not require a defined wage, are portable across sectors, are flexible with regard to contribution timing, and allow a transparent and targeted subsidy to encourage voluntary participation. Concerns about investment risk and provision of ancillary insurance can be addressed with relative ease.

The next section describes a generic MDC scheme and the logical sequence of steps in its design and implementation.

Designing an MDC Scheme

As is the case with traditional mandated pension schemes, the design of an MDC scheme begins with the determination of the target benefit level. Rather than employing a standard replacement rate schedule, however, the MDC target is likely to be aimed at preventing poverty.[4] As discussed in the next section, it may also be part of an integrated strategy that includes social pensions; in this case, target benefit levels would take into account the level and eligibility conditions of the social pension.

For our purposes, we can refer to this target as the minimum consumption target (MCT); see figure 13.1. The target benefit level would involve a payout as a lump sum or as a stream of payments to cover up to 100 percent of the MCT. The premium level is derived through simulations based on assumptions about rates of return on investments and annuity rates.

To illustrate, we take the case of India and set the MCT at the poverty line for India in 2004–05.[5] The monthly poverty lines translate into roughly 4,700 and 6,700 rupees annually for rural and urban areas, respectively. A reasonable target benefit level could be an inflation-indexed annuity equivalent to 100 percent of the MCT—in other words, the absolute poverty line. For the purpose of the illustration, this could be set at around 6,000 rupees per year, or 500 rupees per month. We can now calculate the contribution rate required to reach this target.[6]

The contribution rate required to generate the target pension depends on the rate of return on the invested funds after charges, the number of years of accumulation, and life expectancy. Shah (2005) calculates that under the most conservative investment portfolio, 100 percent government bonds, an Indian worker contributing from age 24 to age 60 at a rate of 10 rupees per day would have a 90 percent probability of achieving the balance required to finance a pension of between 1,000 and 2,000 rupees per month.[7] Roughly, then, a contribution of 5 rupees per day, or 1,825 rupees per year, would ensure that the defined contribution scheme would at least reach our lower target benefit.[8]

FIGURE 13.1 **Steps in determining the parameters and costs of the matching defined contribution (MDC)**

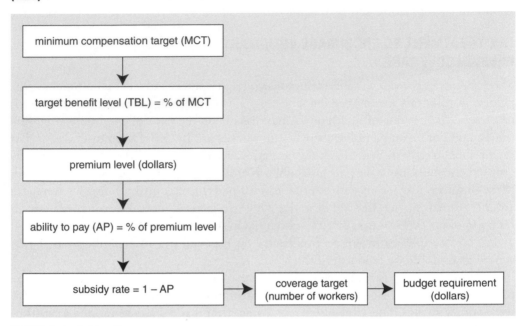

SOURCE: Authors' elaboration.

The final step in this process is to determine the subsidy. As figure 13.1 shows, that involves first assessing the ability to pay, to determine the subsidy for the premium. In the context of a large informal sector, ability to pay will vary significantly across workers and households. It may be useful therefore to target certain segments of the informal sector workforce on the basis of criteria such as need or ease of implementation.[9]

The budget requirement for the MDC program will then be a function of the total potential pool of participants, the amount of the matching contribution, and the take-up rate. The take-up, or enrollment, rate is, in turn, a function of the size of the match. Another important consideration, then, is the elasticity of take-up to different levels of subsidy or matching contribution (the take-up rate/matching elasticity, discussed below).

Unfortunately, there is very limited evidence on the value of this elasticity, particularly in the case of middle- and low-income countries. Indeed, most of the experience with financial incentives to expand pension coverage and increase savings, such as tax incentives and matching contributions, refers to high-income countries and, in particular, the United States. Still, there are important lessons for the design of MDCs, and these are discussed next.

Incentives to Contribute: Experiences with Tax Exemptions and MDCs

Expanding coverage through any type of financial incentive (e.g., tax exemptions or matching contributions) is costly. In order for policy makers to make informed decisions about the adoption of these programs, it is necessary to understand the effects of the incentive on take-up rates, contribution densities, fiscal costs, and income distribution. This section briefly reviews some relevant experiences in member countries of the Organisation for Economic Co-operation and Development (OECD).

TAX TREATMENT TO ENCOURAGE VOLUNTARY PENSION COVERAGE

Many countries provide tax incentives to encourage workers and their employers to participate in voluntary private pension schemes. As with matching contributions, the idea is to increase the net rate of return on savings, usually on the basis of conditions regarding the duration of savings and how benefits are withdrawn. In OECD countries the level of exemptions relative to benchmark savings (typically, a bank deposit) varies from 40 percent of contributions in the Czech Republic to around zero in Mexico and New Zealand. Most countries provide incentives of at least 10 percent of contributions; the average is around 20 percent (see Yoo and de Serres 2004). In general, incentives come at a cost in the form of tax expenditures that are substantial in some OECD countries. In the United States, for example, estimated pension-related tax expenditures are typically about 1 percent of gross domestic product (GDP).

Although there is some evidence that these programs improve participation, the impact on savings is empirically ambiguous. Exemptions increase net rates of return relative to other savings. This creates both an income effect that reduces saving and a substitution effect that increases savings. Thus, the empirical literature offers mixed evidence. (For a review, see Hubbard and Skinner 1996.) Depending on data sources and methodology, some studies find a large effect on saving, while others find little effect. Nonetheless, a consensus seems to emerge that tax exemptions do increase saving among low-income individuals or low savers. (For studies related to 401[k] plans in the United States, see Engen and Gale 2000; Benjamin 2003.)

An issue with these programs, however, is that, given progressive tax schedules, subsidies in the form of tax deductions or exemptions tend to benefit higher-income workers disproportionately. In developing countries these issues are even more important because relatively few people pay income taxes, and these taxpayers tend to be concentrated in the highest quintile of the income distribution. Many of these workers are already in the formal sector and are covered by mandated pension schemes, so that there is little chance of expanding pension coverage by this method. The fact that these are higher-income workers also makes it more likely that savings are shifted from one type of investment to pensions, with little or no incremental effect on total saving. In short, there is less justification for tax-favored, voluntary pension savings in lower-income countries.

MATCHING CONTRIBUTIONS AND TAKE-UP RATES

Chapter 10 provided some insights about the impact of MDCs on contribution densities, based on theory and on simulations with a life-cycle behavioral model. The analysis showed that among "good planners," matching contributions can significantly increase the density of contributions to a pension system. Theoretical take-up rate/matching elasticities tend to be below 0.2 and vary considerably with individual preferences. The analysis also emphasized that ultimately, the impact of the matching program (or any other retirement income transfers) on behaviors depends on the level of the transfer in relation to individual earnings. A "nontrivial" transfer is very likely to change behaviors. In fact, there is considerable empirical evidence that other forms of conditional cash transfers (CCTs) have been very successful in changing behaviors related to investments in education and health (see Grosh et al. 2008).

Most of the literature on the effect of matching contributions, however, is based on U.S. experience—in particular, experience with matching contributions in 401(k) plans, a form of occupational defined contribution scheme that now covers more than one-quarter of the labor force (see Engelhardt and Kumar 2004). There is also evidence based on matching contributions to the tax-preferred defined contribution pension option for the self-employed (Duflo et al. 2005). Perhaps the most relevant study is that of Duflo and coauthors, who conducted an experiment with low- and middle-income households in the United States. Out of 14,000 tax filers, three groups were randomly selected and provided with no match, a 20 percent match, or a 50 percent match. Take-up rates were 3, 8, and 14 percent, respectively—roughly, a 1.5 percentage point increase in the take-up rate for each 10 percentage point increase in the level of matching. The relationship between the amount of the match and the amount of voluntary contributions is less clear, suggesting that there are offsetting income and substitution effects.

The study also showed that information and counseling are important influences on choices about whether to enroll in the matching contribution program. Differences in how information is communicated to potential beneficiaries explain, for instance, differences in responses in relation to another program (saver's credit) that provides essentially similar incentives. The authors conclude that there is no such a thing as a "structural parameter" capturing individual preferences that, given incentives, would determine outcomes. How individuals react to incentives depends not only on how the incentives are framed and communicated but also on the presence of advisory and counseling services that improve access to information and allow for better understanding of the pros and cons of the program (see Bertrand et al. 2005).

Two other factors that seem to affect incentives to enroll in voluntary saving plans are the liquidity of savings and access to credit. Individuals value the liquidity of their savings. For instance, in the United States half of all workers take cash out of their savings plans when changing jobs, although about 80 percent of the money is ultimately saved for retirement purposes (see Hinz 2008). Studies also show that having access to loans can increase saving rates (see Munnell, Sunden, and Taylor 2001). These results are relevant for the design of voluntary programs in middle- and low-income countries. They suggest that it is important to provide flexibility in the withdrawal of savings above a certain threshold and probably also to allow individuals to have access to credit. One possibility, for example, would be to link MDCs with microfinance programs.

The results discussed here cannot yield any general lessons as to behavior, especially for developing countries. They do suggest, however, that MDCs have the potential to increase contribution densities. Moreover, in contrast to incentives on tax treatment, these expenditures can be targeted to the bottom part of the income distribution and may actually increase pension coverage. Because lower-income workers have less scope for offsetting their long-term savings by reducing other types of saving or borrowing, the likelihood of a positive savings effect increases. In fact, one way to finance MDCs would be to shift resources away from tax expenditures of the type used in OECD countries.

Fiscal Impact of MDCs and Social Pensions in a Dynamic Framework

The fiscal impact of matching programs will depend on three main factors: (a) policy choices regarding the level of matching (expected contributions and matching rates by income group and maximum transferable capital); (b) the take-up rate/matching elasticity, which determines contribution densities in the MDC program; and (c) the effect that additional contributions to the pension system have on future demand for social pensions or other transfer programs for preventing poverty during old age. This implies that the design of MDCs needs to be coordinated with the design of ex post retirement transfers in the context of a dynamic strategy for expanding coverage.

In this section we discuss what would be an "optimal" combination of MDCs and social pensions to reach maximum coverage and prevent old-age poverty while minimizing fiscal costs. The central idea is that social pensions would be used to guarantee the minimum consumption target (MCT) over the short run, while a contributory pension scheme based on MDCs targets the same minimum in the long run.[10] As the contributory scheme matures and coverage expands, the role of social pensions would be reduced. In other words, as contribution densities in the contributory scheme increase, in part driven by incentives linked to MDCs, long-term expenditures in social pensions or other transfers to the elderly are expected to decline.[11]

MODELING THE IMPACT OF MDCS ON CONTRIBUTION DENSITIES

Aggregate take-up rates in an MDC program ultimately depend on the probability that individuals will make a contribution to the system within a given period of time (say, one month). In turn, these probabilities are likely to depend on individual characteristics such as employment status, income, age, gender, and educational level, as well as on the size of the matching contribution relative to earnings. As discussed in previous sections, other things being equal, we would expect that the higher the level of matching relative to earnings, the higher the probability of contributing.

Formally, the probability that an individual i in a targeted group j will contribute to an MDC program during time t can be written as:

$$P\left(c_{it} \mid w_{it} > 0\right) = \frac{e^{z_{it}}}{1 - e^{z_{it}}}$$

$$z_{it} = b_j X_{it} + \eta_j \frac{m_{it}}{w_{it}}; \quad i \in j \tag{13.1}$$

where w_{it} represents the earnings of the individual at time t; c_{it} is equal to 1 if the individual makes a contribution at time t (zero otherwise); X_i is a vector of individual characteristics (e.g., age, gender, and education); m is the absolute level of the matching received by the individual; and b_j and η_j are parameters that need to be estimated.[12]

The rationale for MDC programs is that when $m = 0$, the probability of contributing would be too low to finance an adequate level of income during old age.[13] In the absence of MDCs, the government would need to implement some form of retirement income transfer (e.g., social pensions) to prevent poverty during old age. But that could be more expensive than encouraging contributions and saving during active life and targeting social pensions only to the long-term poor (with no saving capacity) or to those who were unable to accumulate a sufficient level of savings because of idiosyncratic shocks that resulted in long periods of inactivity or unemployment.

As discussed above, no empirical estimates or priors about the parameters of equation (13.1) exist. In our analysis, therefore, we explore different combinations of plausible values. We consider two baseline probabilities of contributing when $m = 0$: 3 percent, as in the Duflo et al. (2005) experiment, and 10 percent. These would reflect different b_js and X_js for different targeted groups j. We also assume two contribution rates (5 and 10 percent of GDP per capita) and six matching levels: 0, 0.5, 1.5, 2.0, 2.5, and 3.0 times the individual contribution. Regarding the condition $w_{it} > 0$, we assume that when individuals are working, they face a 5 percent probability of unemployment ($w_{it} < 0$) each month.[14] When they are unemployed, we consider two unemployment durations: three months and six months.[15] Finally, we consider 15 values (between 0.025 and 0.35) for the take-up rate/matching elasiticity η_j, which is the principal uncertainty in the case of middle- and low-income countries.

Figure 13.2 illustrates the link between this elasticity and the take-up rate. When $\eta_j = 0.025$, the matching has little or no effect on the take-up rate. For $\eta_j = 0.15$, a matching of one and two times the individual contribution can increase the take-up rate from 3 to 10 percent and from 3 to 30 percent, respectively. Finally, when $\eta_j = 0.35$ (the implicit value in Duflo et al. 2005), a one-time matching would be enough to increase the take-up rate to 50 percent.

We use the model to simulate the careers, contributions, and pensions of 1,000 representative individuals with earnings equal to GDP per capita in a given country. Each individual is followed on a monthly basis between age 25 and age 65, the assumed retirement age. Each month, individuals can be unemployed (and not contributing to the MDC), working but not contributing, or working and contributing. The transition between states is driven by idiosyncratic shocks and the value of the parameters of equation (13.1).

Our interest is in the present value of costs related to (a) an MDC program and (b) a program that pays a flat pension (social pension) to those individuals older than age 65 who are not able to generate a contributory pension above a given poverty line. Two

FIGURE 13.2 **Take-up rate and matching contributions**

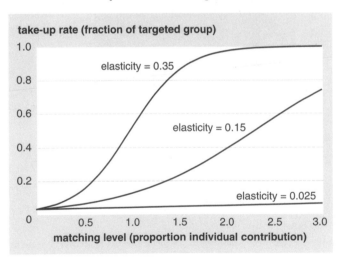

SOURCE: Authors' calculations.

NOTE: The take-up rate is defined as $TR = \exp(z)/(1 - +\exp(z))$ where $z = -3.45 + b * (0.05*m)$, $b/100$ is the take-up rate matching elasticity, and m is the level of matching. In this example, 0.05 refers to the contribution rate (expressed as a share of GDP per capita). The income of the individual is normalized to 1, equivalent to GDP per capita. The parameter -3.45 was calibrated to reproduce a take-up rate of 3 percent when $m = 0$.

poverty lines are considered in the analysis: 30 and 50 percent of income per capita. The underlying assumption in the simulations is that the MDC program is the only source of savings for retirement. This is a reasonable assumption, since the MDC program would offer a higher net rate of return on savings. Hence, if individuals are willing to save, they would be better off saving in the MDC program.

FIGURE 13.3 Fiscal impact of matching contributions with baseline contribution density of 3 percent

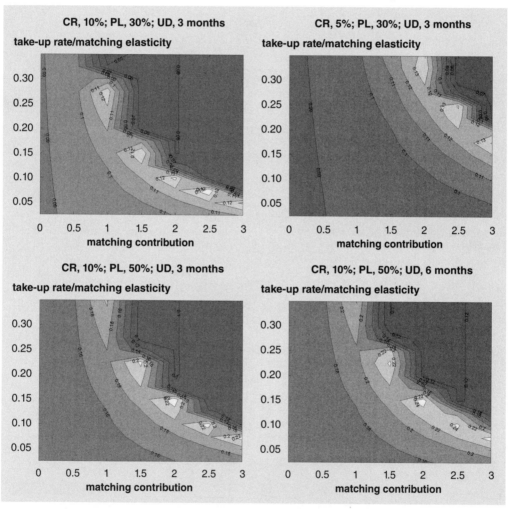

SOURCE: Authors' calculations.

NOTE: GDP, gross domestic product; CR, contribution rate (percent of GDP per capita); PL, poverty line (percent of GDP per capita); UD, unemployment duration. The simulations refer to a group of 1,000 eligible individuals with wages equal to 50 percent of average earnings. These individuals are followed for 480 months (40 years) between age 25 (when they enter the labor force) and age 65 (when they retire). Every month they face a certain probability of being unemployed or working, and if they work, they face a given probability of contributing to the matching system or not. This probability depends on the value of the matching benefit relative to individual earnings and the take-up rate/matching elasticity. Each panel presents the present value of the total costs of matching contributions and social pensions (for individuals who end up with a pension below the poverty line) as a function of the elasticity and the level of matching. Costs are expressed as the present value of total earnings among eligible individuals. Each panel refers to a given level of the contribution rate (CR), the poverty line (PL), and the duration of a spell of unemployment (UD). The probability of becoming unemployed if employed is 5 percent.

MAIN RESULTS

The results are summarized in figures 13.3 and 13.4, which refer to the baseline contribution densities (3 and 10 percent, respectively). Each of the four panels in each figure presents a given combination of the contribution rate, the poverty line, and the duration of unemployment. The horizontal axis gives the level of the matching contribution, and the vertical axis gives the value of the take-up rate/matching elasticity (η_j). The figures show the present value of the total costs of matching contributions and social pensions for 1,000 individuals, expressed as a share of the present value of total earnings. The main insights can be summarized as follows.

1. Matching contributions combined with social pensions have the potential to be cost-effective interventions as long as the take-up rate/matching elasticity and the

FIGURE 13.4 **Fiscal impact of matching contributions with baseline contribution density of 10 percent**

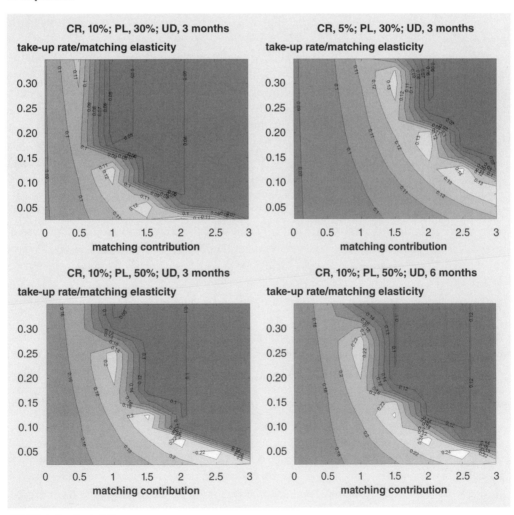

SOURCE: Authors' calculations.

NOTE: GDP, gross domestic product; CR, contribution rate (percent of GDP per capita); PL, poverty line (percent of GDP per capita); UD, unemployment duration. For details of simulation, see notes to figure 13.3.

individual contribution rate are not too low. The level of the minimum required elasticity will depend on the minimum level of the individual contribution. Hence, in our example, while a pure social pension for those with pensions below the minimum would cost 9 to 10 percent of aggregate earnings (depending on the initial contribution densities, contribution rates, and the poverty line), matching contributions could cost between 5 and 10 percent of aggregate earnings.

2. The level of the matching is an important policy choice, and its "optimal" level is quite sensitive to the take-up rate/matching elasticity. In general, matching levels that are too low (below 0.5 or even below 1) would fail to achieve the necessary saving and could cost more than pure social pensions. The explanation is simple. A matching level that is too low will not induce sufficient contributions for individuals to have a pension above the poverty line, and so transfers to these individuals during old age would still be required. Total costs would then depend on how the social pension is designed. If the social pension pays a top-up over the contributory pension, matching contributions would still be less expensive, since at least part of the targeted minimum pension would have been financed by the individual. But if the social pension takes the form of a flat payment equal to the poverty line, the matching would result in additional, wasteful, expenditures.

3. As the take-up rate/matching elasticity declines, the optimal level of matching needs to increase. For instance, in the top left-hand panel of figure 13.3, when the elasticity is equal to 0.35, the optimal level of the matching is equal to 1. For an elasticity equal to 0.15, the optimal level of matching is equal or above 2. Again, if the elasticity is too low, even high matching levels would not make a major difference to contribution densities and could increase costs.[16]

Clearly, the fiscal impact of the MDCs is quite sensitive to the individual contribution rate, the poverty line, the duration of unemployment, and the baseline probability of contributing. The top right-hand panel of figure 13.3 shows that if the individual contribution rate decreases from 10 to 5 percent of GDP per capita, matching levels would need to be more than 2.5 times the individual contribution to make a difference. For take-up rate/matching elasticities below 0.2, matching contributions are unlikely to be effective. Similar results are observed in the case of the 10 percent baseline contribution density for a take-up rate/matching elasticity below 0.10 (see figure 13.4).

A higher poverty line raises the cost of social pensions under no matching but also increases the savings from setting the proper matching rate. Thus, in the case of a poverty line equal to 30 percent of income per capita, moving from no match to the optimal match (which depends on the take-up rate or matching elasticity) reduces costs from 9–10 percent of aggregate earnings (depending on the level of the baseline contribution density) to 6 percent. For a poverty line equal to 50 percent of income per capita, costs drop from 16 percent to 10 percent of aggregate earnings (see the bottom left-hand panels of figures 13.3 and 13.4).

The increase in the duration of the unemployment spell from 3 to 6 months does not significantly affect the optimal level of matching for a given take-up rate/matching elasticity, but it does increase costs. This can be seen in the bottom left and right panels of figures 13.3 and 13.4. Costs under the optimal matching are less than 10 percent of aggregate earnings when the duration of the unemployment spell is 3 months (bottom left-hand panels), but they increase to 12 percent when the duration of the spell is 6 months. This is to be expected, since workers spend less time working and therefore are more likely to end up with pensions below the poverty line. It is also interesting to observe that with longer unemployment duration, the cost of having the "wrong" matching increase from 20 percent of aggregate earnings to 22 percent.

Finally, increasing the baseline contribution density from 3 to 10 percent reduces the level of matching needed for any level of the take-up rate/matching elasticity (compare panels of figure 3.3 with their respective panels in figure 3.4). The implication is that as contribution densities increase over time, presumably driven by economic diversification and labor productivity growth that increase incomes and reduce the sizes of the agriculture and informal sectors, the level of the matching could be reduced. At the same time, even if social pensions are indexed by a measure of average standards of living (e.g., economywide average earnings in the economy), fewer individuals would become eligible. Thus, the aggregate cost of MDCs and social pensions would decline.

Conclusions

Expansion of pension coverage to the informal sector in low- and middle-income countries requires new thinking on pension system design. By definition, mandates are not possible. Given high discount rates and myopia, workers will have to be given some incentive to defer some consumption until old age. In addition, the design of the scheme cannot rely on a steady income stream that can be tracked. Portability of pension wealth for this population is also important, in light of changing occupations and migration. We have argued that a matching defined contribution scheme is a useful approach for addressing these challenges.

Designing an MDC would entail several steps, beginning with the definition of the target pension level, most likely in relation to some objective measure of poverty. This target benefit would, in turn, be used to calculate the contribution amount required. Finally, the share of the contribution that would take the form of a matching contribution from the government would have to be determined.

Setting the correct level for the matching contribution is difficult because little is known ex ante about the elasticity of take-up to different matching amounts. Understanding the behavioral response of informal sector workers will be important in assessing whether the cost of an MDC is acceptable. It is very likely that MDCs are a better use of fiscal resources for old-age income security in low-income countries than income tax deductions would be. The comparison with social pensions, however, is not as clear. If take-up is high for a relatively small match, the long-run cost may be lower than an equivalent benefit paid through a social pension. But if take-up/matching elasticities are low, MDCs would have little effects on contribution densities and would likely increase costs.

Nonetheless, the evidence from high-income countries and experiences with other forms of conditional cash transfers suggest that MDCs can have meaningful effects on behavior. In this case MDCs can be combined with social pensions in the context of a long-term policy strategy to expand coverage and prevent old-age poverty. In essence, poverty among the elderly over the short run would be prevented through social pensions and, for the future elderly, through MDCs. This integrated policy approach could significantly reduce the financial burden of population aging without compromising the government's primary policy objective of minimizing poverty in old age.

Notes

1. This chapter focuses on old-age pensions, but the matching approach would also allow for life, disability, and even health insurance to be added, possibly with subsidized premiums.

2. Other modules that could be incorporated are health and unemployment benefits. For health, this could be done through medical savings accounts combined with catastrophic health insurance, as in the case of Singapore. For unemployment benefits, unemployment individual savings accounts can be combined with matching contributions or unemployment assistance programs. (See Robalino et al., forthcoming, ch. 5.)

3. See Pension Reform Primer Note, "Guarantees," www.worldbank.org/pensions.

4. See Whitehouse (2007) for more than 50 country-specific replacement rate schedules.

5. The calculation is made by adjusting the 1999–2000 poverty line for inflation. Inflation rates were taken from the International Monetary Fund, *World Economic Outlook 2003.*

6. The principle would be the same for the group insurance schemes (disability, survivor, and health): the financing should be set at a sustainable level, and the cost should be transparent, even if a subsidy is to be granted. As mentioned, the defined contribution scheme is the logical first step in design, particularly if the survivor and disability insurance will be tied to the individual account balance.

7. Among other assumptions, Shah (2005) assumes 200 basis points for administrative charges on assets.

8. For the moment, we focus on an individual. The levels here would have to be adjusted according to household size, as the poverty line is a per capita measure.

9. For example, members of groups such as microfinance institutions (MFIs) may be more easily incorporated into the scheme through lower transaction costs and preexisting recordkeeping machinery.

10. See also Palacios, Sluchynsky, and Biletsky (forthcoming) for a discussion of a dynamic approach to social pensions in combination with a gradually expanding contributory scheme.

11. One question is, why would individuals contribute to a matching program if a social pension is available? Indeed, the present value of the social pension should be at least as high as, if not higher than, the present value of the matching. This question is addressed in chapter 10 in this volume, which shows that for some individuals to be eligible for the minimum pension, they would need to overconsume while young. Matching contributions allow for a more flexible distribution of consumption between the present and the future.

12. With appropriate data, the estimation could be done, for instance, by estimating the logit regression:

$$\log\left(\frac{P_i}{1-P_i}\right) = b_j X_i + \eta_j \frac{m_i}{w_i} + \varepsilon_i; \quad \varepsilon \sim N\left(0, \sigma_\varepsilon\right)$$

13. Clearly, to define what we mean by "too low," a reference is needed that will depend on the individual's income level. For instance, take the case of an individual with earnings equal to GDP per capita, and assume that the pension at retirement needs to represent at least 40 percent of income per capita to avoid poverty during old age. This implies financing a 40 percent replacement rate, which could require a 12 percent contribution rate over a period of 40 years. A worker contributing only half of the time would need to double the contribution rate. In Argentina, Chile, and Uruguay, to give an instance, plan members in the lowest income quintile have contribution densities in the 20–40 percent range. Contribution densities in the third quintile are in the 50–60 percent range (see chapters 2 and 10 in this volume).

14. The probability of unemployment chosen is the average in Brazil for individuals earning 50 percent of average earnings (or close to GDP per capita).

15. As a reference, average unemployment durations in Latin American countries vary between 0.9 months in El Salvador and 18 months in Brazil. Unemployment durations are shorter for low-income workers and the unskilled.

16. It is also important to notice that aggregate costs with MDCs reach their highest level when the matching level is close to the optimal, given the take-up rate/matching elasticity (say, 1.5 times instead of 2). In this case, individuals contribute enough to increase the costs of the matching but not enough to save on social pensions.

References

Agnew, Julie R., Lisa Szykman, Stephen Utkus, and Jean Young. 2007. " Literacy, Trust and 401k Savings Behavior." CRR Working Paper 2007-10, Center for Retirement Research at Boston College, Chestnut Hill, MA.

Benjamin, Daniel J. 2003. "Does 401(k) Eligibility Increase Saving? Evidence from Propensity Score Subclassification." *Journal of Public Economics* 87 (5–6): 1259–90.

Bertrand, Marianne, Dean Karlan, Sendhil Mullainathan, Eldar Shafir, and Jonathan Zinman. 2005. "What's Psychology Worth? A Field Experiment in the Consumer Credit Market." NBER Working Paper No. 11892. Cambridge, MA: National Bureau of Economic Research.

Breashears, John, James J. Choi, David Laibson, and Brigitte C. Madrian. 2007. "The Impact of Employer Matching on Savings Plan Participation under Automatic Enrollment." NBER Working Paper 13352, National Bureau of Economic Research, Cambridge, MA.

Duflo, Esther, William Gale, Jeffrey Liebman, Peter Orszag, and Emmanual Saez. 2005. "Savings Incentives for Low and Middle Income Families: Evidence from a Field Experiment with H & R Block." NBER Working Paper 11680, National Bureau of Economic Research, Cambridge, MA.

Engelhardt, Gary, and A. Kumar. 2004. "Employer Matching and 401(k) Saving: Evidence from the Health and Retirement Survey." Working Paper 2004-18, Center for Retirement Research at Boston College, Chestnut Hill, MA.

Engen, Eric M., and William G. Gale. 2000. "The Effects of 401(k) Plans on Household Wealth: Differences across Earnings Groups." NBER Working Paper 8032, National Bureau of Economic Research, Cambridge, MA.

Eriyagama, Vindya, and Ravi P. Rannan-Eliya. 2003." Farmers' and Fishermen's Pension and Social Security Benefit Scheme: Final Report." Health Policy Programme 99, Institute of Policy Studies of Sri Lanka, Colombo.

Grosh, Margaret, Carlo del Ninno, Emil Tesliuc, and Azedine Ouerghi. 2008. *For Protection and Promotion: The Design and Implementation of Effective Safety Nets*. Directions in Development Series. Washington, DC: World Bank.

Hinz, Richard. 2008. "Voluntary Retirement Savings: Motivations, Incentives and Design." Human Development Network, Social Protection (HDNSP), World Bank, Washington, DC.

Hubbard, R. G., and J. S. Skinner. 1996. "Assessing the Effectiveness of Saving Incentives." *Journal of Economic Perspectives* 10 (4): 73–90.

IMF (International Monetary Fund). 2003. *World Economic Outlook 2003*. Washington, DC: IMF.

Levy, Santiago. 2006. *Good Intentions, Bad Outcomes: Social Policy, Informality and Economic Growth in Mexico*. Washington, DC: Brookings Institution Press.

Lussardi, Annamarie. 2004. "Savings and Effectiveness of Financial Education." In *Pension Design and Structure: New Lessons from Behavioral Finance*, ed. Olivia S. Mitchell and Stephen P. Utkus. Oxford: Oxford University Press

Munnell, Alicia, Annika Sunden, and Catherine Taylor. 2001. "What Determines 401k Participation and Contributions?" *Social Security Bulletin* 64 (3): 12–25.

OECD (Organisation for Economic Co-operation and Development). 2007. "Filling the Pension Gap: Coverage and Value of Voluntary Retirement Savings." DAF/AS/PEN/WD(2007)23, OECD, Paris.

Palacios, Robert, Oleksiy Sluchynsky, and Sergiy Biletsky. Forthcoming. "Social Pensions Part II: Their Design and Implementation." Social Protection Discussion Paper, World Bank, Washington, DC.

Perry, Guillermo E., William Maloney, Omar S. Arias, Pablo Fajnzylber, Andrew D. Mason, and Jaime Saavedra-Chanduvi. 2007. *Informality: Exit and Exclusion*. World Bank Latin American and Caribbean Studies, Washington, DC: World Bank.

Robalino, David, and András Bodor. 2007. "On the Financial Sustainability of Earnings-Related Pension Schemes with 'Pay-as-You-Go' Financing and the Role of Government-Indexed Bonds." *Journal of Pension Economics and Finance* 8 (2, April): 153–87.

Robalino David, Andrew Mason, Helena Ribe, and Ian Walker. Forthcoming. "The Future of Social Protection in LAC: Extending Coverage to All by Adapting Programs to Labor Markets and Rethinking the Allocation and Financing of Transfers." World Bank, Washington, DC.

Shah, Ajay. 2005. "Pension Outcomes Associated with Alternative Asset Allocations under the New Pension System." National Institute for Public Finance and Policy, New Delhi.

Whitehouse, E. R. 2007. "Pensions Panorama: Retirement-Income Systems in 53 Countries." World Bank, Washington, DC.

Yoo, Kwang Yeol, and Alain de Serres. 2004. "Tax Treatment of Private Pension Savings in OECD Countries." *OECD Economic Studies* 39 (2): 73–110.

CHAPTER 14

Administration of
Social Pension Programs

Oleksiy Sluchynsky

This chapter provides an overview of practices for the implementation and administration of retirement income transfers. It emphasizes the need to give careful attention to the choice of the administering agency and to base decisions on a detailed assessment of the local systems that will support the implementation and operation of the programs. Where existing mechanisms and systems are strong, they should be utilized, but often, new devices will be needed. The chapter argues that even when institutional capacity is weak, it is possible to correct it and exploit a number of promising operational innovations that are transferable and scalable to the context of a new country or a new program. Finally, where the resources to sustain a universal elderly benefit scheme are limited, a well-designed targeting mechanism should be implemented. Proxy means tests (PMTs) appear to be the most efficient alternative for achieving this. Simple and clear rules, as well as well-defined roles, can make means testing very efficient while keeping the operational cost low.

This chapter discusses key aspects of the policy, implementation planning, and administration of retirement income transfers. It takes stock of international experiences in operational design and administration and develops recommendations pertaining to the operational efficiency of such programs. It identifies some of the best practices in institutional and operational organization, taking into account the country-specific context. Finally, it sets out a simple analytical framework for developing administrative cost measures and assessing the relative operational efficiency of retirement income transfers.

The sections that follow discuss options in institutional and operational design and then examine interactions with contributory pensions and targeting methods. Methods and practices of benefit delivery are outlined, and a framework for developing cost measures is introduced. The final section summarizes the main messages of the chapter.

Implementation Planning and the Administering Agency

Implementation of a social pension program requires careful forethought and planning to balance multiple objectives. These objectives include providing easy access to the potentially eligible population, minimizing leakage, ensuring transparent management, providing smooth interface with other public benefit schemes, and achieving reasonable operational cost. The choice of the administering agency is very important. Local capacity and institutional conditions will often uniquely determine the efficient implementation program and effective management arrangements of the new scheme.

Where existing administrative structures (e.g., various public benefit payment systems) are in place, they need to be assessed as to whether and to what extent they can be utilized to run the new program. If existing systems and institutions are strong, using them would be an obvious choice and could make for greater public sector efficiency and transparency. For beneficiaries, as well, such a setup may be of value, as it could offer a one-stop shop for various programs and benefits provided by the public sector. An important question is whether the new program could better be implemented by an existing pension agency or by a general welfare agency. If the new program involves broad targeting, the choice of a general welfare agency would be more appealing. If both contributory and noncontributory programs provide for a significant degree of interrelations, the pension agency could better fit the bill.

When existing systems are weak or narrow, new institutions may need to be established to administer the new program. For example, when the existing contributory pension program provides for very low coverage or operates using outdated mechanisms, it may be safer for the new program to operate under separate administrative machinery. Establishing a new agency could also help focus operational efforts on the new program, although economies of scope would not be realized.

Implementation decisions in situations where existing systems are broad but mediocre are not clear-cut. If the new social pension program is introduced in the context of a comprehensive reform of pensions or the social assistance system, its administration is likely to be placed under the umbrella of an existing agency that is about to undergo the reform. Such an arrangement may benefit both the old and the new program. If the new program is simply an add-on to the existing range of public benefit provisions, some with broad coverage but with inefficient and nontransparent management, how to administer a new program will require more careful thinking.

In summary, the availability and quality of other institutions and programs influence the design and operation of the social pension administration, its operational costs, and whether it will ultimately be a success. Whereas more developed countries generally have stronger systems with wider coverage, less developed countries face greater implementation challenges but also have opportunities to utilize best practices tested elsewhere.

Program Design

The new program will require clear definition of the benefit eligibility criteria. These generally include age, residency, or citizenship and, in the case of means-tested approaches, limited resources or ineligibility for other programs.

Although these conditions seem simple to define, there are important caveats on how they are implemented in practice. Often, lack of attention to details puts the reform program at considerable risk. Where formal birth and death records exist as part of national identification systems such as the civil register or the voter registration system, those mechanisms can not only help in verifying identity but would also assist in establishing eligibility (i.e., age and residence). There are limitations, however. Certain program designs would require an extended period of residence in the country prior to the benefit claim. For example, in the Nordic countries, the full basic pension benefit is generally paid only to those who can prove residence in the country for the 40 years preceding retirement. The systems and records for validating and enforcing such a requirement may be in place in more developed countries, but in less developed countries that would be a challenge, and more modest requirements will have to be applied. For example, the national identification system often requires periodic certification, on three- or five-year cycles. An individual who claims the benefit and can present a valid national identification document would implicitly meet the condition of residence as defined by the national registration system. In countries with less developed infrastructure and record-keeping systems, it may be advisable not to expand the definition of residence under the basic benefit program beyond the existing national registration system.

Overall, if the national identification document meets some core criteria, including clear photo identification and unique numbering, there may be no need for the new program to issue any new identification document. For example, in Kosovo, as part of the implementation program for a new basic pension program in 2002, policy makers decided to use the civil register identification as the sole and sufficient proof of identity, age, and residence. The residence criteria were explicitly referenced to the preexisting legal framework. In Nepal, to obtain access to the old-age allowance program, elderly persons had first to apply for citizenship certificates to verify their age and residence.

Thus, it is important to survey the legal and operational framework of existing identification schemes to identify how they could be utilized most effectively to support implementation of the new pension program. In some countries, existing registration systems will suffice to track eligibility and payments under the new program. In cases where consolidated national databases of civil records do not exist (the situation in, for example, India), new and sometimes separate procedures will have to be established for personal identification, age verification, and proof of residence.

Posteligibility verification mechanisms need to be in place too, to ensure adequate operational and financial controls. Efficient death-screening mechanisms would be needed to ensure that payments do not go to deceased members. Some countries operate efficient national death registration systems, while in others the information is not consolidated, and enforcement of death registration is weak. To address these deficiencies, programs often adopt life certification mechanisms under which periodic appearances of the beneficiary in person are required if benefit payments are to continue. Selective audits, with home visits of the elderly, represent another alternative. Finally, solutions involving biometric identification for benefit payment are increasingly used as this technology becomes more affordable.

If the benefit depends on the civil or cohabitation status of the recipient (the case, for example, in New Zealand, the United States, and some Nordic countries), another group of life events—marriages and divorces—will have to be captured and monitored by the pension agency. For countries with weak civil record systems, effective implementation of this provision may be challenging, as some marriages would go unregistered, and the costs of registering a fictitious divorce may be low.

Interaction with Contributory Programs

Countries that operate contributory schemes with significant coverage and extensive networks of offices have a considerable operational advantage in implementing universal social pensions, since the main institutional preconditions and infrastructure elements are already in place. For example, where contributory schemes exist, information exchanges with those programs could be very useful. Most contributory schemes operate posteligibility verification mechanisms to determine deaths, both explicitly and implicitly (e.g., survivor benefits or funeral grants), and those could be utilized to administer the basic pension, as well. A very simple means test might be a contributory pension eligibility test.[1] There are, however, several caveats with respect to the interaction of the universal pension with the contributory schemes.

First, the benefit rate of the social pension needs to be harmonized with the minimum benefit offered by the contributory program, and ideally with other public assistance schemes. It may simply be administratively inefficient to top-up benefits from one scheme with a very small benefit from another. Second, indexation policies need to be well coordinated, again, to avoid administrative inefficiencies. Finally, in the case of a pension-tested basic benefit, it is important to define efficient interaction with the early or deferred contributory benefit in order to avoid perverse incentives and ensure equity. For example, early retirement could lead to a smaller monthly contributory benefit but also to a higher present value of the pension-tested social pension payment. Similarly, depending on the nature of the offset in the social pension and the actuarial adjustment of the deferred retirement pension, individuals may choose to postpone claiming contributory pensions to maximize payouts from both systems.

Targeting

Certain eligibility provisions for basic pension programs are intended to reduce transfers to persons who do not need them by excluding those with higher incomes or assets. This can reduce the overall cost of the program, but a robust mechanism for applying such means tests will have to be put in place.

In New Zealand, for example, universal basic pension payments are subject to a general progressive income tax, so those with higher incomes have their basic benefit reduced at a higher rate. Most developing countries, however, do not have broad and well-functioning income tax collection systems, and only a very small percentage of elderly beneficiaries would pay taxes. While such policies can be considered in the long run, some countries seek to incorporate means-testing provisions in their social pension program in more direct and explicit ways.

Australia, South Africa, and the Nordic countries, for example, operate basic pension programs with some means testing. There are differences as to the income included under the testing rules; it may include earned income, pensions, or unearned income.

Although efficient comprehensive means testing may not be feasible in some countries, some simplified categorical rules may be workable. For example, in some remote or rural communities, eligibility could be linked to residence. Alternatively, the program could pay benefits to those who are generally not eligible for benefits from any of the state public benefit programs (including contributory pensions). Going beyond that perhaps would be difficult without an extensive administrative machinery or significant involvement of local community assessment mechanisms.

Some programs grant new benefits under quotas for the number of beneficiaries. Higher quotas can be assigned to relatively poorer and more populous communities. Quotas are used, for example, in the basic pension programs in India and Bangladesh, where they are administered with the involvement of the local grassroots institutions.

Pressure from individuals in the same community who are placed on a waiting list may help in efficiently enforcing the entitlement. More generally, quotas help reduce perverse incentives, as they add a stochastic element to future eligibility determination (Valdés-Prieto 2002).

Another very promising, nondiscretionary approach is the use of proxy means tests (PMTs). The premise of the system is that it is difficult to quantify and verify income for workers in the informal sector, household enterprises, and small farming, but that household welfare can be predicted with fair accuracy on the basis of a rather small number of easy-to-measure and often easy-to-verify indicators (or proxies) of individuals' characteristics and their consumption or ownership of various goods and assets (see chapter 12 in this volume). Thus, representative household consumption (income) surveys are used to estimate the parameters of a formula that, given the observed value of the indicators or proxies for a household or individual, predicts consumption (income). Potential beneficiaries who apply to receive the transfer fill out a questionnaire containing perhaps two to three dozen questions asking for information about the necessary indicators. The application of the formula to the questionnaire permits determination of whether the household or individual is eligible for the transfer. As discussed in chapter 12, PMTs are affected by inclusion and exclusion errors, but these can be controlled or minimized by adjusting the indicators and the estimation methods.[2] PMTs have been applied successfully to the implementation of so-called conditional cash transfers (CCTs) around the world (see Grosh et al. 2008).

In all cases, close attention needs to be paid to the cultural and political environment where the new program is being introduced. Targeting can often be seen as stigmatizing program beneficiaries, and it could thus discourage otherwise eligible claimants, resulting in underutilization of the old-age minimum income scheme. Similarly, sometimes significant discretion with respect to eligibility rules or decisions is placed in the hands of local politicians, which could lead to patronage to gain popular support at the cost of exclusion of some needy and eligible individuals. Fair and transparent mechanisms of eligibility verification and approval are crucial.

Program Access and Payment Systems

It is important to recognize and strategically address potential obstacles to the extension of coverage of the new program. Those include both individual characteristics of the elderly and, possibly, the remoteness and poor infrastructure of certain communities.

The elderly population is not homogeneous; it includes illiterate, disabled, and visually impaired individuals; some cannot sign for themselves. In certain communities, multiple languages are common. These needs will require special attention when it comes to filing applications. Generally, simplified but well-structured application forms reduce ambiguity and discretion in decision making regarding the claim. A study of the social pension payments in the Indian state of Karnataka (Murgai et al. 2006), reports that high transaction costs are incurred during an application process that involves producing several proofs and certificates to be submitted to a village accountant. The study shows that a not insignificant share of applicants (especially illiterate elderly persons and widows) choose to rely on a middleman to prepare their applications, help arrange the required certification, and file the claim.

Extending the opportunity to apply and providing ongoing payment services in some remote and rural communities often pose challenges. In more developed countries, the use of banking services for pension benefit payments would be an obvious choice. The U.S. Social Security Administration reports that a growing number of beneficiaries choose to receive retirement benefits via direct deposit to their bank accounts. In Ukraine payment of pensions via banks yields administrative savings to the pension agency, which does not have to pay the cover cost typically associated with postal delivery. Developing countries, however, often do not enjoy the benefits of a developed and distributed payment infrastructure, and they have resorted to various alternatives and experiments for benefit delivery systems, some at a relatively high cost. For example, in the Zambian pilot social cash transfer scheme, beneficiaries living within 15 kilometers of a designated bank branch were required to open accounts at that bank. For others, special pay points were established at rural health centers and schools (Schubert 2005).

In South Africa mobile van pay points were deployed to facilitate distribution of pensions to remote communities. Today, over 2 million beneficiaries are collecting their pension payments through this system, which utilizes 500 mobile vans that make regular trips to remote villages. The vans are equipped with ATM-style machines and fingerprint readers, facilitating the smart card identification system (see Identix 2004).

In Namibia the universal pension scheme pays about 25 Namibian dollars monthly to all individuals age 60 and over. In 1996 the cash payments were outsourced, and a system of mobile banks was introduced (Schleberger 2002). Every pensioner was issued an electronic identification card with PIN number and fingerprint identification readable by ATMs. Mobile teams were trained and deployed to areas where cash pay points were set up. As a general rule, the aim was that beneficiaries would not have to travel more than 10 kilometers to the collection stations. As result, only 15 percent of all payments went through the post office or banks, as against 85 percent disbursed through the cash pay points. The quality of services increased significantly, but so did the cost, as special security arrangements were required.

In Kosovo, as part of the implementation of the basic pension in areas that at the time were without banking coverage, several mobile bank branches were licensed. These provided scheduled services primarily to the otherwise excluded ethnic minority areas. Retirees were required to use existing bank accounts or to open new ones following regular bank procedures. The combination of easy-to -read bank coverage maps, joint account options, and complementary mobile bank services proved to be a success. Today, coverage of the program is almost universal among the eligible population, all payments are made through banks, and banks have established a permanent presence in the previously excluded communities.

As an alternative to the mobile bank model and to the conventional financial services network, special point-of-service (POS) devices have been widely utilized in Brazil. Using a regular debit card, individuals can access their bank accounts and perform various financial transactions, perhaps while shopping at a local drugstore. Local providers have to be licensed by the host commercial bank, have a telephone line, and be equipped with a card-reading device connecting in dial-up sessions to the remote bank's server. Such simple and accessible systems could be effectively used for payment of pensions.

Power of attorney is another common instrument for facilitating payment delivery to elderly persons with limited mobility; it allows relatives to collect benefits on their behalf. When payments are made through the banking system, allowing joint accounts for the receipt of benefits is another accepted practice. To limit the risk of frauds in which the benefits are collected after the death of the legitimate beneficiary, power of attorney should have a limited duration and be subject to recertification.

Identification of the recipient at the time of payment is also important. As discussed above, where robust national identification systems exist, these could be used to identify members of the program for payment. In the absence of such robust universal identification, the pension agency may be prompted to establish its own identification mechanisms to track postretirement eligibility and screen for illegitimate payments.

The spectrum of observed solutions here ranges from the simplest paper beneficiary card to multipurpose plastic cards. The latter can contain an electronic chip that facilitates biometric identification and perhaps can store benefit payment transactions. With such technology, the member can enter into an offline transaction in the most remote areas. This would require a special hand-held device. Such technology allows for storing and managing, in an electronic offline mode, a whole spectrum of information on multiple programs and benefits. "Smart cards" and biometric identification systems are becoming increasingly common across the globe in applications to various public benefit programs, including both universal and earnings-related pensions.

As an example, in 2001 the government of South Africa, as part of the mobile pension payment services, required individuals to provide their fingerprints and other identification information, which were encrypted and stored on a special card (SCSSA 2004). Use of smart cards is very common in India, where, for example, the state of Andhra Pradesh sanctioned use of the new card as part of the administration of the universal national old-age pension scheme (NOAPS). In the country as a whole, it is seen that the new technology would provide a general platform to which multiple applications could eventually be added, cutting down the cost of delivery of benefits to communities otherwise without banking services.

Under any payment and identification model, proper record keeping, accounting, and monitoring remain the core of a robust administrative system. Under certain circumstances, some components of the operation, such as benefit delivery, can be outsourced to the private sector. That may help expand coverage and improve service quality. Proper cost-benefit analysis will be required to assess the trade-offs of various operational elements such as alternative payment modes and means testing.

Administrative Costs of the Social Pension Programs

The cost of administration is an important factor in designing a new program. Benchmarking and comparison of costs across various programs, however, pose challenges, given the underlying heterogeneity of institutional setups and operational provisions, For example, in addition to an old-age benefit, some programs may provide payments to groups such as widows and the disabled. Presumably, additional administrative resources would be required to assess eligibility in those cases. Separate indicators of efficiency would typically not be available, given that resources are shared. Similarly, operational synergies may exist with other public programs (e.g., contributory pension schemes or general social assistance); premises or staff might be shared with other programs, in which case operational cross-subsidies would be difficult to account for.

In general, the following considerations should be taken into account when assessing administrative costs:

- Programs vary in coverage, so spreading the same costs among a greater number of participants generally should yield economies of scale and lead to lower expenses per participant or as a share of the total budget.

- The generosity of the benefit may often mask administrative inefficiencies if simple generic measures such as costs expressed as a share of the total budget are applied. Use of some kind of cost indicator per beneficiary may help avoid this bias.

- Programs that require means testing or involve assessment of more complex categorical eligibility of various applicants would presumably cost more.

- Finally, service quality comes at a cost. Higher operational expenses may reflect better services provided—more frequent and direct communications with clients, faster processing of benefit claims, alternative payment methods, and so on. (See table 14.1 for alternative indicators of the operational costs of some social pension programs.)

The data presented here come from too restricted a sample of plans to permit definitive conclusions, but some general observations can be instructive:

- New Zealand, with its absolute costs per beneficiary at the higher end of our sample, is nevertheless quite efficient if costs are adjusted for per capita GDP. An important point is that while there is no means testing for most beneficiaries of the New Zealand program, some provisions make significant demands on administrative resources. In particular, claims have to be differentiated with respect to the civil and cohabitation status of the applicants, and the benefits of certain categories of married beneficiaries may be subject to an income test. Furthermore, the responsible agency manages numerous payment cases of individuals who retire overseas, and there are several categories of cases that need to be differentiated, depending on the arrangements New Zealand has with foreign

TABLE 14.1 **Administrative costs of selected social pension programs**

Economy and year	Number of beneficiaries	Beneficiaries as percent of population	Cost as percent of transfers	Cost per beneficiary (US$)	Cost per beneficiary as percent of GDP per capita
Botswana (1999)	71,000	4.1	4.5	15	0.4
Kosovo (2006)	130,000	6.5	1.5	9	0.6
Mauritius (1999)	109,000	9.3	2.5	17	0.5
Namibia (1999)	82,000	4.4	15.0	51	2.5
New Zealand (2005/6)	488,000	11.9	0.5	48	0.2

SOURCE: Authors' calculations based on ILO (1999), MFE Kosovo, Statistics New Zealand, and New Zealand MSD (2005/2006). GDP per capita estimates from http://www.econstats.com/ except IMF for Kosovo. Population estimates from World Bank Institutional Database.

NOTE: GDP. gross domestic product. For Botswana, Mauritius, and Namibia, beneficiaries other than old-age beneficiaries are excluded.

states. Given all these issues, the scheme in New Zealand stands out as an efficient operation. Perhaps to a significant extent this is a result of the high coverage and the corresponding economies of scale.

- Kosovo's plan, the least expensive program per member in absolute terms, does not stand out as especially efficient when costs are adjusted for income. That may seem surprising, given that operationally, this is perhaps one of the simplest programs and one that enjoys a favorable institutional environment. The plan pays an absolutely flat benefit to one well-defined group of the population. It takes advantage of external identification mechanisms and disburses all payments in an automated centralized process.[3] Kosovo is very densely populated, with relatively good penetration by the infrastructure of public and private services. Coverage that is lower than in New Zealand, and hence a relative lack of economies of scale, may be part of the explanation for the relatively low levels of efficiency.

- Mauritius compares well with Kosovo in many ways, and it enjoys both relatively good infrastructure and a high concentration of population. Coverage numbers are comparable, as well. Adjusted cost indicators are of the same magnitude.

- For similar levels of coverage, there is a significant variation in costs between Namibia and a group that includes Botswana, Kosovo, and Mauritius. Schleberger (2002) notes that after privatization of payment services in Namibia, costs increased considerably, with no action on downsizing the public administration that used to support such services. Although the cost of outsourcing consumes more than half of the total administrative budget in Namibia, Schleberger observes that service quality has improved considerably.

The comparative analysis outlined above is a type of framework that should apply to assessment of the costs of any such program.

It is unfortunate that the available sample limits our capacity to further assess important trade-offs involved in the design of the schemes with means testing. To fill this gap, we draw some observations from available studies on targeting and means testing within general assistance schemes.

Besley (1990) sets out a framework for analyzing and comparing the cost-efficiency of means-testing and universal benefit provisions. The main assumption is that means testing involves additional costs and that the same resources could be used for a universal program, with the disadvantage that some resources will be transferred to the nonpoor. Besley's model suggests that universal schemes should be preferred in societies with greater proportions of the poor or with a broader income distribution, where the objective of policy is to reduce the income dispersion of the poor. Otherwise, a means-testing approach should generally be favored, unless exclusion error produces significant inequality among those eligible but excluded. Analysis of an extreme case of the adverse incentive effects of means testing points to an even greater preference for the universal schemes.

Coady, Grosh, and Hoddinott (2002) differentiate among and discuss the administrative, private, incentive, social, and political costs of targeting, noting the varying incidence of each of these cost components under different targeting methods. The authors set out important caveats regarding measurement of the administrative costs of targeting. Under certain assumptions, with finer targeting that leads to a smaller population of beneficiaries and requires less administrative machinery, the administrative costs ratio may be lower for means-tested programs than for universal ones. In view of the potential economies of scale in administration, the authors suggest favoring means testing in programs that cover significant populations or provide for large benefits and, of course, in countries with high administrative capacity, stronger record-keeping traditions, and better accountability.

Coady, Grosh, and Hoddinott (2002) note that under certain circumstances, community-based targeting could be a cost saver because of the supposedly more accurate local knowledge of the situation of the benefit claimants. Indeed, in South Asia local organizations such as local public administration units, village development committees, and ad hoc committees often play a primary role in application processing and eligibility screening for the universal pension programs: this is the case in India and Nepal and in a pilot program in Pakistan. There are trade-offs, however. The absence of a specialized agency may lead to a diffused operational focus and, ultimately, to poor services or low awareness of the program. This would typically be the case when the same officer is put in charge of running multiple operations of the local community and has to struggle to keep up with diverse and competing priorities. Furthermore, as noted above, in a decentralized setting where significant decision-making authority over eligibility criteria or the beneficiary lists resides locally, the program may easily be hijacked by agendas of local politicians seeking to be reelected to office.

Grosh et al. (2008) summarize the findings of various studies that report on targeting costs, including outreach to beneficiaries, determination of eligibility, home visits, verification of information, and maintenance of databases. In a sample of the means-tested and proxy means-tested assistance programs in some former socialist countries of Europe and Central Asia, such costs are found to run from one-quarter to about three-quarters of the total administrative budget.

In summary, the design of a social pension program should carefully balance policy objectives, budgetary constraints, institutional capacity, and operational efficiency. Administration may fail to support ambitious objectives by proving too costly, generating various hidden costs, or allowing leakages. If effective targeting imposes high operational demand on the narrow resource base (possibly eating up any budgetary advantage of payment to a downsized population of beneficiaries), or if significant leakages or considerable exclusion errors persist, serious consideration should be given to a universal benefit.

Conclusion

This chapter has provided an overview of practices for the implementation and administration of retirement income transfers. Social pensions and other retirement income transfers may vary in their objectives and design, but their ultimate success will depend greatly on thorough planning, well thought-out implementation, and good administration. Three main messages emerge from the analysis. First, careful attention needs to be given to the choice of the administering agency, based on a detailed assessment of the local systems that will support the implementation and operation of the programs. In particular, the mechanisms of individual identification, eligibility verification, benefit delivery, and interaction with other public benefit programs need to be carefully analyzed. Where existing mechanisms and systems are strong, they should be utilized—but new devices will often have to be put in place.

Second, it is common to encounter limitations of infrastructure and institutional capacity that pose significant implementation challenges. There are, however, a number of very promising operational innovations that are transferable and scalable to the context of a new country or a new program. Weak institutions should therefore not be taken as a fixed and immovable constraint that precludes the implementation of retirement income transfers.

Third, where the resources to sustain a universal elderly benefit scheme are limited, a well-designed targeting mechanism should be implemented. Proxy means tests appear to be the most promising alternative. The evidence suggests that the costs of administering a targeting scheme are low in relation to the benefits in terms of poverty impact and efficiency in public expenditures. Simple and clear rules, as well as well-defined roles, can make means testing very efficient while keeping the operational cost low.

Notes

1. Many counties operate separate special schemes that include various centrally and locally managed civil service retirement schemes, military retirement provisions, and special opt-out regimes. To ensure fair treatment on the pension test, the same provisions would perhaps have to apply to beneficiaries of these mandatory schemes administered by agencies other than the national pension agency. Data exchange mechanisms and selective and random audits could help contain the growth of ineligible claims.

2. An inclusion error means that someone who is not eligible is selected as a beneficiary. Exclusion error is more worrisome; it means that someone who is eligible is excluded from the program.

3. What remains uncertain is whether commercial banks will continue assessing 5 euros per account per year, under an agreement made at the outset of the scheme (see Gubbels, Snelbecker, and Zezulin 2007); whether the government will continue to subsidize this fee (about 1 percent of total spending); and whether the fee is included in the data that were available to us for this analysis.

References

Besley, Timothy. 1990. "Means Testing versus Universal Provisions in Poverty Alleviation Programs." *Economica*, n.s., 57 (225, February): 119–29.

Coady, David, Margaret Grosh, and John Hoddinott. 2002. "The Targeting of Transfers in Developing Countries: Review of Experience and Lessons." World Bank, Washington, DC.

Fultz, Elaine, and Bodhi Pieris. 1999. "Social Security Schemes in Southern Africa: An Overview and Proposals for Future Development." Discussion Paper 11, International Labour Office, Geneva.

Grosh, Margaret, Carlo del Ninno, Emil Tesliuc, and Azedine Ouerghi. 2008. *For Protection and Promotion: The Design and Implementation of Effective Safety Nets.* Directions in Development Series. Washington, DC: World Bank.

Gubbels, John, David Snelbecker, and Lena Zezulin. 2007. "The Kosovo Pension Reform: Achievements and Lessons." Social Protection Discussion Paper 0707, World Bank, Washington, DC.

Identix. 2004. "South African National Pension Payout Program: Facilitating Entitlement Distribution." Case Study, IBIA (International Biometric Industry Association), Washington, DC.

Murgai, Rinku, Salman Zaidi, Arindam Nandi, and Juan Munoz. 2006. "Do Public Funds Reach the Destitute? Assessment of Leakages and Targeting of Social Pension Programs in Karnataka." South Asia Poverty Reduction and Economic Management unit, World Bank, Washington, DC.

New Zealand, Ministry of Social Development. 2005/6. *Annual Report, 2005/2006.* Wellington: Ministry of Social Development.

Palacios, Robert, Oleksiy Sluchynsky, and Sergiy Biletsky. Forthcoming. "Social Pensions Part II: Their Design and Implementation." Social Protection Discussion Paper, World Bank, Washington, DC.

Schleberger, Eckard. 2002. "Namibia's Universal Pension Scheme: Trends and Challenges." International Labour Office, Geneva.

Schubert, Bernd. 2005. "The Pilot Social Cash Transfer Scheme, Kalomo District—Zambia." CPRC Working Paper 52, Chronic Poverty Research Centre, University of Manchester, Manchester, U.K.

SCSSA (Smart Card Society of Southern Africa). 2004. "Smart Card Trends and Deployment in SA 2004." SCSSA, Johannesburg.

Valdés-Prieto, Salvador. 2002. "Social Security Coverage in Chile, 1990–2001." Background paper for "Keeping the Promise of Old-Age Income Security in Latin America." Office of the Chief Economist, Latin America and the Caribbean Region, World Bank, Washington, DC. http://www-wds.worldbank.org/servlet/WDSContentServer/WDSP/IB/2004/11/12/000090341_20041112151220/Rendered/PDF/304950SValdes1CoverageChile.pdf.

Index

b,f, n, and *t* denote *box, figure, note,* and *table.*

ECO-AUDIT
Environmental Benefits Statement

The World Bank is committed to preserving endangered forests and natural resources. *Closing the Coverage Gap: The Role of Social Pensions and Other Retirement Income Transfers* is printed on recycled paper made with 30 percent post-consumer waste. The Office of the Publisher follows the recommended standards for paper usage set by the Green Press Initiative, a nonprofit program supporting publishers in using fiber that is not sourced from endangered forests. For more information, visit www. greenpressinitiative.org.

Saved:

- 7 trees
- 5 million BTUs of total energy
- 584 lb. of net greenhouse gases
- 2,644 gallons of waste water
- 308 pounds of solid waste

green press
INITIATIVE